PENSIONS AS PROPERTY

This book explores the impact of the European Convention on Human Rights (ECHR) when defining and protecting pension entitlements as property rights.

The sustainability of pension systems in Europe is threatened by mounting public debt and demographic shifts. In recent decades, governments have addressed these challenges by implementing reforms to balance financial stability and guarantee adequate retirement benefits. Many of these reforms have faced legal challenges from activists and lawyers in domestic courts, based on 'stand-still' and 'non-retrogression' constitutional principles. However, Article 1 of Protocol No. 1 of the ECHR offers an alternative approach that protects social security entitlements, including pensions, as private property, deserving of protection against unjustified state interference.

This book explores the historical legal rationale employed by the Court to establish social security entitlements as private property. It further examines how the Court has assessed reforms through a proportionality assessment that weights public interests against individual rights. This analysis distils key principles such as reasonableness, non-discrimination, and fair distribution of burdens that can guide policymakers towards responsible, rights-compliant reform.

Hartmann-Cortés prompts critical inquiry into an often-overlooked framework that will be of interest to policymakers, legal scholars, and anyone engaged in debates at the intersection of pension law, property rights, and social welfare law.

Pensions as Property

Insights from the European Convention on Human Rights

Kevin Hartmann-Cortés

• HART •
OXFORD • LONDON • NEW YORK • NEW DELHI • SYDNEY

HART PUBLISHING

Bloomsbury Publishing Plc

Kemp House, Chawley Park, Cumnor Hill, Oxford, OX2 9PH, UK

1385 Broadway, New York, NY 10018, USA

Bloomsbury Publishing Ireland Limited, 29 Earlsfort Terrace, Dublin 2, D02 AY28, Ireland

HART PUBLISHING, the Hart/Stag logo, BLOOMSBURY and the Diana logo are trademarks of Bloomsbury Publishing Plc

First published in Great Britain 2026

A catalogue record for this book is available from the British Library.

A catalogue record for this book is available from the Library of Congress.

ISBN: HB: 978-1-50998-602-6
ePDF: 978-1-50998-604-0
ePub: 978-1-50998-603-3

Typeset by Compuscript Ltd, Shannon

For product safety related questions contact productsafety@bloomsbury.com

For Lily, with my love and thanks

FOREWORD

This book by Kevin Hartmann-Cortés – a brilliant young researcher – is the result of his PhD research defended in 2023 at UC Louvain. The author examines how the European Court of Human Rights protects pensions as property under Article 1 of Protocol N° 1 (A1P1) and how this framing has shaped pension reform throughout Europe.

One could argue that the main question of the book deals with the kind of legal protection, if any, pension entitlements receive when pension reforms occur. The central claim is that, although property protection under A1P1 is limited and qualified, the principles developed in the Court's jurisprudence have distributive implications. The author claims that the ECtHR has interpreted A1P1 in such a way that it grants stronger protection to the most vulnerable retirees from the heaviest burdens of reform.

It is exactly this analysis which should inspire pension reforms. Property rights under A1P1 do not overrule pension reforms but delimit clear borders. After all, most pension reforms provoke political tension leading to legal mobilization by individuals or groups who consider their rights infringed or violated.

The analysis of the author is more than outstanding. Out of the case-law he distills a coherent theory whereby the essence of A1P1 is defined contextually by three factors: (i) the scale of the interference of the reform, (ii) the nature of the pension entitlement, and (iii) the vulnerability of the claimant. The conclusion is clear the property right on pensions under A1P1 is not a fixed, abstract threshold. Hence reforms are more likely to be compatible with A1P1 when they are temporary, moderate in scope, applied broadly, and preserve a basic level of income. Even reforms establishing permanent cuts to benefits may be permissible if reductions are modest and individuals retain meaningful financial autonomy. Even certain aggravating factors, such as retroactivity, can be tolerated when joined by mitigating elements like modest reductions, broad distribution, or the preservation of income security. The overall assessment depends on how these features interact in a given case. Yet there is a hard limit: once a reform deprives individuals of the means to secure a basic livelihood, the "essence" of the right is considered undermined, and no other configuration can justify the measure.

My conclusion is clear. This book is an absolute must-read for both policymakers and pension lawyers. Policymakers can learn from it how far they can go when implementing pension reforms. Pension lawyers will find practical tools in it to test the extent to which pension reforms are permitted under A1P1.

This book is the culmination of Kevin Hartmann-Cortés's extensive work. At the time of writing this foreword, it was unclear what the future held for Kevin. But one thing is certain: this young man has a very bright future ahead of him. Rarely have I had the opportunity to work with someone so talented, honest and intelligent. But above all, he is a very nice person.

Leuven, Yves Stevens, 16 November 2025
Yves Stevens is a full professor of pension law at the KULeuven.

ACKNOWLEDGEMENTS

This book is largely based on the first section of the PhD thesis that I defended on 27 November 2023 at UCLouvain in Louvain-la-Neuve, Belgium. It is the culmination of six years' work, including one doctoral and two postdoctoral fellowships, funded and supported by the ARC Pension Reform Project 'Sustainable, Adequate and Safe Pensions (2018–2023)', the *Chaire d'excellence Ethias sur les pensions complémentaires* and the OFP-Prolocus Postdoctoral Research Agreement. I am grateful to these institutions for their support, and also to my two academic homes over these years, UCLouvain and KULeuven.

At UCLouvain, both the *Centre de recherche interdisciplinaire Droit, Entreprise et Société* (CRIDES) of the Faculty of Law and Criminology and the *Chaire Hoover d'éthique économique et sociale* of the Faculty of Economic, Social, Political Sciences and Communication provided an outstanding academic environment for the development of my ideas. I am grateful to the current and former members of the academic, scientific, and administrative staff in both centres, including Adrián Herranz, Alejandro Berrotaran, Amaël Maskens, Andrés Salazar, Ariane Robyn, Arno Baurin, Aurélie Frankart, Auriane Lamine, Camille Pascal, Catarina Neves, Catherine Vanderlinden, Cédric Henet, Céline Wattecamps, Diana Piroli, Dina Geron, Edoardo Traversa, Elena Masseglia Miszczyszyn, Elliot Coubbaut, Eric Boot, Filip Dorssemont, Fotios Bregiannis, Francesca Raimondo, Grégory Pontière, Henri Coulot, Hervé Pourtois, Jean-Michel Chaumont, Jens Jørund Tyssedal, John Pitseys, Kebadu Mekonnen, Keivan Diakité, Marc Morsa, Maria Cristina Degoli, Marie Bastin, Maxime Lambrecht, Niko Väänänen, Nunzio Alì, Olivier Malay, Pablo Benito, Pablo Magaña, Philippe Lambrecht, Philippe Van Parijs, Pierre André, Pierre Devolder, Pierre-Etienne Vandamme, Pietro Intropi, Quentin Detienne, Refia Kaya, Rossana Ducato, Sacha Henet, Sara Suárez Gonzalo, Sefane Çetin, Steve Gilson, Vincent Vandenberghe, and Yannick Vanderborght. I am also grateful for the input of Damien Piron, Jean Hindriks, and Elena-Simina Tănăsescu.

At KULeuven, I had the privilege of working as a postdoctoral researcher at the *Instituut voor Sociaal Recht*, thanks to the generosity of Peter Sommen, Ria Janvier, and Inger De Wilde. I also owe a debt of gratitude to Hans van Meerten from Utrecht University, and to Jorik van Zanden and John Mitchem from the Jasper Forum, for their collegiality and for the discussions that helped shape my thinking on the concept of property in pensions. Thanks to Verity Stuart, my editor at Hart Publishing, for her patience, professionalism, and steady guidance throughout the preparation of this book.

Special mention should be reserved for five special people. The support, friendship, advice and intellectual stimulation of Juan Olano has been invaluable. Manuel Valente witnessed the genesis of this book since its very beginning and has heard, read and commented on most of this text. His attentive readings and comments have helped improve it significantly. Axel Gosseries and Alexia Autenne have been exceptional mentors. They have challenged me with rigor while supporting me with constancy, availability and care. Their guidance has been decisive in the intellectual and personal growth that this work aspires to reflect. Yves Stevens, who generously agreed to write the foreword to this book, has been a constant source of intellectual and professional inspiration. I owe him a particular debt of gratitude for his generosity, his rigor, and his confidence in my work.

Much of what I have been able to accomplish is owed to my family, Frederic Muzel, Martin Muzel, Eliana Muzel, Stephanny Hartmann, Joe Hartmann and Maria Fabiola Cortes. Above all, I would like to thank Lily Bernal, to whom this book is dedicated. Her loving support, patience, and care sustained me through the demanding years of writing. What this book owes to her goes far beyond what can be acknowledged here.

CONTENTS

TABLE OF CASES

Introduction

Pension systems are at the heart of modern welfare states. They provide a stable stream of income in old age,[1] precisely at a phase of heightened vulnerability.[2] Pension benefits amount to 72–85 per cent of the total income share of the elderly population in Europe.[3] Yet, these systems face mounting pressures. Demographic ageing,[4] fiscal constraints,[5] labour-market changes[6] and increased reliance on financial markets[7] pose persistent challenges to their sustainability[8] and adequacy.[9]

[1] From an individual perspective, pensions serve as both a mechanism for consumption smoothing and means of insurance. Nicholas Barr and Peter Diamond, 'The Economics of Pensions' (2006) 22 *Oxford Review of Economic Policy* 15, 16.

[2] For a socio-historical overview of social security mechanisms such as old-age retirement pensions, Robert Castel, *L'insécurité Sociale: Qu'est-Ce Qu'être Protégé?* (Seuil 2004); Robert Castel, *La Montée Des Incertitudes: Travail, Protections, Statut de l'individu* (Seuil 2009) 11–65; Robin Blackburn, *Banking on Death: Or, Investing in Life: The History and Future of Pensions* (Verso Books 2002); Gøsta Esping-Andersen, *The Three Worlds of Welfare Capitalism* (Polity 1990).

[3] The percentage depends on whether we count survivors' pensions which are usually held by women. See Social Protection Committee, 'The 2018 Pension Adequacy Report: Current and Future Income Adequacy in Old Age in the EU. Volume I'.

[4] Donald T Rowland, 'Global Population Aging: History and Prospects' in Peter Uhlenberg (ed) *International Handbook of Population Aging* (Springer 2009); Karl Hinrichs, 'Recent Pension Reforms in Europe: More Challenges, New Directions. An Overview' (2021) 55 *Social Policy & Administration* 409; Bernhard Ebbinghaus and Tobias Wiß, 'The Political Economy of Pension Policy' in Bent Greve, Amílcar Moreira and Minna van Gerven (eds), *Handbook on the Political Economy of Social Policy* (Edward Elgar Publishing 2024).

[5] Anke Hassel, Marek Naczyk and Tobias Wiß, 'The Political Economy of Pension Financialisation: Public Policy Responses to the Crisis' Anke Hassel and Tobias Wiß (eds), *The Political Economy of Pension Financialisation* (Routledge 2020).

[6] Karl Hinrichs and Matteo Jessoula, *Labour Market Flexibility and Pension Reforms: Flexible Today, Secure Tomorrow?* (Springer 2012).

[7] Marek Naczyk and Bruno Palier, 'Feed the Beast: Finance Capitalism and the Spread of Pension Privatisation in Europe' [2014] Available at SSRN 2551521; Marek Naczyk and Stefan Domonkos, 'The Financial Crisis and Varieties of Pension Privatization Reversals in Eastern Europe' (2016) 29 *Governance* 167; Hassel, Naczyk and Wiß (n 5).

[8] The question of sustainability is complex. It begins with a definitional challenge: in public economics, sustainability typically refers to a system's capacity to fund pension payments through contributions alone, without additional transfers Aaron George Grech, 'Assessing the Sustainability of Pension Reforms in Europe' (2013) 29 *Journal of International and Comparative Social Policy* 143. This narrow definition is contested, as it can tolerate or even encourage high inequalities in pension benefits. Some argue that any meaningful definition must also include adequacy. Aaron G Grech, 'What Makes Pension Reforms Sustainable?' (2018) 10 *Sustainability* 1. However, this broader definition is relevant only insofar as it illuminates the justifications states advance for their pension systems, and whether these meet the standards set by the European Convention on Human Rights. Beyond that, it lies outside this book's scope.

[9] Grech, 'What Makes Pension Reforms Sustainable?' (n 8); Grech, 'Assessing the Sustainability of Pension Reforms in Europe' (n 8).

In response, most states adopted wide-ranging reforms[10] that triggered intense political debate and social conflict, eventually giving rise to legal disputes.[11]

These legal disputes revolve around a central issue: What form of legal protection, if any, should pension entitlements receive? Answering this question requires examining how given legal frameworks classify such entitlements.[12] That classification determines both the degree of protection pensions enjoy and the limits of state discretion in reforming their systems.

Among the available legal frameworks for adjudicating pension disputes, the human right to property is both prominent and yet insufficiently explored in the literature.[13] This book examines what it means to conceive pensions as private property

[10] According to the OECD: 'Over the last 50 years, pension rules have changed in all OECD countries'. OECD, 'Pensions at Glance 2019: OECD and G20 Indicators' (OECD 2019) 37. Giuseppe Carone and others, 'Pension Reforms in the EU since the Early 2000's: Achievements and Challenges Ahead' [2016] European economy discussion paper 4. Beyond the European sphere, see Carmelo Mesa-Lago, *Evaluación de cuatro décadas de privatización de pensiones en América Latina (1980–2020): Promesas y realidades* (Friedrich Ebert Stiftung, FES 2020).

[11] These legal disputes have been a source of rich literature regarding the degrees to which judges are capable of deciding upon socio-economic matters, and the degrees to which these rights are justiciable and what follows for the role of the judge in those cases. See César Rodríguez-Garavito, 'Empowered Participatory Jurisprudence: Experimentation, Deliberation and Norms in Socioeconomic Rights Adjudication' in Katharine G Young (ed), *The Future of Economic and Social Rights* (Cambridge University Press 2019) 233; Malcolm Langford, 'Judicial Politics and Social Rights' in Katharine G Young (ed), *The Future of Economic and Social Rights* (Cambridge University Press 2019) 66; Malcolm Langford, 'The Impact of Public Interest Litigation: The Case of Socio-Economic Rights' (2021) 27 *Australian Journal of Human Rights* 505; David Bilchitz, 'Socio-Economic Rights, Economic Crisis, and Legal Doctrine' (2014) 12 *International Journal of Constitutional Law* 710; David Landau, 'The Reality of Social Rights Enforcement' (2012) 53 *Harvard International Law Journal* 189. The discussion of the place of judges, in general, and international judges in particular in judging these types of reform will be mentioned later on in the introduction.

[12] The classical approach to these questions is the lens provided by the constitutional or international protection of socio-economic rights: Rodríguez-Garavito (n 11); Samantha Besson, 'In What Sense Are Economic Rights Human Rights? Departing from Their Naturalistic Reading in International Human Rights Law' in Jahel Queralt and Bas van der Vossen (eds), *Economic Liberties and Human Rights* (Routledge, 2019) 45–68; Nikolaos A Papadopoulos, 'Paving the Way for Effective Socio-Economic Rights? The Domestic Enforcement of the European Social Charter System in Light of Recent Judicial Practice' in Claire Boost, Andrea Broderik, Fons Coomans and Roland Moerland (eds), *Myth or Lived Reality: On the (In) Effectiveness of Human Rights* (Springer, 2021) 99; B Goldblatt, 'The Right to Social Security' in Malcolm Langford and Katharine G Young (eds) *The Oxford Handbook of Economic and Social Rights* (Oxford University Press, 2022).

[13] There is great literature that has touched upon the question of the scope and extent of A1P1 like Egon Schwelb, 'The Protection of the Right of Property of Nationals under the First Protocol to the European Convention on Human Rights' [1964] *The American Journal of Comparative Law* 518; A Riza Çoban, *Protection of Property Rights within the European Convention on Human Rights* (Ashgate 2003); Camilo Basilio Schutte, *The European Fundamental Right of Property: Article 1 of Protocol No. 1 to the European Convention on Human Rights: Its Origins, Its Working, and Its Impact on National Legal Orders* (Kluwer 2004); Douglas Maxwell, *The Human Right to Property: A Practical Approach to Article 1 of Protocol No. 1 to the ECHR* (Bloomsbury Publishing 2022). Moreover, there are works regarding socio-economic rights and A1P1, like Ingrid Leijten, *Core Socio-Economic Rights and the European Court of Human Rights* (Cambridge University Press 2018); Ingrid Leijten, 'The Right to Minimum Subsistence and Property Protection under the ECHR: Never the Twain Shall Meet?' (2019) 21 *European Journal of Social Security* 307. Finally, there have been also other works touching on the right to social security and A1P1 in specific Ingrid Leijten, 'From Stec to Valkov: Possessions and Margins in the Social Security Case Law of the European Court of Human Rights' (2013) 13 *Human*

and what kind of protection arises from that characterisation. It further considers what this perspective reveals about the meaning, scope and limits of property protection in the pension context. To do so, it appeals to the framework provided by Article 1 of Protocol No. 1 (A1P1) of the European Convention on Human Rights (ECHR).[14]

Since the 1970s, A1P1 has given rise to a substantial body of jurisprudence, as residents across Europe have challenged pension reforms before the European Court of Human Rights (ECtHR) for breaching the right to the peaceful enjoyment of possessions. This jurisprudence has developed a set of rules, normative requirements and constraints that Council of Europe Member States are expected to observe.

The central claim of this book is that, although property protection under A1P1 is limited and qualified, the principles developed in the Court's jurisprudence have significant distributive implications. The ECtHR has interpreted A1P1 in a way that grants stronger protection to the most vulnerable retirees from the burdens of reform. These are individuals whose pensions are near subsistence level and who depend on them for survival. This distributive logic obliges policymakers to prioritise such retirees when designing reforms to comply with the Convention. It also shapes how property protection allocates burdens and gains of pension reforms and the extent to which it is concerned with intergenerational fairness.

I. Disputing Pension Reforms

Pension reforms are highly contested because they distribute resources across time.[15] Since there is no such thing as a 'neutral' distribution of resources,[16] reforms inevitably shift burdens and benefits,[17] reshaping inequalities within and between

Rights Law Review 309; Klaus Kapuy, 'Social Security and the European Convention on Human Rights: How an Odd Couple Has Become Presentable' (2007) 9 *European Journal of Social Security* 221; Ellie Palmer, 'Protecting Socio-Economic Rights through the European Convention on Human Rights: Trends and Developments in the European Court of Human Rights' (2009) 2 *Erasmus Law Review* 397; Mel Cousins, 'Legitimate Expectation and Social Security Law Under the European Convention of Human Rights' (2021) 23 *European Journal of Social Security* 24. However, this is the first book in which pensions are the core object of study under the private property framework of A1P1.

[14] *X v the Netherlands* App no 4130/69 (EComHR, 1971), Yearbook of the European Convention on Human Rights 224.

[15] Bernhard Ebbinghaus and Katja Möhring, 'Studying the Politics of Pension Reforms and Their Social Consequences' in Kenneth Nelson, Rense Nieuwenhuis and Mara Yerkes (eds), *Social Policy in Changing European Societies: Research Agendas for the 21st Century* (Edward Elgar, 2022) 85; Ebbinghaus and Wiß (n 4); Alan M Jacobs, 'The Politics of When: Redistribution, Investment and Policy Making for the Long Term' (2008) 38 *British Journal of Political Science* 193; Miroslav Verbič and Rok Spruk, 'Political Economy of Pension Reforms: An Empirical Investigation' (2019) 47 *European Journal of Law and Economics* 171; Helmuth Cremer and Pierre Pestieau, 'Reforming Our Pension System: Is It a Demographic, Financial or Political Problem?' (2000) 44 *European Economic Review* 974; Hassel, Naczyk and Wiß (n 5).

[16] R Dworkin, *Justice for Hedgehogs* (Harvard University Press 2011) 4.

[17] See Oliver Pamp, *Political Preferences and The Aging of Populations. Political-Economy Explanations of Pension Reform* (Springer VS 2015) 27. The difficulties of introducing compensation policies for distributive measures for transition losers has to do with difficulties associated with time-consistency

generations.[18] Pareto-efficient[19] reforms are rare.[20] Therefore, most reforms create winners and losers, provoking political tension[21] which often leads to legal mobilisation by affected individuals and groups.[22] The 'judicialisation' of socio-economic disputes reflects the centrality of pensions as a component of the social contract as well as the perceived need to secure accrued entitlements against abrupt or arbitrary change.[23] This trend is visible across Europe and beyond.[24]

and 'unobservability' of individual endowments. See R Fernandez and D Rodrik, 'Resistance to Reform: Status Quo Bias in the Presence of Individual-Specific Uncertainty' (1991) 81 *American Economic Review* 1146–55. For the very notion of transitional losers and transitional winners, see the excellent account by A Gosseries and M Hungerbühler, 'Rule Change and Intergenerational Justice' in JC Tremmel (ed), *Handbook of Intergenerational Justice* (Edward Elgar Publishers 2006).

[18] Pamp (n 17) 17.

[19] For a good explanation of Pareto-efficiency, Jean Hindriks and Gareth D Myles, *Intermediate Public Economics* (MIT Press 2013) 31–33.

[20] Pamp (n 17) 3.

[21] Patrik Marier, *Pension Politics: Consensus and Social Conflict in Ageing Societies* (Routledge 2008); Ebbinghaus and Möhring (n 15); Ondrej Schneider, 'Reforming Pensions in Europe: Economic Fundamentals and Political Factors' CESifo Working Paper, No 2572, Center for Economic Studies and ifo Institute (CESifo), Munich.

[22] Margot E Salomon, 'Of Austerity, Human Rights and International Institutions' (2015) 21 *European Law Journal* 521; Joe Wills and Ben TC Warwick, 'Contesting Austerity: The Potential and Pitfalls of Socioeconomic Rights Discourse' (2016) 23 *Indiana Journal of Global Legal Studies* 629; Rodríguez-Garavito (n 11); Langford, 'Judicial Politics and Social Rights' (n 11); Young (n 11); Wills and Warwick; Rodríguez-Garavito (n 11); Langford, 'Judicial Politics and Social Rights' (n 11); Dafni Diliagka, *The Legality of Public Pension Reforms in Times of Financial Crisis: The Case of Greece* (Nomos Verlagsgesellschaft mbH & Co KG 2018) <www.nomos-elibrary.de/index.php?doi=10.5771/9783845291574>; Elaine Dewhurst and Dafni Diliagka, 'Increasing Pension Ages in Greece and Ireland: A Question of Legitimate Expectations' (2014) 16 *European Journal of Social Security* 225.

[23] I need to be explicit about an assumption I will make about judicial review. I will assume that the ECtHR is sufficiently legitimate and well-placed to perform the task of ensuring the compliance of the ECHR. This is based on Andreas Follesdal, 'The Legitimacy of International Human Rights Review: The Case of the European Court of Human Rights' (2009) 40 *Journal of Social Philosophy* 595. I am aware of the unsettled debate around the question of whether judges are well-placed or legitimate to discuss distributive justice problems regarding benefits and burdens of socio-economic policies like pension reforms. Jeremy Waldron, 'The Core of the Case Against Judicial Review' (2006) 6 *The Yale Law Journal* 1346; Mark Tushnet, *Weak Courts, Strong Rights: Judicial Review and Social Welfare Rights in Comparative Constitutional Law* (Princeton University Press 2009); Doreen Lustig and Joseph HH Weiler, 'Judicial Review in the Contemporary World: Retrospective and Prospective' (2018) 16 *International Journal of Constitutional Law* 315; Caleb Nelson, 'Judicial Review of Legislative Purpose' (2008) 83 *NYU Law Review* 1784; David S Law, 'A Theory of Judicial Power and Judicial Review' (2008) 97 *Georgetown Law Journal* 723. With my assumption I do not intend to undermine the relevance or importance of these discussions, as they provide valuable insights into the complexities of the doctrine of separation of powers. However, they will be set aside from this book. I am more interested in understanding the standards used and set by the ECtHR bodies to assess the compliance of a given reform with A1P1. These standards and the reasons that justify them is what shapes its conception of the human right to a pension as property. Therefore, I will assume that these bodies are sufficiently legitimate to make these interpretations and establish them as normative standards that legislators must adhere to.

[24] Tushnet (n 23); Tara J Melish, 'Rethinking the Less as More Thesis: Supranational Litigation of Economic, Social, and Cultural Rights in the Americas' (2006) 39 *NYU Journal of International Law & Policy* 171; Oliver Gerstenberg, 'The Justiciability of Socio-Economic Rights, European Solidarity, and the Role of the Court of Justice of the EU' (2014) 33 *Yearbook of European Law* 245; Frank I Michelman, 'Socioeconomic Rights in Constitutional Law: Explaining America Away' (2008) 6 *International Journal of Constitutional Law* 663; Landau (n 11); César Rodríguez-Garavito, 'Beyond the Courtroom: The Impact of Judicial Activism on Socioeconomic Rights in Latin America' (2010) 89 *Texas Law Review* 1669; James Fowkes, 'Normal Rights, Just New: Understanding the Judicial Enforcement of Socioeconomic Rights' (2020) 68 *The American Journal of Comparative Law* 722.

Legal disputes about pension reforms engage questions about the permissible scope of legislative discretion, the degree to which participants should enjoy legal certainty and the protection of their expectations. Pension entitlements, after all, have long served as a central mechanism for shielding older cohorts from poverty, particularly during periods of economic crisis.[25]

To adjudicate pension disputes, courts must first determine the legal nature of the entitlements at stake.[26] The standard framework for thinking about pensions is the 'multi-pillar' model: statutory (first pillar), occupational or supplementary (second pillar) and voluntary savings (third pillar).[27] However, while helpful for comparative analysis, this model offers little guidance to a judge. It oversimplifies the institutional diversity of pension systems and does not capture the legal complexity of entitlements themselves.[28]

Pension systems are path-dependent[29] and shaped by political decisions on solidarity and risk-sharing.[30] In a sense, they have different 'identities'.[31] Therefore, even if most legislations and legal orders include the word 'pension' or even 'right to a pension', they can convey different things.[32] For instance, the right to rest,[33] a compensation for withdrawal from the labour market,[34] a part of the wage structure,[35]

[25] Tingyun Chen and others, *Inequality and Poverty across Generations in the European Union* (International Monetary Fund 2018) 5–6.

[26] From an etymological definition, the word 'Pension', in that account, comes from the Latin '*pensio*' or '*pensionem*' which in turn is a by-product of '*pendere*' which means to pay or to weigh. In fact, only from about 1391 onwards, the expression '*pencion*' in old French started to take modern notes by denoting an annuity. Kim De Witte, *De juridische kwalificatie van het recht op pensioen* (KULeuven 2017) 23.

[27] World Bank, *Averting the Old Age Crisis: Policies to Protect the Old and Promote Growth. Summary* (The World Bank 1994). Bruno Palier shows how that model was inspired by the Swiss system already in place since the 1970s. Bruno Palier, *Réformer Les Retraites* (Presses de Sciences Po 2021) 70. This model has been subject of great controversy over time. Peter R Orszag and Joseph E Stiglitz, 'Rethinking Pension Reform: Ten Myths about Social Security Systems' in Robert Holzmann and Joseph E Stiglitz (eds), *New Ideas About Old Age Security* (The World Bank, 2001) 17–57; Hervé Boulhol and Marius Lüske, 'What's New in the Debate About Pay-as-You-Go Versus Funded Pensions?' in Nazare da Costa Cabral and Nuno Cunha Rodrigues (eds), *The Future of Pension Plans in the EU Internal Market: Coping with Trade-Offs Between Social Rights and Capital Markets* (Springer, 2019) 37.

[28] Yves Stevens, *EU Pension Law* (Edward Elgar Publishing 2022); Yves Stevens, 'The Role of the Government in Creating or Enhancing the Access to Funded or Unfunded Pensions in the Modern Welfare State' in Nazare da Costa Cabral and Nuno Cunha Rodrigues (eds), *The Future of Pension Plans in the EU Internal Market: Coping with Trade-Offs Between Social Rights and Capital Markets* (Springer, 2019) 55; De Witte (n 27).

[29] Robert Holzmann, Richard Paul Hinz and Mark Dorfman, 'Pension Systems and Reform Conceptual Framework' (2008) 824 World Bank Discussion Paper; Mesa-Lago (n 10); Stevens, 'The Role of the Government in Creating or Enhancing the Access to Funded or Unfunded Pensions in the Modern Welfare State' (n 28).

[30] Erik Schokkaert and Philippe Van Parijs, 'Just Pensions: Reply to Myles, Oksanen and Fornero' (2003) 13 *Journal of European Social Policy* 276; Mark Hyde and John Dixon, 'A Just Retirement Pension System: Beyond Neoliberalism' (2009) 1 *Poverty & Public Policy* 1; Mark Hyde and Rory Shand, *Retirement, Pensions and Justice: A Philosophical Analysis* (Springer 2017).

[31] Stevens, *EU Pension Law* (n 28) 9–10.

[32] That is why there appear to be few, if any, purely *legal* typologies in the literature. ibid 8–9; De Witte (n 26).

[33] Stevens, *EU Pension Law* (n 28) 8–9.

[34] ibid.

[35] ibid.

deferred salary,[36] reward for services,[37] a form of savings,[38] a collective insurance,[39] a social insurance,[40] a form of shared citizenship,[41] or, as it will be explored in this book, a form of private property. Given this diversity of approaches, pensions are best seen, at the abstract level, as multi-dimensional constructs that combine institutional design with individual legal rights.[42] For courts, appealing to one or another conception would shape their expectations about the security of accrued rights, the distribution of risk between state and individual and the degrees of state discretion to adjust these entitlements.[43]

[36] For this, see the work by B Friot on how should we see the right to a pension as a deferred salary as opposed to a deferred compensation which is considered as a conception functional to a capitalist mode of production. Bernard Friot, *Le Travail, Enjeu Des Retraites* (Dispute (La) 2019). Moreover, in the legal literature, De Witte defends the idea of pensions as deferred salary as follows holds: 'pensions should aim at maintaining the standard of living that is threatened by the loss of income from work. Benefits that only aim at protecting the elderly from the state of need are not considered to be pensions'; De Witte (n 26) 26 (own translation from Dutch).

[37] This was one of the original conceptions of the right to a pension which was strictly linked with the schemes in place for the military in the modern states, especially in the new American republics after their independence. Ana María Muñoz Segura, *La Pensión de Vejez En Colombia. El Recorrido Histórico Entre La Exclusión y La Universalidad* (Universidad de los Andres 2019). We may also trace back the origins of a pension as a reward already in the Roman Empire with the guarantee of a piece of land after military campaigns, Yves Stevens, 'The Silent Pension Pillar Implosion' (2017) 19 *European Journal of Social Security* 98. Moreover, and on a literary note, that was the conception of the pension in Garcia Marquez's *No One Writes to the Colonel*. In a dialogue of the novel, the wife of the old colonel tells him 'You were also entitled to the veteran's pension after risking your neck in the civil war. Now everybody has his future assured and you're dying of hunger, completely alone.' Gabriel García Márquez, *No One Writes to the Colonel* (Penguin UK 2014) 57.

[38] This conception is overall used by those defending the individual accounts funded schemes. On that note see, for instance James A Dorn, 'Pension Reform in China: A Question of Property Rights' (2003) 23 *Cato Journal* 433, 434.

[39] This is one of the requirements set by the European Social Charter on how should states design their pension schemes: Frans Pennings and Gijsbert Vonk, *Research Handbook on European Social Security Law* (Edward Elgar Publishing 2023).

[40] This is usually the position taken by the ILO in multiple reports, starting from the standards-setting approach Albrecht Otting, 'International Labour Standards: A Framework for Social Security' (1993) 132 *International Labour Review* 163.

[41] A shared citizenship comes usually from the idea of the Beveridge Report that inspires non-contributory systems.

[42] Y Stevens has argued ever since his PhD thesis that it is a 'multidimensional hypernym'. A hypernym is a word that names a broad category that includes other words. 'Primate', for instance, is a hypernym for both 'chimpanzee' and 'human'. Stevens, 'The Role of the Government in Creating or Enhancing the Access to Funded or Unfunded Pensions in the Modern Welfare State' (n 28) 61–63.

[43] This also relates to the broader discussion on whether the Court takes a human rights or a standard-based approach. For a description of each approach, see Sol Minoldo and Enrique Peláez, 'What Should Guarantee Pensions Systems Designed with a Human Rights Approach?' in Fermina Rojo-Pérez and Gloria Fernández-Mayoralas (eds), *Handbook of Active Ageing and Quality of Life: From Concepts to Applications* (Springer, 2021) 201, 215; Krzysztof Hagemejer and Valérie Schmitt, 'Providing Social Security in Old Age: The International Labour Organization View' in SW Handayani and B Babajanian (eds), *Social Protection for Older Persons: Social Pension in Asia* (Asian Development Bank 2012); Krzysztof Hagemejer, 'Rights-Based Approach to Social Security Coverage Expansion. Closing the Coverage Gap: The Role of Social Pensions and Other Retirement Income Transfers' (2009) 57 World Bank.

II. Analytical Framework: Private Property under A1P1

This book adopts the right to property under A1P1 of the ECHR as the analytical framework for examining pensions and pension reforms' litigation. Justifying this choice requires addressing two separate questions. The first considers why property provides an appropriate conceptual lens for analysing pension entitlements. The second consists of why A1P1, in particular, provides an interesting framework for the study of pensions and for engaging into broader debates on social policy, resource distribution and pension design. Both of them will be addressed in turn.

A. Why Private Property?

Private property is not an obvious framework for analysing pensions or pension reforms.[44] Three challenges cast doubt on its suitability. First, property protection is often reduced to misleading caricatures that obscure its actual function. Second, there is persistent uncertainty regarding the scope of property protection in pension matters, particularly in the distinction between funded and unfunded schemes. Finally, property competes with other legal frameworks, such as social security or constitutional law, that appear more naturally attuned to pensions. Each will be addressed in turn.

i. Misleading Radical Views of Property

William Blackstone once suggested that '[t]here is nothing which so generally strikes the imagination, and engages the affections of mankind, as the right of property'.[45] This emotional appeal helps explain why, in everyday political discourse, two radical views of property persist: one that casts it in absolutist terms, and another that treats it with scepticism. Both framings raise doubts about whether property can serve as an adequate framework for analysing pensions and pension reforms.

For the absolutist view, which is a form of 'everyday libertarianism',[46] any public redistribution or regulation constitutes 'theft' or represents an illegitimate intrusion on someone's natural property rights.[47] Property becomes a sacrosanct

[44] Marie-Bénédicte Dembour, 'Gaygusuz Revisited: The Limits of the European Court of Human Rights' Equality Agenda' (2012) 12 *Human Rights Law Review* 689, 694.

[45] William Blackstone, *Commentaries on the Laws of England in Four Books. Notes Selected from the Editions of Archibold, Christian, Coleridge, Chitty, Stewart, Kerr, and Others, Barron Field's Analysis, and Additional Notes, and a Life of the Author by George Sharswood. In Two Volumes*, vol 1 (JB Lippincott Co 1893) ch 1.

[46] See ibid.

[47] Everyday libertarianism represents a caricatured understanding of how property, freedom, and their legal protection actually function. See Liam Murphy and Thomas Nagel, *The Myth of Ownership: Taxes and Justice* (Oxford University Press 2002).

right immune to any consideration of social welfare or collective needs.[48] For them, accepting otherwise would render property protection meaningless. On this account, altering existing distributions of resources is deemed unacceptable by definition. This stance rules out property as a helpful analytical framework, since it would condemn virtually any reform in advance.

The sceptic view approaches the property framework with suspicion.[49] Its departing point is assuming that property protection is used to advance a conservative or anti-redistributive agenda. Property law is read as a device that 'codes' existing power relations, thereby prioritising, shielding and hedging the interests of the wealthy against collective claims.[50] This scepticism draws on property law's historical role in entrenching inequality and rests on the assumption that property protection is indifferent to distribution, reproducing existing inequalities without regard to broader social circumstances.[51] From this perspective, property seems too compromised to provide a credible framework for pensions, which are explicitly designed to address distribution and solidarity.

These two sets of views are misleading because both reduce property and its legal protection to caricatures. One of the goals of this book is to show that property protection is more nuanced than those reductive views through the study of the ECtHR's jurisprudence. Against the absolutist view, the ECtHR's jurisprudence shows that property protection is not incompatible with redistribution and regulation. On the contrary, property rights operate within a broad regulatory space, so long as redistributive measures carry democratic legitimacy.[52] Against the sceptical view, the case law shows that property protection is not indifferent to existing inequalities. The Court calibrates the strength of A1P1's protection according to the vulnerability of claimants, giving more weight to those most dependent on their pensions. Ultimately, property protection under A1P1 is neither the rigid shield imagined by absolutists nor the empty tool of domination assumed by sceptics. It functions as a structured and flexible framework that can accommodate various purposes, like welfare and human flourishing,[53] but also redistribution and regulation, while still protecting core entitlements.

[48] See ibid.

[49] Paddy Ireland, 'Law and the Neoliberal Vision: Financial Property, Pension Privatisation and the Ownership Society' (2011) 62 *Northern Ireland Legal Quarterly* 1.

[50] Katharina Pistor, *The Code of Capital: How the Law Creates Wealth and Inequality* (Princeton University Press, Princeton University Press 2019).

[51] Crawford Brough Macpherson, *Property: Mainstream and Critical Positions* (University of Toronto Press 1999); Pistor (n 50).

[52] That is a social democratic vision of property regulation. See Tom Allen, 'Liberalism, Social Democracy and the Value of Property under the European Convention on Human Rights' (2010) 59 *International & Comparative Law Quarterly* 1055.

[53] Eric T Freyfogle, 'Private Ownership and Human Flourishing: An Exploratory Overview' (2013) 24 *Stellenbosch Law Review* 430; Gregory S Alexander, *Property and Human Flourishing* (Oxford University Press 2018). More on this discussion is presented in ch 2.

ii. The Scope Problem: Funded versus Pay-as-You-Go (PAYG)

Whenever it is accepted that the private property framework could be useful to analyse pensions and pension reforms, there is a discussion on the scope of such a framework. The question surrounding that discussion is as follows: Can property protection meaningfully encompass all pension entitlements, or only certain types of them?

This issue emerges from the long-standing debate between funded and PAYG systems.[54] Funded schemes, as opposed to PAYG schemes, are often assumed to create clear property rights through individual accounts or accumulated financial assets that participants 'own' and can defend against governmental interference.[55] This perception is reinforced by the ideal of the 'ownership society', promoting self-reliant 'worker-capitalists' who manage personal risks and accumulate financial assets.[56]

The conventional distinction between funded and unfunded schemes, and its implications for private property, presents itself as both coherent and persuasive. Funded schemes are claimed to create property interests, since their financing creates identifiable assets that belong to participants and therefore attract the protection of property law.[57] In this view, property is understood as a pre-political entitlement,[58] attaching automatically to the assets accumulated in the fund. Because property rights are thought to shield individuals from arbitrary interference, this understanding suggests that participants in funded schemes enjoy greater security than those in PAYG systems, whose entitlements rest on shifting political decisions. Funding, in this case, would hedge individuals from a perceived 'political risk'.[59] Furthermore, it is taken to guarantee more reliable payments in the face of demographic pressures that threaten the sustainability of unfunded pensions. This view, however, collapses under serious legal scrutiny.

The first difficulty of the conventional view is its definitional incoherence. It is highly contested what the relevant 'property' actually is:[60] The underlying assets managed by trustees? The account balance, or the promise of a future benefit?

[54] Didier Blanchet and Bertrand Villeneuve, 'Que Reste-t-Il Du Débat Répartition-Capitalisation?' [1997] *Revue d'économie financière* 157; Jan B Kuné, 'The Controversy of Funding versus Pay-as-You-Go: What Remains of the Debate?' (2001) 26 *The Geneva Papers on Risk and Insurance-Issues and Practice* 418; Boulhol and Lüske (n 27); Torben M Andersen and Joydeep Bhattacharya, 'The Intergenerational Welfare State and the Rise and Fall of Pay-as-You-Go Pensions' (2015) 127 *The Economic Journal* 896.

[55] Kuné (n 54). It is also known as hedging against 'political risk' Nikola Altiparmakov and Milan Nedeljković, '25 Years of Averting the Old Age Crisis in Eastern Europe' (2022) 22 *Global Social Policy* 84.

[56] Ireland (n 49).

[57] ibid.

[58] That is usually the departure point of some liberal (Lockean) and libertarian (Nozickian) approach to property protection: Jeremy Waldron, *The Right to Private Property* (Oxford University Press 1990); Gregory S Alexander and Eduardo M Peñalver, *An Introduction to Property Theory* (Cambridge University Press 2012). These theoretical discussions are described in ch 2.

[59] Kuné (n 54).

[60] Richard Nobles, 'Pensions as Property' (1994) 14 *Legal Studies* 345; Ireland (n 49).

Debates over surplus allocation, employer powers and trustee duties reveal that 'ownership' is intensely mediated, limited, and governed by complex rules that resist simplistic classifications.[61] The participant's relationship to pension assets, therefore, operates through multiple layers of institutional mediation that substantially qualify any straightforward notion of individual control or ownership.[62] Defined Benefit plans illustrate this difficulty. Although funded, they do not confer property rights during the accumulation phase.[63] Beneficiaries are often unaware of the destination of their contributions, since the obligation to pay the promised benefit ultimately rests with the plan sponsor.

The second difficulty concerns a categorical error in defining what makes an entitlement property. The conventional view holds that the method of financing the scheme (funding) transforms an entitlement into property. However, whether an entitlement qualifies as property does not depend on the method of financing of a pension scheme but on its legal recognition. Property is, ultimately, an artefact of law.[64] It is therefore the law that determines, for instance, that Defined Contribution schemes generate property rights over accumulated assets. By the same logic, the law could also recognise other entitlements, such as unfunded schemes, as property and extend similar protection. Economists such as Peter Diamond have long argued that unfunded claims could and should be protected in this way.[65] In practice, this is precisely what happens in various jurisdictions where property clauses already cover PAYG entitlements.[66]

[61] Blackburn (n 2); Nobles (n 60); Ireland (n 49).

[62] Nobles (n 60).

[63] ibid. In the Netherlands there was a debate on whether accruals in funded second pillar plans were property in the context of the new pension reform. Systematically, Dutch Courts have denied such a claim Erik Lutjens, 'Wet Toekomst Pensioenen: Wet Toekomst Pensioenen: Nieuwe Methode Pensioenopbouw – Een Onzekerder Pensioen En Een Fors Aantal Procedures' [2023] *Nederlands Juristenblad*; Erik Lutjens, 'Invaren Pensioen: De Relevantie van Recht Op Eigendom' (2021) 10 *Tijdschrift voor Arbeidsrecht in Context* 3.

[64] As Bentham would beautifully write: 'Property and law are born together, and die together. Before laws were made there was no property; take away laws, and property ceases'; Jeremy Bentham, 'The Theory of Legislation' in John Plamenatz (ed), *Readings from Liberal Writers* (Routledge 1965) 3. Joseph William Singer, 'Property as the Law of Democracy' (2013) 63 *Duke Law Journal* 1287. For further discussion on these points, see ch 2 of this book.

[65] Peter Diamond, 'Insulation of Pensions from Political Risk' in Salvador Valdes-Prieto (ed), *The Economics of Pensions, Principles, Policies and International Experience* (Cambridge University Press 1997); Boulhol and Lüske (n 27).

[66] It is the case of Germany, Hungary, the United States of America and Austria. Pál Sonnevend, *Eigentumsschutz Und Sozialversicherung: Eine Rechtsvergleichende Analyse Anhand Der Rechtsprechung Des Bundesverfassungsgerichts Und Des Ungarischen Verfassungsgerichts*, vol 185 (Springer-Verlag 2007); Charles Reich, 'The New Property' (1964) 73 *Yale Law Journal* 733; Charles A Reich, 'Social Welfare in the Public-Private State' (1965) 114 *University of Pennsylvania Law Review* 487; Charles A Reich, 'Individual Rights and Social Welfare: The Emerging Legal Issues' in Peter Robson (ed), *Welfare Law* (Routledge 2020); Rick J Hecker, 'On the Subject of Property and Social Security: A Traditional Analysis' (2012) 7 *Liberty University Law Review* 143; Danny Pieters, 'Security in Social Security: Reflections from a Legal Point of View' (2012) 67 *Pravnik* 21; Bob De Mars, Pieters, Danny and Schoukens, Paul '"Security"' as General Principle of Social Security Law in Europe: Conclusions on Legislative Aspects' in Bob De Mars, Pieters, Danny and Schoukens, Paul (eds), *Security: A General Principle of Social Security Law in Europe* (Europa Law Publishing, 2010) 605–36. As it will be clear from ch 4 onwards, it is also the case in Europe through A1P1 and the ECtHR.

The third difficulty of the conventional view lies in the illusion that funding ensures security of future benefits. The existence of assets in a funded scheme appears to offer stronger guarantees to beneficiaries when compared to the uncertain willingness of future workers to pay contributions. However, this is nothing but a superficial impression. The assets in funded schemes are not 'bags' of resources waiting to be distributed but financial claims whose value depends on the performance of markets, the solvency of issuers and the readiness of governments and employers to stand behind them. Therefore, both funded and unfunded pensions ultimately amount to claims on future output generated by the labour of future workers.[67] The security of pension promises, hence, rests not on whether the scheme is funded or unfunded, nor on whether entitlements are legally described as property, but on the productive capacity of the economy and the political commitment to sustain intergenerational transfers.[68] To assume that property provides the foundation of security is to confuse appearance with substance, for in practice, property plays little role in ensuring that benefits are actually paid.

Taken together, these flaws reveal that the conventional view on funding, property and pensions is neither a coherent legal principle nor a sound theoretical claim, but rather a rhetorical and political position.[69] The meaningful legal question is not whether the property framework is only relevant to one or another particular scheme. Instead, it is what specific interests and expectations are being protected and how legal frameworks define, allocate and enforce those rights. That is precisely the purpose of this book, which will clarify the scope, limits and conditions under which such property protection exists under A1P1 for pension entitlements.

iii. The Proxy Challenge: Competing Legal Frameworks

The third challenge of adopting this framework goes as follows. Even if one accepts that property analysis can meaningfully apply to all pension entitlements, is private property an adequate conceptual framework for understanding and assessing pensions? After all, pension entitlements are governed by specific legal regimes like social security law,[70] or broader commitments like constitutional guarantees of socio-economic rights[71] and other international human rights instruments

[67] Nicholas Barr, *Economics of the Welfare State* (Oxford University Press, USA 2020); Barr and Diamond (n 1); Nicholas Adrian Barr, *The Welfare State as Piggy Bank: Information, Risk, Uncertainty, and the Role of the State* (Oxford University Press 2001); Nicholas Barr and Peter Diamond, *Reforming Pensions: Principles and Policy Choices* (Oxford University Press 2008); Orszag and Stiglitz (n 27).

[68] Barr, *Economics of the Welfare State* (n 67); Barr and Diamond (n 1); Barr, *The Welfare State as Piggy Bank: Information, Risk, Uncertainty, and the Role of the State* (n 67); Barr and Diamond (n 67); Orszag and Stiglitz (n 27).

[69] Nobles (n 60). There is also a great discussion in the literature about the economic assumptions made by promotors of funding as a superior mechanism within pension systems. See Orszag and Stiglitz (n 28). More recently Altiparmakov and Nedeljković (n 55); Mesa-Lago (n 10).

[70] Pennings and Vonk (n 39); Jean-Jacques Dupeyroux, Michel Borgetto and Robert Lafore, *Droit de La Sécurité Sociale*, vol 18 (Dalloz 2015).

[71] Young (n 22).

of social security.[72] These frameworks often address questions of entitlement security, eligibility, adjustment[73] and reform in ways specifically tailored to the social protection function of pensions. Sceptical views on property could argue that it risks distorting the nature of pensions by importing the logic of individual ownership into a domain rooted in solidarity, collective risk-sharing and social citizenship.[74] From this perspective, property is an unnecessary or even misleading proxy for the real issues at stake.

This critique is important and deserves to be taken seriously. Social security law, constitutional law or human rights law frameworks rightly emphasise collective responsibility, redistribution, and the social contract between generations.[75] They are the obvious framework to address the questions of pension reform, and about sustainability, adequacy and equity in pension design. However, there are at least three reasons to insist on exploring the property approach to pension entitlements.

First, property protection has traditionally functioned as a way of stabilising expectations and securing entitlements against arbitrary interference.[76] By framing pensions as property, legal analysis underscores the normative relevance of both individual security and dependency of beneficiaries. In doing so, it examines what should be the burden that states must provide when justifying reforms affecting accrued rights or expected benefits.

Second, property law is not neutral. Recognising pensions as property forces judges and legal scholars to confront the distributive choices involved in pension reform from the perspective of property: whose security is prioritised, whose interests are weighed and on what grounds interference is justified.[77] It also places reform within a framework of specific legal accountability, subjecting state action to a relatively high standard that is widely accepted and recognised in all liberal-democratic legal systems.[78]

Third, adopting a property framework can also help illuminate the conditions under which pensions can function as reliable sources of income security in old age. It requires specifying what exactly is being protected – accrued benefits, future expectations, underlying assets – and against what forms of interference.[79] This clarity is essential in systems with diverse institutional arrangements and competing policy goals.

[72] De Mars and others (n 66); Pieters (n 66); Isabelle Hachez, *Le Principe de Standstill Dans Le Droit Des Droits Fondamentaux: Une Irréversibilité Relative* (Bruylant 2008).

[73] Hachez (n 72).

[74] Quentin Detienne, *Droit Économique Européen et Systèmes de Pension de Retraite Nationaux. Quelles Influences Pour Quels Résultats?* (Presses Universitaires de Liège 2023).

[75] Dupeyroux, Borgetto and Lafore (n 70); Pennings and Vonk (n 39); Goldblatt (n 12).

[76] James W Ely, *The Guardian of Every Other Right: A Constitutional History of Property Rights* (Oxford University Press 2008).

[77] Hanoch Dagan, *Property: Values and Institutions* (Oxford University Press 2011); David Anderson, 'Compensation for Interference with Property' [1999] *European Human Rights Law Review* 543; George Gretton, 'The Protection of Property Rights' in Chris Himsworth and Alan Boyle (eds), *Human Rights and Scots Law: Comparative Perspectives on the Incorporation of the ECHR* (Hart Publishing 2002).

[78] Gretton (n 68); Ely (n 77); John Kekes, 'The Right to Private Property: A Justification' (2010) 27 *Social Philosophy and Policy* 1.

[79] Sonnevend (n 66).

By addressing these three challenges, the choice of private property as a framework becomes justified. The next step is to explain the value of choosing A1P1 as the property framework for the analysis in this book.

B. Why Article 1 of the First Protocol?

Three reasons justify choosing the framework provided by A1P1. First, A1P1 provides a unified but flexible standard of property protection that applies across the Council of Europe. Second, it allows us to fill a doctrinal gap. Although pensions have long been litigated under A1P1, sustained scholarly analysis of how the property framework operates in this context remains limited. Finally, because the level of analysis is sufficiently broad to set broad normative requirements that apply to all Council of Europe states regardless of their domestic pension model, without prescribing specific institutional design.

i. A Unified and Authoritative Framework

Many legal orders treat pension rights as an interest to be protected under the property clause. In Europe, for instance, the German and Hungarian constitutional courts have interpreted that pensions fall within the realm of property protection.[80] The United Kingdom has also discussed the degrees of property protection provided by its pension plans.[81] Beyond Europe, in the United States, the constitutional doctrine evolved from treating welfare benefits as mere gratuities to recognising statutory entitlements as protected property.[82] Moreover, at the regional human rights level, the Inter-American Court of Human Rights has also interpreted pensions as being protected under the property clause.[83]

One of the strengths of A1P1 is offering a unified and authoritative framework for understanding property relations.[84] It is well known that international human rights law is exerting a growing influence on shaping discussions and understanding rights at the domestic level.[85] Human rights law serves as a robust framework within which interactions between the state and various agents unfold.[86] While debates persist regarding the automatic applicability of international law, including human rights law, in domestic legislation (eg the discussion between monists

[80] ibid.

[81] Nobles (n 60).

[82] Hecker (n 66).

[83] *Case of the Five Pensioners (Cinco Pensionistas) v Peru*, Inter-Am. Ct. H.R., Ser. C No. 98 (28 Feb 2003).

[84] Maxwell (n 13).

[85] Olivier De Schutter, *International Human Rights Law. Cases, Materials, Commentary* 3rd edn (Cambridge University Press 2019).

[86] This is part of the phenomenon of 'internationalisation' of law. For a recent comprehensive account, see Marcelo Dias Varella, *Internationalization of Law Globalization, International Law and Complexity* (Springer International Publishing 2014).

and dualists), the influence of that field is undeniable.[87] The Court's interpretations of the Convention are binding for the 46 Member States of the Council of Europe,[88] providing the leading transnational standard for property protection of pension entitlements across Europe. National courts, and even the Court of Justice of the European Union (CJEU), regularly cite and apply this jurisprudence,[89] and policymakers must anticipate its requirements when designing and implementing reforms.[90] By examining how the ECtHR interprets property to include pensions, this book explores the benefits as well as the limits of individual rights-based approaches to securing pension rights.

ii. Filling a Doctrinal Gap

Much of the existing literature offers valuable insights into socio-economic rights under the Convention,[91] the degrees of positive obligations,[92] general questions about access to justice[93] and the interpretation of property rights more generally.[94] However, there has been less sustained attention to how the property framework operates in the specific context of pensions, what it requires of policymakers and what limits it places on reform. This book aims to address that gap by clarifying the normative commitments embedded in this framework and examining how it can contribute to ensuring security, fairness and predictability in pension policy.

iii. General Standards with Binding Effect

The level of analysis provided by the ECtHR is particularly well-suited to this book because it enables the overcoming of the specific institutional details of

[87] Luzius Wildhaber, 'The European Convention on Human Rights and International Law' (2007) 56 *International & Comparative Law Quarterly* 217.

[88] Samantha Besson, 'The Erga Omnes Effect of Judgments of the European Court of Human Rights: What's in a Name?' in Samantha Besson (ed), *The European Court of Human Rights after Protocol 14* (Schulthess 2011) 125.

[89] Sabrina Praduroux, 'Property and Expropriation: Two Concepts Revisited in the Light of the Case Law of the European Court of Human Rights and the European Court of Justice' (2019) 8 *European Property Law Journal* 172.

[90] Besson (n 88); Oddný Mjöll Arnardóttir, 'Res Interpretata, Erga Omnes Effect and the Role of the Margin of Appreciation in Giving Domestic Effect to the Judgments of the European Court of Human Rights' (2017) 28 *European Journal of International Law* 819.

[91] Leijten, *Core Socio-Economic Rights and the European Court of Human Rights* (n 13); Leijten, 'From Stec to Valkov: Possessions and Margins in the Social Security Case Law of the European Court of Human Rights' (n 13); Leijten, 'The Right to Minimum Subsistence and Property Protection under the ECHR: Never the Twain Shall Meet?' (n 13).

[92] Vladislava Stoyanova, *Positive Obligations under the European Convention on Human Rights: Within and Beyond Boundaries* (Oxford University Press 2023).

[93] Kevin Hartmann-Cortés, 'On Future Retirees' Legal Standing: Rethinking A1P1 Admissibility in Pension Reform Cases' [2025] *The European Convention on Human Rights Law Review*.

[94] Pieter Van Dijk and Godefridus JH Van Hoof, *Theory and Practice of the European Convention on Human Rights* (Martinus Nijhoff Publishers 2023); Maxwell (n 13).

individual pension systems or reforms. Both the text of the Convention and the Court's case law make clear that there is no requirement to adopt any particular financing model, whether contributory or non-contributory, PAYG or funded.[95] Instead, the Convention framework insists that, regardless of the approach, states must comply with specific outcomes, including equality, adequacy and non-discrimination.[96]

Rather than offering a detailed legal analysis of individual national systems or technical design questions, this book focuses on how the Convention can shape and discipline these institutional choices. Its goal is to clarify the legal standards and normative commitments embedded in the ECtHR's property jurisprudence, and to explore how these standards can shape, constrain and potentially improve the distributive outcomes of pension reforms.

That being said, these three reasons also point to the limits of this book. Because the analysis is anchored in the ECHR and the jurisprudence of the ECtHR, its claims remain confined to that legal context. The doctrinal analysis hereby made cannot by itself provide comprehensive answers to the pressing questions of today's reforms. Hence, this book does not address broader policy debates, such as the relative merits of PAYG and funded systems or questions of optimal funding strategies. Those debates involve complex normative and empirical judgements about sustainability, adequacy and intergenerational equity that go beyond the scope of A1P1.[97] What the book does offer is an account of how such debates, and their possible solutions, can be read through the lens of A1P1 protection and of what this framework requires of pension reform.

III. Methodology

This book adopts a doctrinal approach or legal doctrine.[98] Legal doctrine aims to interpret, systematise and clarify the principles and rules of a legal framework on its own terms.[99] It seeks to resolve internal inconsistencies, ensure conceptual coherence and adapt legal reasoning to new social contexts.[100] Despite criticisms of narrowness or abstraction, doctrinal analysis remains essential to legal

[95] See more in ch 4.

[96] ibid.

[97] For a good recapitulation of what is going on with such a debate, see Altiparmakov and Nedeljković (n 55); Boulhol and Lüske (n 27); Mesa-Lago (n 10).

[98] Mark Van Hoecke, 'Legal Doctrine: Which Method (s) for What Kind of Discipline?' in Mark Van Hoecke (ed), *Methodologies of Legal Research: Which Kind of Method for What Kind of Discipline?* (Hart Publishing 2011) 11.

[99] Pauline C Westerman, 'Open or Autonomous? A Debate on Legal Methodology as a Reflection of the Debate on Law' in Mark Van Hoecke (ed), *Methodologies of Legal Research* (Hart Publishing 2010).

[100] James Gordley, 'The State's Private Law and Legal Academia' (2008) 56 *The American Journal of Comparative Law* 639; Jan M Smits, 'What Is Legal Doctrine? On the Aims and Methods of Legal-Dogmatic Research' [2015] *Maastricht European Private Law Institute* 5.

scholarship and practice.[101] It provides the clarity and reliability that courts, legislators and practitioners need when addressing complex legal questions, especially in areas such as pension reform that directly affect individuals' livelihoods.[102]

At its core, this approach treats the law both as the object of study and as the analytical framework.[103] This book focuses on key legal concepts – including property, possessions, equality, legitimate expectations and entitlements – as they are defined and interpreted by the Court. The aim is to make sense of these notions as they function within the legal system itself, rather than imposing external theoretical models.[104] Yet, to avoid a purely 'black-letter' perspective,[105] this book also appeals to the insights from economics, public finance, philosophy and actuarial science literature.

A relevant methodological assumption to state is that this book adopts a functionalist perspective on human rights law.[106] Functionalism contrasts with foundationalist approaches that seek universal moral grounds for rights.[107] Instead, it focuses on their practical roles: defining the requirements of good governance and setting limits on state power in its relationship with individuals.[108] From this perspective, human rights serve both as commitment devices promoting shared well-being[109] and as constraints that protect individuals against disproportionate burdens.[110]

In terms of data, this book analyses primary legal materials, including treaty texts and authoritative interpretations by judicial and quasi-judicial bodies. It examines relevant case law in detail, with particular attention to decisions from the ECtHR available through the HUDOC database.

[101] Westerman (n 99); Van Hoecke (n 98).

[102] Anne Ruth Mackor, 'Explanatory Non-Normative Legal Doctrine. Taking the Distinction between Theoretical and Practical Reason Seriously' in Mark Van Hoecke (ed), *Methodologies of Legal Research. Which Kind of Method for What Kind of Discipline?* (Hart Publishing 2011); Joseph William Singer, 'Normative Methods for Lawyers' (2008) 56 *UCLA Law Review* 899.

[103] Westerman (n 99).

[104] Rob Van Gestel and Hans-Wolfgang Micklitz, 'Why Methods Matter in European Legal Scholarship' (2014) 20 *European Law Journal* 292.

[105] Van Hoecke (n 98).

[106] I take the labelling of both groups from a categorization used by John Tasioulas in John Tasioulas, 'Towards a Philosophy of Human Rights' (2012) 65 *Current Legal Problems* 1. That being said, two caveats. First, this is a simplification of a rich debate which relevance has only increased in the last decade. Second, Tasioulas uses those categories to advance the thesis according to which the current discussion of IHRL has, according to his own terms, regrettably fallen in the allures of 'foundationalism' or 'functionalism'.

[107] ibid.

[108] Laura Valentini, 'In What Sense Are Human Rights Political? A Preliminary Explanation' (2012) 60 *Political Studies* 180.

[109] 'All forms of lawmaking, whether legislative, judicial or other means, should be guided by our shared understanding of the requirements of the good society and that, by way of practical reasoning, we can work out the basic forms of human good'; John Finnis, *Natural Law and Natural Rights* (Oxford University Press 2011) 214.

[110] Conor Gearty, 'Human Rights: The Necessary Quest for Foundations' in Costas Douzinas and Conor Gearty (eds), *The Meanings of Rights: The Philosophy and Social Theory of Human Rights* (Cambridge University Press 2014).

IV. Structure of the Book

The book is structured in six chapters and a conclusion, with each chapter addressing a specific question in the overall analysis. Chapter one situates the ECtHR's institutional role and interpretive method, explaining its authority in defining Convention rights. Chapter two examines the theoretical foundations of property protection under A1P1. Chapter three analyses the notion of 'possessions', focusing on the Court's autonomous definitions and the concept of legitimate expectations. Chapter four traces the Court's earlier formalistic doctrine (1972–96), which constrained protection by relying on distinctions based on funding and contributions. Chapter five explores the shift to a functionalist approach (1996 to the present), which broadened protection to recognise pensions' role as a social security mechanism. Chapter six analyses the acceptability test and proportionality review, arguing that despite the margin of appreciation afforded to states, the Court's reasoning reveals an implicit prioritarian concern with protecting vulnerable retirees. Finally, a general conclusion section brings together the main findings and reflects on their broader policy and judicial implications.

1

How the European Court of Human Rights Interprets the Convention

Introduction

The European Court of Human Rights (ECtHR; the Court) was established in 1959 to enforce the European Convention on Human Rights (ECHR; the Convention), a treaty adopted in 1950 under the auspices of the Council of Europe to protect basic civil and political liberties.[1] While the Convention is formally limited to those rights, the Court has gradually extended its reach by reinterpreting their scope and content to encompass certain socio-economic interests.[2] Notably, it has treated some pension entitlements as possessions under the Convention's property clause set out in Article 1 of Protocol No 1 (A1P1). This development and its implications for pension policy are the main subjects of this book.

This chapter describes the ECtHR's institutional role and interpretative methods. It has two aims. First, to provide the reader with a basic framework for understanding how the Court interprets rights under the Convention. This includes its procedures, its supervisory function and the interpretive techniques it uses to define the content of rights.[3] Introducing them here provides the tools needed to follow the Court's reasoning on private property.[4]

The second aim is to clarify the scope of the book. This is not a broad study of pension systems or social policy design. It is an analysis of how a supranational court, operating within a constrained institutional setting, approaches legal claims involving social and economic issues through the framework of private

[1] Alfred William Brian Simpson, *Human Rights and the End of Empire: Britain and the Genesis of the European Convention* (Oxford University Press, USA 2004).

[2] Birte Wassenberg, *History of the Council of Europe* (Council of Europe 2013); David John Harris and others, *Law of the European Convention on Human Rights* (Oxford University Press 2023).

[3] Samantha Besson, 'The Erga Omnes Effect of Judgments of the European Court of Human Rights: What's in a Name?' in Samantha Besson (ed), *The European Court of Human Rights after Protocol 14* (Schulthess 2011) 125; Rudolf Bernhardt, 'Human Rights and Judicial Review: The European Court of Human Rights' in David M Beatty (ed), *Human Rights and Judicial Review: A Comparative Perspective* (Brill Nijhoff 1994) 297–319.

[4] Douglas Maxwell, *The Human Right to Property: A Practical Approach to Article 1 of Protocol No. 1 to the ECHR* (Bloomsbury Publishing 2022).

property.[5] For that reason, its institutional design plays a central role in this analysis.[6] The individual complaints mechanism, which gives direct access to the Court, is balanced by principles like subsidiarity and the margin of appreciation.[7] These constraints shape the limits of its authority in reviewing domestic policies under the Convention's framework. The Court's evolving jurisprudence reflects the tension between maintaining its legitimacy as an international tribunal while effectively protecting individual rights across diverse legal systems.[8]

This chapter is divided into five sections. Section I traces the historical context of the ECHR and its jurisprudential expansion, examining how the Court's role has evolved from its modest origins to its current position as a key player in the European human rights protection framework. Section II examines the Court's position as guardian of Convention rights through the system for individual complaints. Section III discusses the Court's interpretative methods, which enable adapting Convention provisions to contemporary challenges while maintaining its institutional legitimacy. Section IV examines the Court's structured assessment framework for evaluating rights violations. Finally, section V concludes with an examination of the ECtHR's interaction with national legal systems, focusing on how its jurisprudence influences domestic law and policy-making, particularly in the realm of social protection.

I. Origins and Evolution of the Convention System

A. Post-War Europe and Human Rights

The ECHR emerged from the ruins of World War II as part of Europe's commitment to prevent future atrocities.[9] Signed on 4 November 1950 by the Member States of the newly established Council of Europe, the Convention represented a revolutionary step: for the first time, states committed themselves to a binding system of individual rights protection enforced by a permanent Court.[10]

The Convention's preamble affirms its commitment to values such as individual freedom, political liberty and the rule of law. It also expresses the belief that these principles should contribute to fostering economic and social progress.[11] These values seemingly embody a shared Western European vision meant to

[5] Besson (n 3).

[6] Pieter Van Dijk and Godefridus JH Van Hoof, *Theory and Practice of the European Convention on Human Rights* (Martinus Nijhoff Publishers 2023).

[7] Besson (n 3); Bernhardt (n 3); Maxwell (n 4).

[8] Eileen Denza, 'The Relationship between International and National Law' (2014) 4 *International Law* 412.

[9] It was open for signatures in 1950 and enforceable since September 1953. Simpson (n 1).

[10] Harris and others (n 2).

[11] Statute of the Council of Europe and texts of Statutory Character. London, 5 May 1949. European Treaty Series No 1. Preamble and art 1.

serve as a bulwark against communism.[12] The Council of Europe's institutional framework – including the Committee of Ministers, Consultative Assembly and General Secretariat – was designed to implement this vision through two different yet complementary instruments: the Convention, which protects civil and political rights, and the European Social Charter, which addresses socio-economic rights such as housing, work and social security.[13] While both form part of Europe's human rights architecture, this book focuses exclusively on the Convention and the evolution of its enforcement mechanisms.

The Convention's revolutionary character lies in its enforcement mechanism. For the first time, sovereign states accepted binding obligations to guarantee specific human rights to all residents in their territory, under the supervision of an international court. This institutional innovation established the ECHR as a central instrument in international human rights law, which other regional treaties in Africa and the Americas have replicated.[14]

B. The Convention's Scope and Character

The Convention has a dual nature. On the one hand, it functions as an international treaty, subject to interpretation in accordance with the 1969 Vienna Convention on the Law of Treaties. On the other hand, the Convention is materially constitutional, as it sets out fundamental principles and rights that form the legal foundation for states bound by it.[15] These principles and rights include the right to life, the prohibition of torture, the right to a fair trial and freedoms of thought, conscience and religion.[16]

The Convention's emphasis on civil and political rights rather than broader socio-economic guarantees reflected a strategic choice to adopt a concise and broadly acceptable text.[17] This focus on rights 'essential to a democratic society' has shaped both the Convention's character and the Court's subsequent interpretative role. Initially ratified by 22 states, the Convention has since been accepted by all 46 active members of the Council of Europe, evolving from a post-war agreement into a comprehensive regional framework for human rights protection.[18]

[12] Samuel Moyn, *The Last Utopia: Human Rights in History* (Harvard University Press 2012) 1; Harris and others (n 2) 1.

[13] Wassenberg (n 2).

[14] Harris and others (n 2) 30.

[15] Besson (n 3).

[16] Marie-Bénédicte Dembour, 'Gaygusuz Revisited: The Limits of the European Court of Human Rights' Equality Agenda' (2012) 12 *Human Rights Law Review* 689.

[17] Tom Allen, 'Liberalism, Social Democracy and the Value of Property under the European Convention on Human Rights' (2010) 59 *International & Comparative Law Quarterly* 1055, 1064; Pierre-Henri Teitgen, CE Consult. Ass, Debates, 1st Session, p 408, 19 August 1949, cited in Harris and others (n 2); Kevin Boyle, 'The European Experience: The European Convention on Human Rights' (2009) 40 *Victoria University of Wellington Law Review* 167.

[18] The Council of Europe took the determination to expel Russia after the invasion to Ukraine in February 2022. Therefore, even if ratified by Russia, the Council of Europe only has 46 active members.

C. The ECHR's Focus: Civil and Political Rights

Human rights are traditionally classified into civil and political rights, often referred to as *negative rights*, and socio-economic rights, usually called *positive rights*, depending on the type of obligation they impose on the state.[19] Negative rights, grounded in eighteenth-century natural rights thought, are designed to protect individuals from state interference and typically require governments to abstain from action.[20] In contrast, positive rights emerged in the twentieth century, requiring states to take affirmative steps to provide access to goods and services such as work, housing, education and social security.[21]

Some legal and political discourses draw a hierarchy between civil and political rights and socio-economic rights, often based on perceived differences in their enforceability. In their view, civil and political rights are considered essential to a democratic society, while socio-economic rights are viewed as aspirational policy goals with limited justiciability.[22] This distinction, however, has been severely criticised.[23] Critics contend that the separation is both conceptually weak and practically unworkable. Even the so-called negative rights often require substantial public resources and institutional infrastructure to be effectively enforced. Recognising the positive obligations embedded in all categories of rights challenges the validity of the traditional negative – positive divide.[24]

Historical analysis further undermines the idea that negative rights hold chronological or normative priority over positive rights. The standard narrative suggests that civil and political rights were articulated and accepted earlier, and thus occupy a more fundamental place in human rights law. However, historical evidence shows that the classification of rights into 'negative' and 'positive' did not arise from principled theoretical commitments. Instead, it emerged as a pragmatic solution to diplomatic tensions during United Nations negotiations, particularly

[19] For a classification of human rights as first, second (and so on) generations see Jack Donnelly, *Universal Human Rights in Theory and Practice* (Cornell University Press 2013) 34–37; That discussion has also been framed within the notions of 'liberties and subsidies' in Stephen Holmes and Cass R Sunstein, *The Cost of Rights: Why Liberty Depends on Taxes* (WW Norton & Company 2000) 39; However, a recent book discussing the historical roots of the generational classification strongly disputes its usefulness and accurateness. In fact, it is labelled as 'misguiding' Steven LB Jensen and Charles Walton, *Social Rights and the Politics of Obligation in History* (Cambridge University Press 2022) chs 1 and 12; Cécile Fabre, *Social Rights under the Constitution: Government and the Decent Life* (Oxford University Press 2000) 41.

[20] Harris and others (n 2); Holmes and Sunstein (n 19) 36.

[21] Charles Fried, *Right and Wrong* (Harvard University Press 1978) 110; Eibe H Riedel, *Social Security as a Human Right: Drafting a General Comment on Article 9 ICESCR-Some Challenges*, vol 26 (Springer Science & Business Media 2006) 46; Fabre (n 19) 40.

[22] Harris and others (n 2) 3.

[23] Ellie Palmer, 'Protecting Socio-Economic Rights through the European Convention on Human Rights: Trends and Developments in the European Court of Human Rights' (2009) 2 *Erasmus Law Review* 397.

[24] Jensen and Walton (n 19).

in the drafting of post-war human rights instruments. The distinction reflects political compromise more than any deep normative divide.[25]

Instead of a hierarchy that separates rights based on their enforceability or origin, an alternative view emphasises their interdependence. On this account, the meaningful exercise of civil and political rights depends on the fulfilment of basic socio-economic needs.[26] Human rights demonstrate fundamental interconnections that transcend the formal classification of state obligations. This recognition has led to the development of the doctrine of the indivisibility of human rights, which positions socio-economic rights not as secondary to civil and political freedoms but as integral to a unified rights framework.[27] This conceptual shift has elevated socio-economic rights to the status of legitimate entitlements, while underscoring their instrumental role in sustaining democratic governance and enabling the effective enjoyment of fundamental liberties.[28]

The ECtHR formally acknowledged the interdependence of rights in its landmark 1979 decision *Airey v Ireland*. In that judgment, it recognised that material conditions can fundamentally affect an individual's ability to exercise their Convention rights.[29] However, the Court has carefully circumscribed this recognition by maintaining clear jurisdictional boundaries. In *N v the United Kingdom*, it explicitly stated that '[a]lthough many of the rights it contains have implications of a social or economic nature, the Convention is essentially directed at the protection of *civil and political rights*'.[30]

The Court's acceptance of the interdependence of rights led it to nevertheless require applicants to demonstrate a direct link between their claim and a right explicitly protected by the Convention.[31] This approach enables the Court to address matters not expressly covered by the Convention's text while remaining within its formal mandate. Socio-economic issues, such as retirement pensions, have been incorporated into the Court's jurisprudence through this method by being linked to existing provisions, for instance, through the right to the peaceful enjoyment of possessions as outlined in A1P1.

[25] ibid.

[26] This is one of the premises on which, for instance, Philippe Van Parijs builds his account of 'real freedom' to justify a universal basic income Philippe Van Parijs, *Real Freedom for All: What (If Anything) Can Justify Capitalism?* (Clarendon Press 1995) 3.

[27] The development of this theory took place following the proclamation of the Teheran Declaration in 1968 during the International Conference on Human Rights, where it was asserted that human rights are interdependent and indivisible as follows: 'Since human rights and fundamental freedoms are indivisible, the full realization of civil and political rights without the enjoyment of economic, social and cultural rights is impossible.' Proclamation of Teheran, International Conference on Human Rights, 22 Apr.–13 May 1968, 13, U.N. Doc. A/CONF.32/41 (1968). For further discussion on this theory, see JW Nickel, 'Rethinking Indivisibility: Towards a Theory of Supporting Relations between Human Rights' (2008) 30(4) *Human Rights Quarterly* 984–1001, 985.

[28] Fabre (n 19) 13.

[29] *Airey v Ireland* Series A no 32 (1979) 2 EHRR 305.

[30] *N v United Kingdom* (GC) App no 26565/05 (ECtHR, 2008) §44 (emphasis added).

[31] Maxwell (n 4).

II. The Court as the Guardian of Convention Rights

A. The Individual Complaints System

The ECtHR is the permanent judicial body responsible for interpreting the Convention and adjudicating alleged violations. The Convention sets an individual complaints mechanism, allowing individuals, non-governmental organisations, and groups to bring claims before the Court against member states.[32] The Court's judgments are legally binding, with the Committee of Ministers of the Council of Europe supervising their implementation.[33]

The Court's system of judicial review rests on two features. First, it employs a liability-based model of corrective justice, focusing on specific disputes between individuals and states.[34] This approach requires applicants to demonstrate direct harm by a state's action, distinguishing it from an *actio popularis*, which would allow challenges to legislation without proof of personal harm.[35] This requirement keeps the Court's focus on concrete disputes involving public authority, rather than abstract legislative review or purely private conflicts.[36]

Second, the Court operates under a system of 'weak' judicial review. When the Court finds that a state breached the Convention, this finding *per se* does not automatically invalidate the disputed measure within the domestic legal system.[37] This limitation reflects a careful balance between effective international oversight and respect for national sovereignty, allowing states to maintain their legislative autonomy while remaining accountable for breaches of the Convention.

The Court's system of review operates through a structured procedure that begins with an admissibility assessment governed by Article 35 of the Convention.

[32] Harris and others (n 2).

[33] ibid.

[34] Corrective justice is mainly concerned with the just and fair relationships between two agents, emphasising the principles of reciprocity, equality, and mutual benefit in the exchange of goods, services or rights. Its purpose is to rectify voluntary or involuntary injustices within a given relationship. The applicant's claim reflects the correlative structure of corrective justice, asserting an intrinsic link between the disputed violation and the actions of the respondent state. The idea of corrective justice is found in Aristotle's Nicomachean Ethics, Book V, where he distinguishes between distributive and corrective justice as having different nature. Such idea of corrective justice has gained enormous importance in current theories of private law, especially when it comes to tort law. Ernest J Weinrib, 'Corrective Justice in a Nutshell' (2002) 52 *The University of Toronto Law Journal* 349.

[35] *Valentin Câmpeanu v Romania* App no 47848/08 (ECtHR, 2014) §101. 'The Convention does not provide for the institution of an *actio popularis* … meaning that applicants may not complain against a provision of domestic law, a domestic practice or public acts simply because they appear to contravene the Convention.'

[36] Colm O'Cinneide, 'Taking Horizontal Effect Seriously: Private Law, Constitutional Rights and the European Convention on Human Rights' (2003) 4 *Hibernian Law Journal* 77.

[37] Andreas Follesdal, 'The Legitimacy of International Human Rights Review: The Case of the European Court of Human Rights' (2009) 40 *Journal of Social Philosophy* 595, 595–607; Bernhardt (n 3) 297–319.

Two key requirements must be satisfied at this stage. First, applicants must exhaust all domestic remedies before approaching the ECtHR, a requirement that reflects the principle of subsidiarity outlined in Article 13.[38] This principle recognises national courts as the primary guardians of human rights, positioning the ECtHR as a supervisory mechanism that intervenes only after domestic remedies prove inadequate. Second, Article 35(1) establishes a six-month time limit for applications, calculated from the date of the final domestic decision. This temporal constraint ensures legal certainty, preserves evidentiary integrity and promotes the timely resolution of claims.

Applications that meet these criteria proceed to the adjudication phase. The Court transfers the application to the respondent government for observations, enabling bilateral engagement and allowing the state to present its defence or acknowledge a violation. Following deliberation, the Court issues a binding judgment on the individual case.[39]

B. Judgment and Enforcement

The Court's judgments are declaratory in nature and focus on two elements: first, determining whether the state has engaged in wrongful conduct; and second, formally declaring a violation of the applicant's rights.[40] As established in *Brumarescu v Romani*a, these judgments impose a clear obligation on states to 'put an end to the breach and make reparation for its consequences in such a way as to restore as far as possible the situation existing before the breach'.[41]

While declaratory in nature, the Court may award financial compensation under Article 41 of the Convention. This power applies only if three conditions are met: (i) the Court must first declare a Convention violation; (ii) it must determine the inadequacy of domestic legal remedies; and finally (iii) it must conclude that compensation is necessary given the circumstances.[42] If these criteria are satisfied, the Court may grant 'just satisfaction', including monetary awards and reimbursement of legal costs.

[38] Samantha Besson, 'Subsidiarity in International Human Rights Law: What Is Subsidiary about Human Rights?' (2016) 61 *The American Journal of Jurisprudence* 69; Eva Brems, 'Positive Subsidiarity and Its Implications for the Margin of Appreciation Doctrine' (2019) 37 *Netherlands Quarterly of Human Rights* 210; Sabino Cassese, 'Ruling Indirectly. Judicial Subsidiarity in the ECtHR', paper for the Seminar on 'Subsidiarity: a double sided coin? 1. The role of the Convention mechanism; 2. The role of the national authorities', held to coincide with the ceremony marking the official opening of the judicial year of the European Court of Human Rights, 30 January 2015, Strasbourg; Thomas Kleinlein, 'The Procedural Approach of the European Court of Human Rights: Between Subsidiarity and Dynamic Evolution' (2019) 68 *International & Comparative Law Quarterly* 91.

[39] Van Dijk and Van Hoof (n 6).

[40] Maxwell (n 4) 300.

[41] *Brumarescu v Romania* App no 28342/95 (ECtHR, 1999) §35.

[42] Maxwell (n 4) 316.

This approach highlights that the Convention does not guarantee an automatic right to compensation.[43] Since payments often come from public funds, the Court exercises restraint to avoid imposing disproportionate burdens on states.[44]

Over time, the Court's remedial approach has evolved through the development of pilot judgments, first introduced in *Broniowski v Poland*.[45] These types of judgments aim to move beyond individual redress by addressing structural defects in national legal systems that generate repeated violations.[46] They allow the Court not only to award compensation but also to prescribe general measures, including legislative reforms with prospective application.[47] While the use of pilot judgments has been selective and mainly limited to property rights cases, the Court has not yet applied this approach to pension-related claims.

C. The Court's Authority

The Court's judgments carry both decisional and interpretive authority.[48] This dual system of authority – combining direct force through specific judgments with broader jurisprudential influence – enables the Court to shape domestic public policy while respecting national sovereignty, creating a dynamic system of human rights protection.

Decisional authority, also known as '*res judicata*', refers to the binding effect of judgments on the parties to a specific case.[49] Under the Convention, states are required to execute judgments in accordance with their terms, creating direct obligations through this *inter partes* effect. Interpretive authority or '*res interpretata*' extends beyond individual cases to shape the understanding and application of Convention rights across all Member States. This broader influence arises when a judgment offers clear, coherent reasoning suitable for general application, remains valid without being overruled, and is reaffirmed in at least one subsequent decision.[50] Although the Court is not formally bound by precedent, it adheres closely to its prior rulings to preserve legal certainty and coherence in Convention jurisprudence.[51]

[43] Maxwell (n 4).
[44] Harris and others (n 2) 25; Maxwell (n 4) 316.
[45] *Broniowski v Poland* (GC) (2004) ECHR 2004-V.
[46] In cases concerning the right to property, for instance, the Court has ordered specific types of restitution to remedy the breach of the applicant's right like it was the case in *Brumarescu v Romania* (n 41).
[47] Alec Stone Sweet and Helen Keller, 'The Reception of the ECHR in National Legal Orders' in Hellen Keller and Alec Stone Sweet (eds), *A Europe of Rights: The Impact of the ECHR on National Legal Systems* (Oxford University Press, 2008) 13; Oddný Mjöll Arnardóttir, 'Res Interpretata, Erga Omnes Effect and the Role of the Margin of Appreciation in Giving Domestic Effect to the Judgments of the European Court of Human Rights' (2017) 28 *European Journal of International Law* 819.
[48] Besson (n 3).
[49] ibid 129.
[50] ibid 161.
[51] *Cossey v United Kingdom* App no 10843/84 (ECtHR, 1990) §35.

Departures from precedent occur only with compelling justification, often in response to substantial societal change.[52]

The Court's interpretive authority creates an *erga omnes* effect, influencing all state parties regardless of their involvement in a specific case.[53] This broader influence is particularly evident in the application of the margin of appreciation doctrine, where national authorities are afforded greater discretion when they take into account the Court's interpretation of Convention provisions.[54]

III. Methods of Interpretation

The ECtHR employs various methods of interpretation through two different approaches: judicial restraint and judicial activism.[55] In developing A1P1, the Court has employed all methods interchangeably.[56]

A. Judicial Restraint

Judicial restraint favours a conservative interpretation. This approach includes various methods like textual analysis, intentionalism and the margin of appreciation doctrine.

i. Textual Analysis

As an international treaty, the Convention must be interpreted according to the Vienna Convention on the Law of Treaties (1969), which establishes three fundamental requirements: good faith analysis, understanding of the text in its ordinary meaning and consideration of the broader context to fulfil the treaty's object and purpose. This traditional method, commonly known as 'black letter' or 'textualist' interpretation, represents the Court's primary method for determining the natural and plain meaning of the Convention text.[57]

ii. Intentionalism

When provisions contain deliberately vague or ambiguous language, as in A1P1, textual analysis alone is insufficient. In such cases, the Court initially refers to the

[52] *Chapman v United Kingdom* App no 27238/95 (ECtHR, 2001) §70.
[53] Besson (n 3) 128.
[54] Arnardóttir (n 47) 835–36.
[55] Maxwell (n 4) 30; Maša Marochini, 'The Interpretation of the European Convention on Human Rights' (2014) 51 *Zbornik radova Pravnog fakulteta u Splitu* 63, 63.
[56] Maxwell (n 4) 40–41.
[57] Saadi v United Kingdom App no 13229/03 (ECtHR, 2008) §62.

drafters' original intentions by consulting the *travaux préparatoires*, which record the debates that led to the recognition of the right.[58] However, intentionalism or originalism was short-lived, as the interpretation of Convention rights, including the right to the peaceful enjoyment of property,[59] has considerably evolved beyond their original conception.[60]

iii. The Margin of Appreciation Doctrine

The margin of appreciation doctrine represents a form of judicial restraint in the Court's jurisprudence.[61] In practical terms, it is the leeway granted to national authorities in deciding how to implement Convention rights, especially where those decisions involve complex social, economic or moral questions.[62] It is closely tied to the principle of subsidiarity, which was formally acknowledged in Protocol 15.[63] Although the doctrine does not appear in the Convention text or the *travaux préparatoires*, it has become a central principle in defining the relationship between the Court and Member States.

The scope of the margin varies depending on the subject matter, the right at stake and the broader context. However, the literature identifies a consistent pattern emerging in the case law. The Court is more likely to grant governments a wider margin when they engage seriously with its case law in justifying contested measures.[64] Critics argue that excessive deference of this kind risks introducing a form of relativism that erodes the Convention's normative authority.[65] The case law on pension entitlements under A1P1 illustrates how a generous margin can dilute the Convention's protective force. This effect will be examined in detail in chapter six.

[58] Maxwell (n 4) 31.
[59] Allen (n 17).
[60] Maxwell (n 4) 31.
[61] Steven C Greer, *The Margin of Appreciation: Interpretation and Discretion under the European Convention on Human Rights*, vol 17 (Council of Europe 2000); Arnardóttir (n 47); Brems (n 38); Jan Kratochvíl, 'The Inflation of the Margin of Appreciation by the European Court of Human Rights' (2011) 29 *Netherlands Quarterly of Human Rights* 324; Lorenza Mola, 'The Margin of Appreciation Accorded to States in Times of Economic Crisis. An Analysis of the Decisions by the European Committee of Social Rights and by the European Court of Human Rights on National Austerity Measures' (2015) 5 *Lex Social* 174; James A Sweeney, 'A Margin of Appreciation in the Internal Market: Lessons from the European Court of Human Rights' (2007) 34 *Legal Issues of Economic Integration* 27; Kristina Trykhlib and Vasyl Lemak, 'Autonomous Interpretation by the European Court of Human Rights and Margin of Appreciation' (2022) 22 *International and Comparative Law Review* 135; George Letsas, *A Theory of Interpretation of the European Convention on Human Rights* (Oxford University Press 2007).
[62] Jeffrey A Brauch, 'The Margin of Appreciation and the Jurisprudence of the European Court of Human Rights: Threat to the Rule of Law' (2004) 11 *Columbia Journal of European Law* 113.
[63] Maxwell (n 4) 32.
[64] Kratochvíl (n 61); Harris and others (n 2) 14.
[65] Maxwell (n 4) 36.

B. Judicial Activism

Different from judicial restraint, judicial activism relies on interpretative methods that allow the Court to expand the scope of Convention rights in response to changing legal and social conditions. The three primary approaches are autonomous interpretation, the living instrument doctrine and the principle of effectiveness.

i. Autonomous Interpretation

The autonomous interpretation method is the most prominent driver of expansion in the Court's case law. It allows the ECtHR to define contested legal concepts independently of their domestic meanings.[66] The approach begins with the recognition that domestic legal systems often provide divergent or ambiguous definitions of terms such as property, justice or the rule of law.[67] The Court then develops a Convention-specific meaning that ensures uniform application across Member States.[68]

Critics have described this method as an exercise of 'illegitimate judicial discretion'.[69] However, it is the way found by the Court to guarantee both internal coherence as well as uniform reach of the Convention within a heterogenous landscape of legal systems. The autonomous interpretation method has expanded the understanding of what constitutes private property to protect other instances of wealth, such as retirement pensions, under the property clause.[70]

ii. The Living Instrument Doctrine

The living instrument doctrine, first articulated in *Tyrer v United Kingdom*[71] enables the Court to interpret the Convention in light of present-day conditions rather than remaining bound by historical or originalist understandings.[72] This method seeks to prevent the fossilisation of rights or definitions that are contingent on a historical context. As noted before, while the Court is not formally bound by its own case law (*stare decisis*), it generally adheres to precedent for reasons of legal certainty, departing from established case law only for compelling reasons. This evolutionary interpretation presents a particular challenge in maintaining

[66] Letsas (n 61) 41–43.
[67] Jeremy Waldron, 'Is the Rule of Law an Essentially Contested Concept (in Florida)?' (2002) 21(2) *Law and Philosophy* 137–64.
[68] Letsas (n 61) 83–84.
[69] Maxwell (n 4) 38.
[70] See chs 4 and 5.
[71] Tyrer v United Kingdom Series A no 26 (1980) 2 EHRR 1 §38.
[72] Baroness Hale, 'Common Law and Convention Law: The Limits to Interpretation' [2011] *European Human Rights Law Review* 534.

equilibrium between effectively protecting Convention rights and avoiding undue interference in matters of public debate or policy.[73]

iii. The Principle of Effectiveness

Finally, the principle of effectiveness requires the Court to interpret Convention rights in a way that ensures their practical and effective enjoyment. Under this approach, interpretation must give full meaning to each provision, in line with the Convention's text and broader purpose.[74] This principle has been central to the development of positive obligations, which require states not merely to abstain from interference but to take active steps to protect rights.[75] The effectiveness doctrine reflects the Court's commitment to ensuring that rights are not merely theoretical, but capable of producing concrete legal protection.

IV. The Structure of Rights' Review

A. Overview

The ECtHR applies an 'acceptability test' to determine both the applicability of a provision and whether a violation has occurred.[76] For A1P1, this takes the form of a five-step analysis.[77] While later chapters in this book provide further detail on each step through pension case law, this section outlines the general framework.

The steps are: (i) confirming that the applicant holds a property right; (ii) determining whether there was an interference with that right; (iii) assessing the lawfulness of the measure; (iv) considering whether it pursued a legitimate public interest; and (v) evaluating whether the measure achieved a 'fair balance' between the general interest and the applicant's interests, essentially determining its proportionality.

[73] Maxwell (n 4) 39.

[74] ibid 40.

[75] ibid; Vladislava Stoyanova, 'Causation between State Omission and Harm within the Framework of Positive Obligations under the European Convention on Human Rights' (2018) 18 *Human Rights Law Review* 309.

[76] This was the position held by Judge Gerald Fitzmaurice in his dissenting opinion in *Marckx v Belgium* [1979] European Court of Human Rights (6833/74). 'Only if it is both applicable, and also has been infringed, can the defendant party be held responsible and (as regards the Convention on Human Rights) a Convention-breaker … The foregoing are elementary, standard propositions which should not need stating because they are such as everyone would assent to in principle, – but principle is easily lost sight of when eagerness for specific results – however meritorious they may be in themselves – overreaches the still, small voice of the juridical conscience.'

[77] Camilo Basilio Schutte, *The European Fundamental Right of Property: Article 1 of Protocol No. 1 to the European Convention on Human Rights: Its Origins, Its Working, and Its Impact on National Legal Orders* (Kluwer 2004).

B. The Acceptability Test

i. Demonstrating a Well-Defined Property Right

The first step examines whether the applicant holds an existing, well-defined property right or 'possession'. This filters out claims that fall outside A1P1's scope.[78] Using the autonomous interpretation method, the Court has developed a concept of 'possession' that goes beyond traditional property, such as land, to include interests with economic value, including pension benefits.[79] However, two key limitations apply: the property must be held in a private capacity, as public authorities cannot file applications,[80] and it must exist at the time of application, because A1P1 covers only existing possessions, enforceable claims, not the right to acquire property.[81]

ii. Types of Interferences

Once the Court recognises a possession as sufficiently established, it proceeds to assess whether and how interference with the peaceful enjoyment of property occurred. Following *Sporrong and Lönnroth v Sweden*, the Court distinguishes three types of interference: general interference, deprivation of property and control of use.[82] This classification shapes the intensity of subsequent scrutiny.[83] Deprivation, the most severe form, occurs when the entitlement is extinguished either *de jure*, through formal transfer of title, or *de facto*, by loss of all meaningful use despite retaining legal ownership.[84] Control of use typically preserves both title and the right to sell, even where use is heavily restricted, as in rent control or zoning cases.[85] Interferences that do not clearly fit into either category may be classified as general interference, a residual category that often yields less favourable outcomes for applicants.[86]

Although these distinctions formally guide the Court's analysis, with deprivation triggering a presumption of compensation and control of use placing the burden on the applicant, the boundaries between categories often blur in practice.[87] The Court's method operates more as a sliding scale of severity than a fixed typology, with the intensity of review adjusting to the degree of interference.[88]

[78] Maxwell (n 4) 78.
[79] ibid 79.
[80] ibid. The discussion on how did the Court arrive to such conclusion and what follows for the case law will be discussed in ch 3 of this book.
[81] Maxwell (n 4) 84.
[82] *Sporrong and Lönnroth v Sweden* Series A no 52 (1983) 5 EHRR 35.
[83] Maxwell (n 4) 133–34.
[84] ibid 139–41.
[85] ibid 146.
[86] ibid 159–61.
[87] ibid 133–34.
[88] ibid 169.

iii. Lawfulness

The third step focuses on whether the measure of interference was 'subject to the conditions provided by law' as required by A1P1. The Court interprets this requirement as a lawfulness test that extends beyond formal compliance with domestic rules. Interpreting 'law' in its substantive sense implies examining not only parliamentary statutes but also subordinate legislation, unwritten law and judicial precedents to ensure genuine adherence to the rule of law.[89] These legal sources must be accessible, precise and foreseeable, allowing individuals, with the assistance of legal advice if necessary, to anticipate the consequences of their actions.[90] In practice, the Court determines whether interferences have a basis in domestic law and whether legal provisions meet standards of accessibility and precision.[91]

Guided by the principle of subsidiarity, the Court generally presumes compliance with domestic law and intervenes only in cases of arbitrariness or manifest injustice.[92] Even contested measures, such as retrospective legislation, may satisfy the lawfulness threshold. This deferential approach often shifts the burden of substantive review to later stages, particularly the assessment of proportionality and fair balance.[93]

iv. Justified on Public Interest Reasons

The fourth step considers whether the measure was justified by reasons of 'public interest'. Although this requirement appears straightforward, it proves complex in practice.[94] Since *James v United Kingdom*, the Court has treated 'public interest' and 'general interest' as analogous concepts, despite subtle distinctions in the Convention's different language versions.[95]

The Court grants states considerable deference at this stage, particularly in matters involving economic policy or social welfare. During periods of austerity, financial crisis or economic transformation, states tend to enjoy their widest margin of appreciation.[96] This deferential stance has effectively transformed the public interest requirement into a procedural formality. Some scholars describe it as a 'Paper Tiger'.[97] The Court has occasionally identified public interest justifications even when governments failed to advance them,[98] inferring them from the broader context. While rare exceptions exist where the Court has rejected

[89] ibid 171–72.
[90] ibid 188–89.
[91] *The Sunday Times v United Kingdom (No 1)* Series A no 30 (1979–80) 2 EHRR 245.
[92] Maxwell (n 4) 182.
[93] ibid 192.
[94] ibid 199.
[95] *James and Others v United Kingdom* Series A no 98 (1986) 8 EHRR 123.
[96] Maxwell (n 4) 203; *Ambruosi v Italy* App no 31227/96 (ECtHR, 2000).
[97] Maxwell (n 4) 197.
[98] ibid 203.

public interest arguments, these remain the exception rather than the rule.[99] In practice, substantive scrutiny is deferred mainly to the proportionality stage, making it unlikely that a measure would fail the public interest test but pass proportionality.[100]

The final step assesses proportionality, asking whether a 'fair balance' was struck between the general interest and the applicant's rights. This is the stage where A1P1 'most often bites'.[101]

v. Proportionality

The principle of proportionality is central to the Court's interpretation of the Convention. As stated in *Soering v United Kingdom*, the Court seeks to maintain a 'fair balance between the demands of the general interest of the community and the requirements of the protection of the individual's fundamental rights'.[102] For rights like A1P1, proportionality is particularly relevant, because the Convention explicitly allows for restrictions based on competing values such as the public interest.[103]

To find whether a measure is proportional, the Court examines whether the measure pursues a legitimate aim, whether the means employed are rationally connected to that aim and whether less intrusive alternatives were available. This test assesses the reasonableness of the relationship between the interference and the stated objective.

The intensity of the review also depends on the context of the case. States enjoy broader margins of appreciation in areas such as taxation, environmental protection or welfare policy. By contrast, proportionality plays no role under absolute rights like Article 3, which prohibits torture and inhuman or degrading treatment or punishment.[104]

In the cases involving A1P1, compensation is a key factor in assessing proportionality, particularly in cases of severe harm, like total deprivation of a property right. While A1P1 does not explicitly require compensation,[105] the Court generally views payment 'reasonably related to property value' as a condition of proportionality. Full market value compensation is not always required.[106] In cases where the disputed property is the claimant's main source of income, heightened scrutiny may apply, potentially requiring compensation above market value.[107] However,

[99] *Rosenzweig and Bonded Warehouses Ltd v Poland* App no 51728/99 (ECtHR, 2005); *SA Dangeville v France* App no 36677/97 (ECtHR, 2002).

[100] Maxwell (n 4) 206.

[101] ibid 297.

[102] *Soering v United Kingdom* Series A no 161 (1989) 11 EHRR 439 §161.

[103] Harris and others (n 2) 10.

[104] ibid 11.

[105] Allen (n 17).

[106] ibid; Maxwell (n 4) 242–44.

[107] Maxwell (n 4) 255.

in exceptional circumstances – such as periods of political transition or financial crisis – the Court may accept reduced or no compensation.[108]

V. From Strasbourg to National Legal Orders

A. Monist and Dualist Approaches

While the Convention assigns primary responsibility for its enforcement to the contracting parties, the reception of the Court's interpretative authority varies across national legal systems.[109] Although all 47 Member States have incorporated the Convention's text in some form, the extent to which domestic actors adopt the Court's interpretation – particularly its treatment of pensions as property – differs significantly.

The Convention is not inherently self-executing, and the Court's judgments do not automatically bind national courts outside the case at hand. The domestic effect of the Court's *res interpretata* depends on each legal system's willingness to integrate international norms and allow judges to rely on them in their reasoning.[110] This is often framed through the lens of monist and dualist approaches to international law, a distinction that shapes how Strasbourg jurisprudence influences national legislation and judicial practice.[111]

In monist systems, where international law automatically becomes part of the domestic legal order, the Court's interpretations can have immediate effect without further legislative action. Austria and Switzerland exemplify this model, with domestic judges applying the Court's interpretations of Convention rights, including the classification of certain pension entitlements as property under A1P1.[112] However, even within monist frameworks, the authority granted to Strasbourg jurisprudence varies. Italian courts, for instance, treat the Convention primarily as a tool for guiding legislative policy, rather than a binding source for judicial decisions. Similarly, German courts give primacy to their domestic legislation, treating the Convention as an auxiliary interpretive source.[113]

In dualist systems, international law requires explicit legislative incorporation to have a domestic effect. When the Court develops new interpretations of property rights that affect pensions, dualist systems must actively incorporate these developments through legislative or judicial action.[114] The case of the United

[108] Allen (n 17); Maxwell (n 4) 244.
[109] Article 1 of the Convention establishes the obligation to Member States to 'secure' the rights and freedoms set out in the Convention for all individuals within their jurisdiction.
[110] Denza (n 8).
[111] Harris and others (n 2) 23.
[112] ibid 24–25.
[113] ibid.
[114] Maxwell (n 4).

Kingdom's Human Rights Act 1998 is an interesting example of a dualist approach. The Act allows domestic courts to apply Convention rights and to take Strasbourg jurisprudence into account.[115] This framework has proven successful in reducing applications to Strasbourg by providing effective domestic remedies.[116]

Recent developments have enhanced the interaction between national and European levels of rights protection. Protocol No 15's emphasis on subsidiarity reinforces national authorities' primary role in protecting Convention rights, while Protocol No 16 creates new opportunities for judicial dialogue through its advisory opinion mechanism. These developments are particularly significant for pension rights, where national authorities must balance social policy objectives with property protection standards established by the Court.[117]

B. The Court's Broader Influence

The Court's influence extends beyond formal incorporation into domestic law. Even in systems where the Convention has limited direct effect, national legislators increasingly consider the Court's interpretation of Convention rights during policy debates.[118] This indirect or 'shadow' influence reflects Convention states' efforts to avoid adverse judgments and the Court's practice of affording a wider margin of appreciation to states that engage seriously with Convention principles in their legislative processes.[119] This preventive influence is particularly relevant for pension reform cases, where lawmakers are bounded by both domestic constitutional constraints and the Court's evolving interpretation of property under A1P1. Engaging with these constraints at the design stage helps ensure compatibility with the Convention. These issues will be examined in greater detail in chapter six.

Conclusion

This chapter has traced the evolution of the Convention from its post-war origins to a sophisticated system of human rights protection, focusing on its institutional structure, enforcement mechanisms and interpretative methods. Although initially limited to civil and political rights, the Court has progressively recognised the interdependence of human rights. This development is particularly evident in the expansion of provisions, such as the right to private property, to find ways to address issues beyond their limited scope.

[115] ibid.
[116] Harris and others (n 2) 24–25.
[117] Maxwell (n 4).
[118] Or even in jurisdictions outside the Council of Europe, like the Colombian Constitutional Court. *T-631/2002* (Constitutional Court of Colombia, 2002).
[119] Maxwell (n 4) 368; Kratochvíl (n 61); Trykhlib and Lemak (n 61).

The European Court of Human Rights has developed a distinctive approach to judicial review, striking a balance between international supervision and national sovereignty. This balance operates through the individual complaint mechanism and the principle of subsidiarity, shaping both the Court's authority in specific cases and its broader systemic influence. The Court's interpretative methodology reflects this equilibrium: alongside traditional tools like textual analysis and intentionalism, it employs dynamic methods such as the autonomous interpretation and the living instrument doctrine. The five-step framework guides the Court's assessment of interferences, ensuring a structured review of state measures against Convention standards.

The domestic implementation of Convention rights illustrates the complex interaction between international norms and national legal orders. While formal incorporation varies across member states, the Convention's influence extends into policy-making and legislative decisions. Recent developments indicate an evolving relationship between national and European protection mechanisms, although challenges persist in ensuring effective rights protection across Europe.

These aspects of the Convention system provide the essential context for understanding how the Court has developed its approach to specific rights, particularly its innovative interpretation of property rights under A1P1, which will be examined in detail in the chapters that follow.

2

The Theoretical Architecture of Property Rights in Article 1 Protocol No 1

Introduction

When the Convention's drafters considered including property rights within the original text, they faced questions about the relationship between individual rights, collective interests and the tension between them in the distribution of wealth. For instance, why should property rights merit protection alongside civil rights and liberties? What follows for states recognising private property protection? What underlying values should be protected by property? The resulting text of Article 1 of Protocol No 1 (A1P1) reflects a partial and imperfect answer to these questions. It embodies a series of ideological, political and practical compromises, which deliberately left open the interpretation of its content and scope to be later decided by the European Court of Human Rights (ECtHR, or the Court) in its future jurisprudence.[1]

Understanding how the Court has approached the content and application of A1P1 requires close attention to the concept of property itself. The term 'property' is flexible, contested and politically loaded.[2] It defies a conclusive definition[3] because it encompasses a vast range of rights and objects that have little in common except that they are claimed by individuals and upheld by the state.[4]

[1] Douglas Maxwell, *The Human Right to Property: A Practical Approach to Article 1 of Protocol No. 1 to the ECHR* (Bloomsbury Publishing 2022) 73; Tom Allen, 'Liberalism, Social Democracy and the Value of Property under the European Convention on Human Rights' (2010) 59 *International & Comparative Law Quarterly* 1055.

[2] Jeremy Waldron, 'What Is Private Property' (1985) 5 *Oxford Journal of Legal Studies* 313, 338.

[3] Kevin Gray, 'Property in Thin Air' (1991) 50 *The Cambridge Law Journal* 252.

[4] Waldron, 'What Is Private Property' (n 2) 318; Rachael Walsh, *Property Rights and Social Justice: Progressive Property in Action* (Cambridge University Press 2021); JE Penner, *The Idea of Property In Law* (Clarendon Press 1997); James E Penner, *Property Rights: A Re-Examination* (Oxford University Press, USA 2020); James Penner and Michael Otsuka, *Property Theory: Legal and Political Perspectives* (Cambridge University Press 2018); Gregory S Alexander and Eduardo M Peñalver, *An Introduction to Property Theory* (Cambridge University Press 2012); Frank I Michelman, 'Property as a Constitutional Right' (1981) 38 *Washington & Lee Law Review* 1097; Andries Johannes Van der Walt, *Property in the Margins* (Bloomsbury Publishing 2009); Michael Diamond, 'The Meaning and Nature of Property: Homeownership and Shared Equity in the Context of Poverty' (2009) 29 *Saint Louis University Public Law Review* 85; Jesse Dukeminier and others, *Property* (Aspen

This diversity extends across many dimensions, including duration, structure and function. Some property rights, such as patents, are temporary and conditional. Others, like freehold ownership, are permanent and essentially absolute. Some forms of property are highly personal, such as household belongings, while others, like shares in a corporation, are abstract and impersonal.[5]

This diversity of meanings, types and approaches to property gives rise to deep theoretical disagreements about its nature and purpose.[6] At times, the right to private property gets confused with other values like liberty or the rule of law. For instance, when international organisations construct indicators that claim to quantify and rank degrees of freedom across countries.[7] However, the main disagreement within the literature is whether property rights are best understood as instruments for achieving broader social goals, such as economic efficiency or personal autonomy,[8] or whether they reflect intrinsic moral claims tied to dignity, security or liberty.[9] These competing views shape at least three relevant legal questions for the purposes of this book: (i) which interests should be protected legally, (ii) why they should be protected and, (iii) what kinds of interference with them may be justified.

This chapter examines various theoretical approaches to property law and the protection of private property. It does not aim to resolve enduring debates about the nature or scope of private property, nor will it examine the merits of each approach. Such ambitions lie well beyond the reach of this chapter and, for that matter, this book. Instead, it pursues three more limited objectives. First, it aims to clarify the conceptual framework underlying property protection under A1P1. To do so, it examines how different theoretical perspectives influence the identification of protected 'possessions'. As property takes increasingly diverse forms in modern societies, including traditional assets like land and capital as well as public entitlements such as licences or pensions, it becomes essential for both scholars and practitioners to engage with the theoretical assumptions that underpin legal protection.[10] The second objective is exploring how competing visions of property's function shape the scope and content of protection under A1P1. Finally, it examines how these theoretical perspectives inform the practical limits and obligations that A1P1 imposes on Member States.[11] A consideration that the reader must

Publishing 2017); Jeremy Waldron, *The Right to Private Property* (Oxford University Press 1990); André van der Walt and Rachael Walsh, 'Comparative Constitutional Property Law', *Comparative Property Law* (Edward Elgar Publishing 2017).

[5] James Y Stern, 'Property's Constitution' (2013) 101 *California Law Review* 277, 286.

[6] Waldron, *The Right to Private Property* (n 4); Waldron, 'What Is Private Property' (n 2).

[7] Jeremy Waldron, *The Rule of Law and the Measure of Property* (Cambridge University Press 2012).

[8] Alexander and Peñalver (n 4); Walsh (n 4); van der Walt and Walsh (n 4); Ronald A Cass, 'Property Rights Systems and the Rule of Law' [2003] Available at SSRN 392783.

[9] Friedrich August Hayek, *Law, Legislation and Liberty*, vol 19 (University of Chicago Press 2022); Alexander and Peñalver (n 4); Waldron, *The Right to Private Property* (n 4); Waldron, *The Rule of Law and the Measure of Property* (n 7); van der Walt and Walsh (n 4); Walsh (n 4).

[10] Charles Reich, 'The New Property' (1964) 73 *Yale Law* 733; Crawford Brough Macpherson, 'Capitalism and the Changing Concept of Property' in Eugene Kamenka and Ronald Stanley Neale (eds), *Feudalism, Capitalism and Beyond* (Australian National University Press 1975); Crawford Brough Macpherson, *Property: Mainstream and Critical Positions* (University of Toronto Press 1999).

[11] The relevance of this theoretical debate about A1P1's scope and nature extends beyond Strasbourg. The property framework developed by the ECtHR has become a crucial reference point for

bear in mind is that the main challenge of judicially protecting property rights arises from the concept's inherent diversity and the normative disagreements that surround it.[12]

The chapter is structured as follows. Section I examines the nature of property rights protection and considers how different theoretical approaches conceptualise property within a human rights framework. Section II explores competing visions of property's purpose, including the distinction between instrumental and intrinsic approaches, as well as the distinction between monistic and pluralistic understandings of its value. Section III traces the evolution of A1P1, analysing how theoretical debates shaped both the drafting of the provision and its interpretation by the ECtHR. The chapter concludes by synthesising these insights to outline a framework for understanding how the Court approaches the protection of property rights under A1P1.

I. Conceptualising Property

A. The Nature of Property

A1P1 protects the peaceful enjoyment of *private* property as opposed to other types of property arrangements, like collective or common property.[13] Private property arrangements assign and distribute valuable resources to identifiable individuals who could claim exclusivity in their ownership.[14] In the landmark case *Marckx v Belgium*,[15] the Court held the following:

> By recognising that everyone has the right to the peaceful enjoyment of his possessions, *Article 1 is in substance guaranteeing the right of property*. This is the clear impression left by the word's 'possessions' and 'use of property' (in French: 'biens', 'propriété', 'usage des biens'); the *travaux préparatoires*, for their part, confirm this unequivocally: the drafters continually spoke of 'right of property' or 'right to property' to describe the subject-matter of the successive drafts which were the forerunners of the present Article 1.[16]

Even if the terminology of A1P1 is different in both of the Council of Europe's official languages (English and French), the provision conveys the same meaning: the

understanding property rights in modern European law, influencing both the Court of Justice of the European Union and some national Courts. See Yassin Abdullah Kadi and Al Barakaat International Foundation v Council of the European Union and Commission of the European Communities (GC) Joined Cases C-402/05 P and C-415/05 P, EU:C:2008:461, [2008] ECR I-6351; Pál Sonnevend, *Eigentumsschutz Und Sozialversicherung: Eine Rechtsvergleichende Analyse Anhand Der Rechtsprechung Des Bundesverfassungsgerichts Und Des Ungarischen Verfassungsgerichts*, vol 185 (Springer-Verlag 2007).

[12] Maxwell (n 1) 65–68.

[13] Waldron, 'What Is Private Property' (n 2); Waldron, *The Right to Private Property* (n 4); Penner, *The Idea of Property In Law* (n 4); Penner, *Property Rights: A Re-Examination* (n 4).

[14] Waldron, 'What Is Private Property' (n 2) 327.

[15] *Marckx v Belgium* Series A no 31 (1979) 2 EHRR 330.

[16] ibid §63 (emphasis added).

protection of the peaceful enjoyment of *private* property. Therefore, whenever the term *possessions* appears in the context of the ECtHR's case law, it refers to private property. Schwelb argues that:

> The Protocol, of which the English and French texts are equally authentic, provides in the English version of Art. 1(1) that every natural or legal person is entitled to 'the peaceful enjoyment of his possessions', while the French text says that '*toute personne physique ou morale a droit au respect de ses biens*'. There is no counterpart in the French version to the idea of peaceful enjoyment. The second sentence of the French text does not repeat the term '*biens*', but speaks of '*propriété*' instead. While the English text of the first paragraph uses twice the term 'possessions', the second paragraph speaks of controlling 'the use of property'. The French text renders this by '*reglementer l'usage des biens*'. While normally one ought to assume that the use of different words in a comparatively short treaty provision is intended to convey different meanings, this is obviously not the case here. Nor can the English term 'possessions' be understood in a technical-legal sense, as denoting (factual) possession as distinct from (legal) ownership or property; as the *possessio* of Roman law contrasted to *dominium* or *proprietas;* as the French term possession (the word does not appear in the French version of the Protocol) in contrast to *propriété*; as *Besitz* opposed to *Eigentum*. The only reasonable conclusion which can be drawn from this lack of terminological symmetry and consistency is that for the purposes of the Protocol all the terms employed in Article 1 mean the same, namely 'property', '*proprieté*', and that the use of different expressions is legally irrelevant.[17]

Knowing that the Convention protects private property does not tell us much about what it is, what its nature is, its justification, purpose or limitations. These are, at the core, the questions that mark any discussion concerning property institutions.[18]

In the literature, there is a lack of a generally accepted account of what private property is and how it is to be contrasted with alternative systems of property rules.[19] Some sceptics even go as far as claiming that private property 'defies definition', and therefore, any discussion about such an institution is useless.[20]

The elusive nature of property, however, does not diminish its relevance in everyday legal and political thought. Instead, the complexities of the concept reveal its fundamental characteristics and implications for the law. Property

[17] Egon Schwelb, 'The Protection of the Right of Property of Nationals under the First Protocol to the European Convention on Human Rights' [1964] *The American Journal of Comparative Law* 518, 519–20.

[18] Alexander and Peñalver (n 4) 2.

[19] Waldron, 'What Is Private Property' (n 2). Nevertheless, this claim does not mean that such accounts do not exist. Influential accounts in the Law and Economics literature describe private property as having a dual character: on the one hand, as exclusive control over a thing; on the other, as a set of interpersonal claims concerning its valuable uses. Thomas W Merrill, 'Property and the Right to Exclude' (1998) 77 *Nebraska Law Review* 730; Hanoch Dagan, *Property: Values and Institutions* (Oxford University Press 2011); James W Harris, *Property and Justice* (Oxford University Press 1996).

[20] Waldron, 'What Is Private Property' (n 2).

operates as a recognised human right, enshrined not only in A1P1,[21] but also in various constitutional texts that have brought property rights to the forefront in the midst of ever-growing regulatory control over private ownership.[22] Understanding the theoretical approaches to property sheds light on how the Court navigates the tensions between individual property rights, collective interests and legislative authority, particularly when addressing novel forms of property and regulatory measures that affect their enjoyment.[23] The following section examines how broader philosophical approaches to property assign meaning and value to such claims, which in turn shapes how courts might evaluate them.

B. Property in Legal Theory

The difficulty in clearly defining what private property is arises from its inherent complexity at both conceptual and theoretical levels. At the conceptual level, property operates simultaneously as a direct relationship between people and things, which is the layman's conception of property, and as a system of social relationships mediated through things, which is the sophisticated legal conception.[24] While the common understanding of property as a person-thing relationship captures an essential aspect of ownership, which is the duties imposed on everyone else concerning those rights,[25] legal analysis has developed this into a more complex framework. Such a framework recognises how property rights structure relationships between people regarding things.[26] This legal understanding has traditionally been expressed through the metaphor of a 'bundle of rights'.[27] The metaphor highlights the complex legal relationships that define ownership, describing how these relationships are based on legal rights, and underscores the social role that ownership plays.[28]

The 'bundle of rights' picture remains the most influential characterisation of property in legal theory.[29] Such a picture portrays a flexible array of multiple personal rights between individuals, where each person has correlative duties not to interfere with the owner's rights (such as damaging or stealing their property),[30] and most recently, between the state and individuals, whereby the same duties

[21] Maxwell (n 1) 62.
[22] Walsh (n 4) 4.
[23] Maxwell (n 1) 42; Reich, 'The New Property' (n 10).
[24] Anthony M Honoré, 'Oxford Essays in Jurisprudence' (Oxford University Press, 1961); Waldron, 'What Is Private Property' (n 2) 314.
[25] Alexander and Peñalver (n 4) 2.
[26] Honoré (n 24); Waldron, 'What Is Private Property' (n 2).
[27] Waldron, 'What Is Private Property' (n 2) 314–315.
[28] Gregory S Alexander, *Commodity & Propriety: Competing Visions of Property in American Legal Thought, 1776–1970* (University of Chicago Press 2008).
[29] Alexander and Peñalver (n 4) 3.
[30] James E Penner, 'The Bundle of Rights Picture of Property' (1995) 43 *UCLA Law Review* 711, 712.

emerge for everyone else.[31] These rights include different types (liberties, claim-rights, powers, immunities) and specific incidents (right to possess, use, capital, etc).[32]

Critics of the bundle picture argue that it is 'little more than a slogan' rather than a coherent theoretical framework.[33] The critique departs from the idea that the bundle picture lacks any canonical formulation or clear methodology, merely associating two separate philosophical views without providing real explanatory power about the nature of property itself.[34] From that point, it claims that the bundle picture fails to recognise that property law serves a distinct and unified interest: the interest in exclusively determining the use of things.[35] By treating property as merely a disaggregated collection of rights, critics argue, the bundle theory misses property's conceptual unity and its function in organising how we allocate and control resources.[36] They further hold that such a picture obscures the fundamental connection between rights, objects and individuals.[37]

The debate on the bundle picture reflects the difficulty of clearly defining the nature of property.[38] To overcome this difficulty, the literature offers two approaches. The first approach moves beyond the bundle metaphor by trying to elucidate the necessary and sufficient conditions of property through identifying a specific 'menu' of ownership rights (including possession, use, management, and income rights) that characteristically appear in property systems. While no single right is necessary for ownership, these rights collectively form a recognisable pattern of property.[39] This approach, however, cannot accommodate the heterogeneity of the objects of property. These objects of property vary so fundamentally in legal theory that it becomes rather difficult to apply a unified concept of ownership across all cases.[40] Furthermore, variations in who owns property and what is owned can substantially alter the nature of the property relationship itself.[41]

[31] Reich, 'The New Property' (n 10); Charles A Reich, 'Social Welfare in the Public-Private State' (1965) 114 *University of Pennsylvania Law Review* 487; Charles A Reich, 'Individual Rights and Social Welfare: The Emerging Legal Issues' in P Robson (ed), *Welfare Law* (Routledge 2020).

[32] Penner (n 30); Another way to describe the bundle in analytical terms is provided by Munzer 'The idea of property – or, if you prefer, the sophisticated or legal conception of property-involves a constellation of Hohfeldian elements, correlatives, and opposites; a specification of standard incidents of ownership and other related but less powerful interests; and a catalog of "things" (tangible and intangible) that are the subjects of these incidents. Hohfeld's conceptions are normative modalities. In the more specific form of Honor's incidents, these are the relations that constitute property'. Stephen R Munzer, *A Theory of Property* (Cambridge University Press 1990) 23.

[33] Penner, 'The Bundle of Rights Picture of Property' (n 30) 712.

[34] Penner, *The Idea of Property In Law* (n 4).

[35] ibid.

[36] Penner, 'The Bundle of Rights Picture of Property' (n 30); Penner, *The Idea of Property In Law* (n 4); Penner, *Property Rights: A Re-Examination* (n 4).

[37] Alexander and Peñalver (n 4) 3.

[38] In the literature of Law & Economics, the bundle picture seems to be ultimately developed by them.

[39] Alexander and Peñalver (n 4) 5.

[40] Waldron, 'What Is Private Property' (n 2) 316.

[41] Waldron, 'What Is Private Property' (n 2); Waldron, *The Right to Private Property* (n 4).

The second approach, which is more helpful for this book, abandons the attempt to reveal or define the essential features of property and instead defines property through its societal function: the allocation of material resources.[42] This functional definition focuses on how property law creates rules determining who can access and use which resources, when and for what purposes.[43] In a private property system, rules governing access and control are organised around the concept that resources are separate objects assigned to particular individuals.[44]

The latter functional approach can distinguish property as a legal institution while remaining neutral about both how rights should be structured and what values they should serve. Such simplicity is both its strength and weakness, as it does not provide a normative justification for allocating rights in particular ways, or tell us anything about which human interests or values are relevant in a given property system.[45] To complete this picture, a brief description of the different normative approaches to property is needed, outlining the multiple values that property tends to promote.

Normatively speaking, property operates simultaneously as an idea and as an institution that shapes social relationships and serves one or many values like efficiency, human flourishing, freedom or security.[46] Exploring both the social[47] and value dimensions of property becomes necessary to set the stage for the discussion of how property should be structured to serve them. Such a description provides additional conceptual tools for approaching A1P1.

II. Theoretical Approaches to Property

Is property 'a social function',[48] a subjective pre-political entitlement or just a right with a social aspect?[49] The theoretical discussions surrounding the structure, purpose and societal interests that property rights serve are extensive and multifaceted.[50] The variety of perspectives on those questions highlights deep

[42] Waldron, 'What Is Private Property' (n 2) 319.
[43] Waldron, 'What Is Private Property' (n 2); Waldron, *The Right to Private Property* (n 4).
[44] Waldron, 'What Is Private Property' (n 2).
[45] Alexander and Peñalver (n 4); Waldron, 'What Is Private Property' (n 2).
[46] Alexander and Peñalver (n 4) 6–7.
[47] Walsh (n 4) 5.
[48] Léon Duguit, *Les Transformations Générales Du Droit Privé Depuis Le Code Napoléon* (Falcan 1920).
[49] Honoré (n 24); Walsh (n 4) 2.
[50] Penner and Otsuka (n 4); George Gretton, 'The Protection of Property Rights' in C Himsworth and A Boyle (eds), *Human Rights and Scots Law: Comparative Perspectives on the Incorporation of the ECHR* (Hart Publishing 2002); Tom Allen, *Property and the Human Rights Act 1998* (Hart Publishing 2005); Gregory S Alexander, *Property and Human Flourishing* (Oxford University Press 2018); van der Walt and Walsh (n 4); Penner, *The Idea of Property In Law* (n 4); Penner, *Property Rights: A Re-Examination* (n 4); Honoré (n 24); Penner, 'The Bundle of Rights Picture of Property' (n 30); Waldron, *The Rule of Law and the Measure of Property* (n 7); Walsh (n 4); Henri Lepage, *Pourquoi La Propriété*, vol 287 (Hachette Paris 1985); Jean-Fabien Spitz and others, 'Why Private Property?' (2019) 73 *Raisons politiques* 119; Charles A Reich, 'The New Property' (1964) 73 *Yale Law Journal* 733; Bruce Ackerman,

disagreements about property's role and the proper balance between individual rights and collective interests. Moreover, they reflect disputes over what is the precise content of the right to property and whether its features are exclusive to such a right, or shared with other important objectives relevant for our political morality, like the rule of law.[51] Although this book cannot explore all these perspectives in depth, making sense of this broader landscape is relevant for analysing how the Court will recognise pensions as property.

Organising property theories can be a difficult task given their significant conceptual interrelations. The literature presents various frameworks serving pedagogical purposes: some scholars organise theories into families according to the values they foster,[52] others by the nature of the entitlement[53] and others by their underlying theoretical agenda.[54]

Table 2.1 Theoretical Approaches to Property

	Monistic Theories	**Pluralistic Theories**
Instrumental Value Theories	Utilitarian Kantian	Progressive
Intrinsic Value Theories	Natural Rights/ Libertarian	Hegelian

Source: Own elaboration.

This book organises the most relevant property theories following two axes as seen in Table 2.1. Each of them seeks to illuminate their underlying assumptions and implications, while also revealing their intersections. The first axis distinguishes between instrumental and intrinsic value approaches. Instrumental theories view property as a means to achieve broader societal goals like welfare maximisation, human flourishing or external freedom. In contrast, intrinsic value theories consider property rights as inherently valuable or constitutive of human identity. In terms of rights allocation rules, instrumental theories prioritise the design of rules that effectively achieve designated outcomes,[55] while intrinsic value theories emphasise safeguarding the fundamental nature of property rights.[56]

Private Property and the Constitution (Yale University Press 1977); Elinor Ostrom and Charlotte Hess, 'Private and Common Property Rights' in G De Geest (ed), *Encyclopedia of Law and Economics* (Edward Elgar Publishing Limited 2011); Joseph William Singer, 'Property as the Law of Democracy' (2013) 63 *Duke Law Journal* 1287; Joseph William Singer, 'Democratic Estates: Property Law in a Free and Democratic Society' (2008) 94 *Cornell Law Review* 1009; Gregory S Alexander and others, 'A Statement of Progressive Property' (2008) 94 *Cornell Law Review* 743.

[51] Waldron, *The Rule of Law and the Measure of Property* (n 7).

[52] Alexander and Peñalver (n 4).

[53] Waldron, *The Right to Private Property* (n 4); Penner, *The Idea of Property In Law* (n 4); Penner, *Property Rights: A Re-Examination* (n 4).

[54] Walsh (n 4); Alexander (n 50); Singer, 'Property as the Law of Democracy' (n 50).

[55] Walsh (n 4).

[56] Alexander and Peñalver (n 4).

The second axis examines how theories conceptualise property's relationship to human interests, contrasting monistic approaches that prioritise a single primary function (like welfare or liberty) with pluralistic perspectives that acknowledge multiple, potentially competing interests that property institutions must simultaneously serve. Such division also implies different regard for allocation rules. While monistic approaches advocate for standardised, clear-cut allocation rules, pluralistic frameworks favour adaptable arrangements capable of harmonising diverse interests.

A. Property's Purpose

i. Instrumental Theories

Instrumental theories evaluate property institutions based on their effectiveness in achieving specified ends. The three main instrumental approaches (Utilitarian, Kantian and Progressive) differ in what ends they prioritise, while sharing the view that property's value lies in what it enables to reach rather than what it inherently is.

Utilitarianism stands as the predominant view of property among lawyers today.[57] This approach, encompassing a diverse family of theoretical positions, provides a consequentialist framework for evaluating property institutions.[58] Utilitarians judge the fairness of property institutions by their outcomes.[59] At its core, the utilitarian view advocates for structuring property institutions to maximise aggregate welfare. It understands human interests principally through the lens of individual 'preference satisfaction'.[60] Contemporary utilitarian thinkers, particularly those aligned with the Law and Economics movement, tend to argue that property institutions should be configured to maximise society's net wealth.[61] This theoretical orientation leads to property systems that privilege clear entitlements, especially the right to exclude, viewing these as the most efficient mechanisms for ensuring predictability in property law while facilitating market transactions and reducing coordination or transaction costs.[62]

Kantian theory, while also instrumental, pursues a different end: securing external freedom.[63] This approach shifts the focus of property rights as necessary

[57] ibid 11.
[58] ibid 17.
[59] ibid 11.
[60] ibid 17.
[61] ibid.
[62] Walsh (n 4) 3; Guido Calabresi and A Douglas Melamed, 'Property Rules, Liability Rules, and Inalienability: One View of the Cathedral' in RA Epstein (ed), *Modern Understandings of Liberty and Property* (Routledge 2013). This is also reflected in the new 'information theories'. See Merrill (n 19). On a good account on the questions of property and the differences in terminology in law and economics, see Daniel Alejandro Monroy Cely, *Análisis económico del derecho Fundamentos y escuelas.* (Universidad Externado de Colombia 2023) 181–99.
[63] Alexander and Peñalver (n 4) 74.

tools for efficiency to essential conditions for the meaningful exercise of individual freedom.[64] For Kant, property is a 'noumenon'. That is to say, a concept grasped through reason rather than empirical observation. Through this lens, property rights grant individuals the ability to use external objects in pursuit of their freely defined ends, subject to moral imperatives.[65] Kant views property as an institution capable of regulating interpersonal relationships.[66] As a consequence, allocation rules must follow universal principles that both enable meaningful choice for individuals and preserve reciprocal relations between property holders. The state, in this case, emerges as an intermediary but necessary institution for securing both individual and external freedom.[67]

Progressive property theory presents a third instrumental approach that emphasises the multifaceted nature of property. Progressive theorists conceptualise property both as an abstract idea and as a concrete social institution that serves multiple ends, inter alia, efficiency, individual development, fostering meaningful social relationships and promoting human flourishing.[68] The underlying moral conceptions of just social relationships, distribution and democracy are what inform how property institutions can pursue these various values and therefore shape the allocation rules.[69]

Progressive theorists argue that meaningful human flourishing requires the redistribution of resources from those with means to those who lack them.[70] However, different from utilitarians, progressive theorists are careful in recognising that no discrete group of people should bear disproportionate demands of redistribution for the sake of the community's benefit.[71] In this account, property rights have a fundamental value in articulating social relationships, as they are essential for developing free-thinking individuals and fostering 'social and political competence'.[72] The challenge lies, instead, in knowing how to balance this security with the adaptability needed to promote human flourishing for everyone.[73]

These contrasting instrumental approaches fundamentally shape how a court like the ECtHR can conceptualise and adjudicate property rights. A utilitarian approach will likely prioritise efficient resource allocation and market certainty when determining whether an interest qualifies as property. In contrast, a Kantian framework would lean towards examining whether property rights secure individual autonomy and reciprocal freedoms. Progressive property theory would

[64] ibid 72.
[65] ibid.
[66] ibid 74.
[67] ibid 75.
[68] Walsh (n 4) 23.
[69] ibid; Singer, 'Democratic Estates: Property Law in a Free and Democratic Society' (n 50) 1047.
[70] Walsh (n 4) 29.
[71] Hanoch Dagan, 'The Social Responsibility of Ownership' (2006) 92 *Cornell Law Review* 1255.
[72] Michelman (n 4) 1102.
[73] Eric T Freyfogle, 'Private Ownership and Human Flourishing: An Exploratory Overview' (2013) 24 *Stellenbosch Law Review* 430.

push a court even further, requiring the judge to consider how property recognition and protection can advance multiple social values simultaneously, from individual development to community wellbeing. These theoretical distinctions matter not only for property recognition but also for determining the scope of legitimate interference with a given property right, such as a pension entitlement, and the appropriate balance between individual and collective interests in property disputes.

As will be clear in chapters four and five, the Court adopts an instrumental view of property. Depending on the case, the Court uses different reasons to recognise different entitlements as worthy of property protection, embedded in a broader framework of what property protection is all about under A1P1. Such a framework is what determines the extent to which A1P1 protects them.

ii. *Intrinsic Value Theories*

Intrinsic value theories of property do not see private property as a tool to achieve external objectives, but as something valuable in and of itself. These include natural rights and libertarian traditions, which ground property in individual entitlements, as well as Hegelian theories, which link property to the development and expression of personal identity. Despite their differences, all of these views share the belief that property has intrinsic moral or political worth.

Natural rights or libertarian theories see property as a pre-political right emerging from fundamental moral entitlements that set the boundaries or 'trumps'[74] an individual's position against the government.[75] Under these views, especially those inspired by Locke's account, the value of property rights arises from notions of moral desert.[76] According to them, it is the natural right of individuals to the fruits of their labour, which exist independently of their consequences for social welfare or other ends.[77] In these accounts, law and legal institutions should serve the value of property and not the contrary. Therefore, the current distribution of property must be respected, as it is socially and morally legitimate so long as it is acquired lawfully.[78]

Natural rights theories share with utilitarianism the intuition that individuals are treated as genuine moral agents only when the legal rules governing property are sufficiently predictable and stable. Such conditions enable individuals to make plans, form reasonable expectations about the future, and take responsibility for

[74] Ronald Dworkin, 'Rights as Trumps' in Jeremy Waldron (ed), *Theories of Rights* (Oxford University Press 2009) 157.

[75] Alexander and Peñalver (n 4) 42.

[76] Waldron, *The Right to Private Property* (n 4).

[77] Alexander and Peñalver (n 4) 36–38. The Lockean vision of property was functional both in England to secure the intertemporality of ownership and for colonizers in America to take over the land of indigenous tribes. For further discussion on the usage of these theories, see Katharina Pistor, *The Code of Capital: How the Law Creates Wealth and Inequality* (Princeton University Press 2019).

[78] Van der Walt (n 4) viii.

the choices – such as investments – they make within a given legal framework.[79] In this tradition, the protection of private property is closely tied to the enjoyment of individual freedom and the rule of law,[80] both of which are viewed as first-order values in a political community. On this account, property becomes a precondition for liberty.

The natural rights' reading of private property implies a strong suspicion towards any (re)distribution attempts guided or commanded by the state. In these views, changing the legal structures that govern these relations might lead to harmful consequences. Hayek, for instance, considered that legislation, mainly when it disturbed private property relations (market relations), was driven by a managerial mentality of politicians, which could have shattering consequences for liberty.[81] In this view, legal institutions should be an instrument at the service of property stability, which is, in turn, conceived as the right of rights, or 'the guardian of every other right'.[82] As a result, changes to property structures might be seen not only as inefficient but as a direct threat to individual freedom and political legitimacy.

Hegelian theory offers a more complex account of property's normative function. For Hegel, property is 'the relation of personality to the external sphere of things, understood in terms of free will'.[83] Like other property theories, it acknowledges the social dimension of ownership and the way it structures relationships among individuals.[84] However, while it shares with natural rights theorists the idea that property promotes individual freedom, it grounds that freedom in property's essential role in personality formation and self-realisation.[85] On this view, property is not simply a means to secure autonomy but a necessary condition for becoming a self-determining person.[86] For this account, property is constitutive of human identity and development, and for that reason, is understood as intrinsically valuable.[87]

The contrast between natural rights and Hegelian approaches reveals fundamentally different understandings of when property rights can legitimately be limited or regulated. Natural rights theorists, who view property as a pre-political right emerging from a moral desert, require a strong justification for any state interference with property. They typically require explicit consent or truly compelling public necessity. Hegelian theory, while also treating property as intrinsically valuable, offers a more nuanced framework that can accommodate different levels

[79] Jeremy Waldron, 'The Rule of Law in Public Law' in M Elliot and D Feldman (eds), *The Cambridge Companion to Public Law* (Cambridge University Press 2015) 58.

[80] Like Locke and Hayek. See Waldron, *The Rule of Law and the Measure of Property* (n 7) 7; Cass (n 8).

[81] Hayek (n 9) 123–78.

[82] James W Ely, *The Guardian of Every Other Right: A Constitutional History of Property Rights* (Oxford University Press 2008).

[83] Penner, *The Idea of Property In Law* (n 4) 173.

[84] Alexander and Peñalver (n 4) 68.

[85] ibid 65.

[86] Margaret Jane Radin, 'Property and Personhood' [1982] *Stanford Law Review* 957.

[87] Alexander and Peñalver (n 4) 65.

of protection based on property's role in personality development. This suggests that for Hegelian theory, the degree of protection might vary. Its intensity might be a function of how central a particular property is to personal identity and self-realisation.[88] That view would therefore allow for more flexible regulation of property that is less connected to personhood, while maintaining robust protection for property that is central to individual development.

While theoretically valuable, these intrinsic value approaches rarely surface in ECtHR litigation, largely because A1P1's text aligns more closely with an instrumentalist perspective by explicitly recognising that property rights may be constrained for public interest reasons. Nevertheless, applicants occasionally advance arguments drawing from intrinsic value theories to strengthen their positions. The natural rights view emerges strategically in cases where applicants seek to characterise state action as a deprivation or expropriation, either to prevent regulatory measures from taking effect or to secure compensation.[89] In cases concerning pension entitlements, a notable example arose during the Hungarian pension reforms, where an applicant contended that their social security contributions constituted an inviolable property right that could not be modified by subsequent redistributive regulation without amounting to a substantial deprivation of rights.[90] The Court, however, rejected this argument at the admissibility stage, concluding that the applicant failed to demonstrate the existence of a legitimate proprietary interest that would qualify for protection under A1P1.

Arguments echoing Hegelian property theory have emerged in cases concerning the restitution of property confiscated during the communist era in post-Soviet states. In these cases, applicants have contended that certain items merit A1P1 protection specifically because they are constitutive of the applicant's personal or familial identity.[91] The core argument asserts that these possessions hold particular meaning beyond their economic value, thereby deserving their complete restitution due to their role in personal and family heritage. While such personality-based arguments occasionally influence how cases are framed and may strengthen certain aspects of applications, they find limited success in the Court. A1P1's text and its jurisprudence do not explicitly recognise or incorporate Hegelian conceptions of property's relationship to personal identity, but rather view property as fungible, so that compensation measures could substitute in cases of interference.

B. Property's Values

Property theories can also be categorised by their understanding of what human values property institutions should serve. These different understandings influence

[88] Radin (n 86).
[89] *Anheuser-Busch Inc v Portugal* (GC) ECHR 2007-I (2007) 44 EHRR 42.
[90] *EB v Hungary App no 34929/11* (ECtHR, 2013).
[91] *Prince Hans-Adam II of Liechtenstein v Germany* (GC) ECHR 2001-VIII.

how legal systems approach resource allocation and property protection, even when such theoretical frameworks remain implicit in judicial reasoning.[92] It is the case, for instance, when the ECtHR must decide whether the interest at stake should be treated as a property right deserving the protection of A1P1.

Monistic approaches identify a single primary interest that property institutions should serve. These theories attempt to reduce all property considerations to a unitary metric or value. Utilitarianism represents the clearest example. For this view, all relevant considerations of property institutions are reduced to their ability to enhance welfare, efficiency, or preference satisfaction.[93] This single-minded focus offers analytical clarity but raises questions about whether important human interests are being overlooked or improperly reduced to a single measure. Moreover, it tells us little about whether unfair burden distribution can exist as a result of reallocating individual property rights.

Similar monistic tendencies appear in libertarian theories, which prioritise individual liberty above all other values. Libertarian approaches view property rights as fundamental moral claims that exist prior to and independent from their social consequences.[94] In their most extreme interpretations, any regulatory interference with property constitutes a *de facto* reduction of individual liberty.[95] This emphasis on pre-political property rights effectively aims at freezing any attempt to reform existing distributions of property, framing public regulation as an impermissible interference with liberty. However, in practice, such radical claims find little traction when confronted with texts like A1P1, which explicitly recognises the legitimacy of property regulation subject to specific conditions. As discussed earlier, these libertarian arguments tend to emerge strategically in applications to characterise interferences as deprivations, thereby strengthening compensation claims.[96]

Kantian theory, while more sophisticated, also displays monistic features in its focus on external freedom as the primary interest that property serves. Although this approach recognises multiple aspects of freedom, it ultimately reduces property's relevance to its role in enabling independence from others' choices. Therefore, it struggles to fully capture the property's multifaceted social role, which has been widely recognised even in the most individualistic societies.[97]

In contrast, pluralistic accounts contend that property serves multiple human interests that resist reduction to a single metric.[98] Progressive property theorists explicitly recognise property's role in serving various incommensurable values, ranging from physical security and economic efficiency to human flourishing and

[92] Walsh (n 4) 43.
[93] Alexander and Peñalver (n 4) 13.
[94] Richard A Epstein, *Takings: Private Property and the Power of Eminent Domain* (Harvard University Press 1985).
[95] Liam Murphy and Thomas Nagel, *The Myth of Ownership: Taxes and Justice* (Oxford University Press 2002).
[96] Maxwell (n 1) 134.
[97] Walsh (n 4) 1–2.
[98] Dagan (n 19) 3–27; Alexander and Peñalver (n 4).

development.[99] This pluralistic understanding usually demands more nuanced allocation rules that balance competing interests rather than optimising for a single value.[100] The relevant values at stake are highly context-dependent. Recognising proprietary interests in land, for instance, primarily serves efficiency goals, while protecting pension entitlements could advance individual autonomy.[101] This context-sensitive approach to property's multiple values, though not explicitly acknowledged, characterises the ECtHR's jurisprudential development in recognising diverse proprietary interests under A1P1.

The Hegelian Approach also adopts a pluralistic view. However, it conveys a very different meaning to the plurality of interests served by property. This approach acknowledges that property's role in personality development cannot be reduced to a single dimension, but involves multiple aspects of human life and social relationships.[102] In this view, property can be classified into personal and fungible, each serving different values or interests.[103] The first one is bound to an individual in the constitutive sense, meaning that it is a type of property that allows them to determine their own personhood, self-identification and promote healthy self-development. The second one is a type of property that helps to achieve personal freedom, but the loss of which could be substituted.[104]

The Court's jurisprudence reflects an ongoing tension between monistic approaches, usually advanced by applicants disputing various types of measures that seek clear, rule-based criteria and pluralistic approaches, which recognise multiple bases for property protection.[105] This tension is relevant for understanding the debate surrounding the recognition of welfare entitlements as property in the evolution of the ECtHR's case law.[106] The next section traces how the normative debates surrounding property shaped A1P1's text and how its drafters tasked the ECtHR with the management of those tensions through judicial interpretation.

III. The Development and Evolution of A1P1

A. The Making of A1P1

A1P1 has been catalogued as one of the Convention's most controversial and obscure provisions.[107] It is the 'problem child' of the European family of rights and

[99] Walsh (n 4) 23.
[100] Freyfogle (n 73); Alexander (n 50).
[101] Singer, 'Property as the Law of Democracy' (n 50).
[102] Alexander and Peñalver (n 4) 65.
[103] Radin (n 86).
[104] ibid; Alexander and Peñalver (n 4) 66–67.
[105] *James and Others v United Kingdom* Series A no 98 (1986) 8 EHRR 123.
[106] See chs 4 and 5.
[107] A Riza Çoban, *Protection of Property Rights within the European Convention on Human Rights* (Ashgate 2003) 124.

freedoms.[108] There are two reasons for such a description. First, because it does not provide a direct statement of rights.[109] Namely, it does not adhere to the formula of other articles in the Convention, like 'everyone has the right to X', followed by a substantive characterisation of the right.[110] Second, because there is a distinction between the title of the article, 'Protection of Property', and the body of the article, where the word 'property' does not appear, thereby creating unnecessary ambiguity.[111] These two aspects render A1P1 open for interpretation, but simultaneously, vulnerable to misunderstanding and opportunistic usage.

Drawing on Article 17 of the Universal Declaration of Human Rights, the drafters sought to establish property rights protection that would shield individuals from arbitrary dispossession.[112] During initial discussions, the Council of Europe's Committee on Legal Affairs and Human Rights endorsed including property rights in the Convention, notwithstanding concerns about incorporating what many viewed as socio-economic rather than civil rights. The Committee ultimately concluded that property rights protection was fundamental to securing personal and family independence.[113]

The debate focused on the nature and scope of the right. Critics questioned why a socio-economic right like property was prioritised over others, such as the right to work or an adequate standard of living.[114] To many drafters, socio-economic rights, such as fair wages or the right to work, seemed equally, if not more, fundamental than the right to property.[115] The British delegate, Lord Layton, viewed the inclusion as a zero-sum game, asserting that either all such rights should be included or none at all. Some other delegations pointed to the vagueness of the concept, arguing that property was too difficult to define at the Convention's level, hence arguing for toning down its strength and purpose.[116]

Political concerns also shaped the debate. Some feared that enshrining property rights would send the wrong message to those without substantial property, as it might appear to protect the interests of the wealthy at the expense of the poor.[117] There was also apprehension that such a provision could transform into a straitjacket for governments that would obstruct their ability to tax or nationalise property for the sake of societal good.[118] Concerns were also raised about

[108] ibid.

[109] David Anderson, 'Compensation for Interference with Property' [1999] *European Human Rights Law Review* 543, 543.

[110] For instance, Article 2 on the right to life: 'Everyone's right to life shall be protected by law. No one shall be deprived of his life intentionally save in the execution of a sentence of a court following his conviction of a crime for which this penalty is provided by law'.

[111] Gretton (n 50) 275.

[112] Maxwell (n 1) 66.

[113] ibid 65–68.

[114] Jim L Murdoch, *Reed and Murdoch: Human Rights Law in Scotland* 4th edn (Bloomsbury Publishing 2017) 960.

[115] Maxwell (n 1) 65–68.

[116] ibid.

[117] ibid.

[118] ibid.

the enforceability and justiciability of the right in judicial proceedings. These arguments led to the exclusion of the right in the initial draft of the Convention.[119]

The proponents of property rights persisted in their advocacy even after the Convention's approval, campaigning for its inclusion in an additional protocol. They emphasised property's dual role: as a means for individual self-fulfilment and its function as a bulwark against totalitarian state power. The powerfully resonated during the drafting, given the recent memory of Jewish property confiscations during World War II.[120]

The final text of A1P1 emerged as a compromise between a robust conception of property rights protection and complete exclusion.[121] The text's deliberate ambiguity reflects the fundamental ideological tension between liberal and social democratic conceptions of property rights prevalent in post-war Europe.[122] The liberal perspective conceptualised property as a pre-political natural right, arguing that state interference necessarily required market-value compensation to mirror voluntary private transactions. In contrast, the social democratic perspective saw property regulation as a normal state of affairs in rights-respecting nations, with compensation being a matter of distributive justice rather than corrective justice.[123] These competing visions were particularly evident in post-war European constitutions, such as those of Italy, Ireland and Germany, which protected property rights while explicitly recognising property's social function.[124]

At the core of the debate is the question of whether states are required to provide direct market-value compensation to individuals whose property is taken. The final text of A1P1 represented an uneasy compromise between these competing views,[125] suggesting that it was never intended to convey an overly libertarian[126] conception of property rights.[127] Although the provision conceives of property regulation as an interference with individual entitlement, it leaves legislatures significant discretion in matters of expropriation and regulation, reflecting social democratic thinking.[128] It also removed any requirement of compensation in cases of regulation or deprivation of property. In this respect, A1P1 sets out a 'weak right'[129] that provides procedural guarantees to individuals when a state interferes with their property, and, in conjunction with Article 14, a guarantee that entitlements are allocated and administered without discrimination.[130]

[119] ibid.
[120] ibid 66.
[121] ibid 73; Allen (n 1).
[122] Allen (n 1); Riza Çoban (n 106) 125.
[123] Allen (n 1) 1058.
[124] ibid 1062.
[125] ibid 1064.
[126] Or an 'every-day libertarian' account. See Murphy and Nagel (n 95).
[127] Maxwell (n 1) 49.
[128] Allen (n 1) 1064.
[129] Maxwell (n 1) 2.
[130] Allen (n 1) 1064.

Drafting an ambiguous text like A1P1 amounted to an implicit delegation to the ECtHR to define the scope, limits, and exceptions of the right through its case law.[131] In exercising this interpretive role, however, the Court moved beyond the original compromise reflected in the text. Despite the Protocol's deliberate omission of any compensation requirement, the Court held that expropriation without fair compensation constitutes a violation of A1P1, with market value established as the primary standard for assessing compliance.[132]

Since the 1980s, the Court's jurisprudence has increasingly reflected core liberal principles, particularly in cases involving traditional forms of property such as land. This approach rests on three key ideas. First, the value of property is determined by market conditions. Second, state intervention is treated as a disruption of a natural economic order and must therefore be subject to robust justification. Third, such interference is considered legitimate only if it preserves the owner's position in a way that is broadly comparable to a voluntary transaction.[133]

When addressing novel forms of property, such as social security entitlements, however, the Court's jurisprudence retains various elements of social democratic thinking.[134] This translates into two aspects. First, the Court's acceptance of departures from market-value compensation required by economic restructuring or social justice goals. Second, the recognition that property rights can serve purposes related to individual dependency and welfare protection.

B. Content and Duties

While property rights traditionally function as a 'trump' against governmental interference,[135] the precise scope of 'peaceful enjoyment' under A1P1 required judicial clarification. This issue emerged in *Powell and Rayner v United Kingdom*,[136] where the applicant argued that 'peaceful enjoyment' encompassed his right to a quiet environment on his land. This conception arises as a result of the disruptions of his quiet environment by aircraft noise following the modification of Heathrow Airport's flight pathways.[137]

After reviewing the admissibility of the case, the Court rejected the applicant's interpretation of the expression 'peaceful enjoyment' established in A1P1. Instead, what 'peaceful' enjoyment of private property conveys is a duty for governments

[131] Maxwell (n 1) 76–77.
[132] Allen (n 1); Maxwell (n 1) 2.
[133] Allen (n 1).
[134] See ch 6.
[135] Dworkin (n 74) 157.
[136] *Powell and Rayner v United Kingdom* Series A no 172 (1990) 12 EHRR 355.
[137] ibid.

to abstain from disturbing the enjoyment of the myriad of property rights that individuals might have over their 'possessions'.[138]

The scope of state duties in ensuring 'peaceful enjoyment' has expanded over time to encompass positive obligations, which require various forms of active state intervention.[139] The least controversial of these obligations requires states to take active measures to protect individual property through the correct application of the rule of law in property-related procedures.[140] More complex obligations have emerged, including the duty to act diligently to prevent potential property deprivations. In *Öneryildiz v Turkey*,[141] the Court established that mere abstention from interference may not suffice to fulfil state obligations under A1P1:

> [A]fter emphasising the key importance of the right enshrined in Article 1 of Protocol No. 1, considered that genuine, effective exercise of that right did not depend merely on the State's duty not to interfere *and could require positive measures of protection [of the property]*.[142]

The case involved applicants who challenged state negligence in addressing risks at a garbage collection site. The subsequent explosion caused both loss of life and destruction of property in the surrounding area. The Court held that this incident constituted an interference with the applicants' property rights under the first sentence of A1P1.[143] Moreover, it established that ensuring the peaceful enjoyment of possessions may require proactive measures to protect property integrity. The Court clarified, however, that such positive obligations arise only under specific

[138] 'The Convention's drafters recognized that democratic governments need leeway to adopt or modify economic and social policies implicating private property without, in every instance, compensating adversely affected owners. On the other hand, the drafters also understood that the rule of law in general and the stability and predictability of property rights in particular would be undermined if governments could arbitrarily deprive owners of their possessions. In attempting to reconcile these competing perspectives, the European Court and Commission have created a complex and intricate jurisprudence interpreting the right of property'; Laurence R Helfer, 'The New Innovation Frontier-Intellectual Property and the European Court of Human Rights' (2008) 49 *Harvard International Law Journal* 1, 8.

[139] Vladislava Stoyanova, 'Causation between State Omission and Harm within the Framework of Positive Obligations under the European Convention on Human Rights' (2018) 18 *Human Rights Law Review* 309; Vladislava Stoyanova, 'Causation between State Omission and Harm within the Framework of Positive Obligations under the European Convention on Human Rights' (2018) 18 *Human Rights Law Review* 309; Vladislava Stoyanova, 'The Disjunctive Structure of Positive Rights under the European Convention on Human Rights' (2018) 87 *Nordic Journal of International Law* 344; Vladislava Stoyanova, 'Fault, Knowledge and Risk within the Framework of Positive Obligations under the European Convention on Human Rights' (2020) 33 *Leiden Journal of International Law* 601; Vladislava Stoyanova, 'Framing Positive Obligations under the European Convention on Human Rights Law: Mediating between the Abstract and the Concrete' (2023) 23 *Human Rights Law Review* 1; Vladislava Stoyanova, *Positive Obligations under the European Convention on Human Rights: Within and Beyond Boundaries* (Oxford University Press 2023).

[140] Pieter Van Dijk and Godefridus JH Van Hoof, *Theory and Practice of the European Convention on Human Rights* (Martinus Nijhoff Publishers 2023) 804.

[141] *Öneryıldız v Turkey* (GC) ECHR 2004-XII (2005) 41 EHRR 20.

[142] ibid 130 (emphasis added).

[143] ibid 133.

conditions and vary in intensity depending on circumstances.[144] The key determinant is whether applicants could 'legitimately expect' such protective action from public authorities: '[T]here is a direct link between the measures an applicant *may legitimately expect* from the authorities and his effective enjoyment of his possessions'.[145]

The legitimacy of expected positive measures depends on the individual's relationship with the state, particularly whether a 'special tie' exists.[146] Prisoners represent the paradigmatic example, because their unique dependency creates a 'special status' and corresponding ties with the state. Additionally, individual vulnerability, whether arising from an omission or inherent condition, may establish such special 'ties'.[147] These vulnerabilities manifest in two forms: innate vulnerabilities, exemplified by children or persons with disabilities, and social vulnerabilities, encompassing religious minorities or victims of domestic violence.[148] I have argued elsewhere that this framework of positive obligations could require governments to index certain welfare benefits, particularly for individuals who heavily depend on such entitlements and maintain special ties with the state, given that these benefits often constitute their primary or sole wealth.[149]

C. A1P1's Purpose

The purpose of A1P1 is to ensure a reasonable understanding of the stability and predictability of property relations between individuals and governments in matters related to the control of resources.[150] The heart of A1P1 is to protect the individual entitlement to property, and therefore places an obligation on states to justify interferences in a particular way.[151] A1P1 appears to act only in the aftermath of a disputed interference to obtain some form of monetary and declaratory redress.[152] This goes in line with the reflection of Judge Fitzmaurice in his dissenting opinion in *Marckx v Belgium*:[153] '[T]he chief if not the only object of A1P1 was to prevent the arbitrary seizures, confiscations, expropriations, extorsions or other

[144] Elsewhere I argued that such principle can also be applied in cases concerning inflation and welfare benefit entitlements. Kevin Hartmann-Cortés, 'Should We Uprate Social Benefits for Inflation as a Matter of Article 1 Protocol 1?' (2022) 24 *European Journal of Social Security* 319.

[145] *Öneryıldız v Turkey* (n 140) §134 (emphasis added); Dabić v Croatia App no 49001/14 (ECtHR, 2021) §51; Broniowski v Poland (GC) (2004) ECHR 2004-V §143.

[146] Stoyanova, 'Causation between State Omission and Harm within the Framework of Positive Obligations under the European Convention on Human Rights' (n 138) 330.

[147] ibid 331; Hartmann-Cortés (n 143).

[148] Stoyanova, 'Causation between State Omission and Harm within the Framework of Positive Obligations under the European Convention on Human Rights' (n 138) 331.

[149] Hartmann-Cortés (n 143).

[150] Allen (n 50) 185.

[151] Maxwell (n 1) 62.

[152] ibid 50.

[153] *Marckx v Belgium* (n 15).

capricious interferences with peaceful enjoyment that many governments are – or frequently have been – all too prone to resort to'.[154]

A1P1's protective capacity lies in its capacity to scrutinise state actions that might 'go too far'[155] in regulating property, thereby constraining governments' ability to implement drastic property redistribution without significant public expenditure.[156] This does not preclude governments from modifying or adjusting property regulations when necessary. Importantly, contrary to 'everyday libertarian' interpretations, the right to peaceful enjoyment of property holds no special status within the Convention's framework. The Convention establishes no hierarchy among rights, nor does it recognise any right as absolute or predominant.[157] Instead, Convention rights exist in parallel, requiring careful balancing when they intersect.

More recent interpretations have expanded A1P1's purposes. In his dissenting opinion in *Konyv-Tár KFT v Hungary*,[158] Judge Wojtyczek argued that A1P1 serves to protect economic freedom by limiting governmental interference with private property.[159] This view suggests additional purposes for A1P1: ensuring procedural fairness, protecting individual autonomy and safeguarding human dignity.[160] Through its protection of private property rights, A1P1 fulfils a 'double' protective function, securing both specific entitlements and the broader liberal institution of private ownership.[161]

This multifaceted approach becomes particularly evident in cases concerning pensions and welfare benefits. As will become clear in chapter six, A1P1 protects vulnerable individuals' autonomy by preserving their position within the social security system. This diversity of protected interests reflects A1P1's pluralistic approach to property, with the precise balance of values varying according to the type of entitlement at issue.

Conclusions

This chapter has examined how certain theoretical foundations influence the protection of property rights under A1P1 of the European Convention on Human Rights. Property emerges as both a legal concept and a social institution,

[154] ibid. Dissenting opinion of Judge Fitzmaurice, §20.

[155] I am drawing a parallel between the 'test' used by the United States Supreme Court concerning the Fifth Amendment of the United States Constitution, where Justice Oliver Wendell Holmes famously stated that a regulation constitutes a taking when it 'goes too far'. *Pennsylvania Coal Co v Mahon* (1922) 260 393 (United States Supreme Court).

[156] Maxwell (n 1) 50.

[157] Tom Bingham, *The Rule of Law* (Allen Lane 2010) 82–83.

[158] *Konyv-Tár KFT v Hungary* App no 21623/13 (ECtHR, 2018).

[159] ibid. Dissenting Opinion of Judge Wojtyczek, §5.

[160] Allen (n 50) 283–93.

[161] AJ Van der Walt, '"Double" Property Guarantees: A Structural and Comparative Analysis' (1998) 14 *South African Journal on Human Rights* 560, 560.

functioning not merely as a relationship between people and things, but as a sophisticated system of mediated social relationships. The analysis reveals a fundamental tension between instrumental and intrinsic approaches to property rights protection. Instrumental theories, which evaluate property based on its capacity to achieve specific ends, offer courts flexible frameworks for adjusting property rights as social conditions evolve. Intrinsic value theories, by contrast, view certain property rights as fundamental regardless of consequences, pushing toward more rigid protection of core interests. This theoretical tension helps explain the fluctuation in property law between the demand for clear rules or flexible standards, particularly in cases where courts must balance individual rights against collective needs.

A1P1's framework encompasses diverse entitlements and imposes dual obligations on states. For individuals, it guarantees the unconstrained exercise of property rights over 'possessions' without undue governmental interference. For states, it requires both restraint from unjustified interference and, in certain circumstances, active protection of individual property rights. The evolution of these positive obligations reflects the provision's adaptability to changing social conditions and recognition of varying vulnerabilities among property holders. Notably, the intensity of these obligations varies according to beneficiaries' vulnerability and their relationship with the state, demonstrating A1P1's capacity to accommodate different levels of protection based on social context and individual circumstances.

The Court's case law demonstrates a sophisticated understanding of property's role in modern society. Property serves many functions: protecting individual autonomy, fostering social relationships, enabling economic activity and promoting human flourishing. Such a pluralistic understanding has enabled the Court to extend protection to non-traditional forms of property while maintaining coherent standards of review.

The theoretical foundation laid out in this chapter helps explain how the Court determines which interests merit protection and which limitations are justified. The framework developed here suggests that property functions both as an instrument for advancing social goals and as a safeguard of individual autonomy. Effective protection requires principles that are flexible enough to respond to evolving social needs yet robust enough to secure meaningful individual rights, all while maintaining coherence in protection standards.

3

What Counts as Property under Article 1 of Protocol No 1?

Introduction

Article 1 of Protocol No 1 (A1P1) protects the right to private property. That much is settled. But when it comes to defining what exactly is protected under that article precisely, ambiguity arises. As chapter two showed, A1P1's ambiguous drafting was not accidental. It was the result of an ideological compromise which tried to accommodate competing views on the role of property within the Convention system.[1] Moreover, it was a way to leave to the European Court of Human Rights (ECtHR) the responsibility to define the content and scope of that article through judicial interpretation.

One of the first tasks of the Court was to define the object of A1P1's protection. The English version of the norm speaks of protecting 'possessions', which is an uncommon term in Anglo-Saxon legal traditions to refer to private property.[2] The French version offers no more clarity, treating *biens* and *propriété* interchangeably.[3] Yet, understanding what a 'possession' is ultimately defines the operational limits of A1P1.

This chapter aims to engage with the content, scope and boundaries of A1P1. The guiding questions are four: (i) what are the necessary and sufficient conditions for a legal interest to qualify as a 'possession' under the Court's? (ii) How has this definition expanded the traditional boundaries of private property protection? (iii) What temporal requirements must an interest meet to fall within the scope of A1P1? And finally, (iv) what role does the doctrine of legitimate expectations play in extending protection to forward-looking claims such as pensions?

[1] A Riza Çoban, *Protection of Property Rights within the European Convention on Human Rights* (Ashgate 2003); Tom Allen, 'Liberalism, Social Democracy and the Value of Property under the European Convention on Human Rights' (2010) 59 *International & Comparative Law Quarterly* 1055; Douglas Maxwell, *The Human Right to Property: A Practical Approach to Article 1 of Protocol No. 1 to the ECHR* (Bloomsbury Publishing 2022); Laurence R Helfer, 'The New Innovation Frontier-Intellectual Property and the European Court of Human Rights' (2008) 49 *Harvard International Law Journal* 1; Pieter Van Dijk and Godefridus JH Van Hoof, *Theory and Practice of the European Convention on Human Rights* (Martinus Nijhoff Publishers 2023).

[2] Maxwell (n 1) 79.

[3] Dissenting opinion of Judge Fitzmaurice in *Marckx v Belgium* Series A no 31 (1979) 2 EHRR 330.

The reader must always bear in mind that this is not a general study of A1P1, but one explicitly concerned with its application to pension entitlements.[4] Therefore, some dimensions of the right to property will be underscored more explicitly, as they are more relevant for the protection of pensions.

The chapter is divided into three sections. Section I examines the Court's construction of the autonomous approach to define what is a possession and how it has evolved to encompass modern forms of economic interest. Section II turns to the temporal dimension of A1P1, focusing on the distinction between existing possessions and future entitlements, which is an issue that plays a decisive role in pension-related litigation. Section III addresses the doctrine of legitimate expectations and explores how it enables the Court to protect specific disputed claims while maintaining coherent boundaries on the reach of A1P1. Together, these sections provide the conceptual groundwork for the detailed analysis of pension benefits as property that follows in the following chapters.

I. What Makes Something a 'Possession'?

The most fundamental question for any case under A1P1 is defining whether the applicant holds a 'possession'. The concept of 'possessions' defines the outer boundary of A1P1. Only the objects, rights, or interests that qualify as 'possessions' engage the Convention's protection. If the interest at stake does not qualify as a possession, the case is rejected *ratione materiae*.

Determining what qualifies as a 'possession' poses a challenge for a regional court, especially within the Council of Europe, where the two principal legal traditions coexist and where Member States differ not only in their conceptions of property but also in the regulation of its acquisition, use and protection. In the civil law tradition, property is classically defined as a real right over a thing (*droit réel*), which, in turn, is typically subdivided into three 'incidents':[5] use, enjoyment and ownership.[6] These types of rights create a relationship between the right holder and the rest of the world. That is to say, the owner's right over the thing is enforceable against any third party, including the State. In contrast, personal rights (*droits personnels*) establish claims against specific individuals.[7] A pension entitlement, for example, is usually treated as a personal right created by statute, not as real property in the strict sense.

[4] For a sustained and longer description of other dimensions of A1P1, see Maxwell (n 1).

[5] By incidents I am referring to the classical categorisation used by Anthony M Honoré, *Ownership* (Oxford University Press, 1961) 112–24.

[6] François Terré, 'L'évolution Du Droit de Propriété Depuis Le Code Civil' [1985] *Droits* 33.

[7] ibid; Georges Ripert, Jean-Claude Boulanger and Marcel Planiol, 'Traité de Droit Civil, d'après Le Traité de Planiol' in G. Ripert and J. Boulanger (eds), *Obligations, contrat, responsabilité, droits réels, biens, propriété*, vol 2 (Librairie Générale de Droit et de Jurisprudence, 1957).

The English common law divides property into real and personal categories: land on the one hand, and everything else, including equity, on the other.[8] It further distinguishes between rights *in rem* and *in personam*. Rights *in rem* attach to things and are enforceable against third parties.[9] The archetypal example of a right *in rem* is a piece of land. Rights *in personam*, which are also labelled as *choses in action*, are relational and enforceable only between identified persons.[10] The archetypal example of a right *in personam* is a debt (or 'claim' (*créances*)).[11]

Under classical common law doctrine, *choses in action* – debts, claims, contractual entitlements – were not considered property.[12] They were conceived as purely relational rights between two (or more) people. Put differently, 'a right to prosecute a legal relation by bringing a Court action against some other person or persons'.[13] The defining feature of these rights was that they were unopposed to third parties different from those within the legal relation at stake. More recent doctrine, however, classifies them in the category of property as well.[14] Choses in action became unique objects of property,[15] because unlike rights *in rem*, which exist independently of the law, rights *in personam* are created and shaped only by the law itself.[16]

The doctrinal discussions about the property nature of claims like licences, regulatory benefits or pension entitlements show that there is still debate on how to treat them legally. Some domestic legislations classify them as property.[17] Others treat them as expectations or administrative gratuities.[18] The same variation applies to the degree of constitutional or statutory protection afforded to property

[8] JE Penner, *The Idea of Property In Law* (Clarendon Press 1997) ch 5.

[9] ibid; Charles Sweet, 'Choses in Action' (1894) 10 *Law Quarterly Review* 303.

[10] Wesley Newcomb Hohfeld, 'Fundamental Legal Conceptions as Applied in Judicial Reasoning' (1917) 26 *The Yale Law Journal* 710.

[11] René Savatier, 'Les Métamorphoses Économiques et Sociales Du Droit Privé d'aujourd'hui' in R Savatier (ed), *Approfondissement d'un droit renouvelé* (Dalloz 1959) 146; Jean Carbonnier, 'Les Biens: Monnaie, Immeubles, Meubles' in *Droit Civil*, vol 3, 21st edn (Presses Universitaires de France 2000) 71.

[12] Alan Brudner, James Penner and H Smith, 'Private Property and Public Welfare' in James Penner and Henry Smith (eds), *Philosophical Foundations of Property Law* (Dalloz 2013) 68, 87–90.

[13] Penner (n 8) 107.

[14] Jeremy Waldron, 'Property Law' in Dennis Michael Patterson (ed), *A Companion to Philosophy of Law and Legal Theory* (Wiley Online Library 2010) 10.

[15] Penner (n 8); Sweet (n 12).

[16] Waldron (n 14) 10.

[17] Danny Pieters, 'Security in Social Security: Reflections from a Legal Point of View' (2012) 67 *Pravnik* 21. For a discussion outside of Europe; C. Reich, 'The New Property' (1964) 73 Yale Law 733; Charles A Reich, 'Social Welfare in the Public-Private State' (1965) 114 *University of Pennsylvania Law Review* 487; Charles A Reich, 'Individual Rights and Social Welfare: The Emerging Legal Issues' in *Welfare Law* (Routledge 2020); Rick J Hecker, 'On the Subject of Property and Social Security: A Traditional Analysis' (2012) 7 *Liberty University Law Review* 143.

[18] Pieters (n 17). For a discussion outside of Europe see Reich, 'The New Property' (n 17); Reich, 'Social Welfare in the Public-Private State' (n 17); Reich, 'Individual Rights and Social Welfare: The Emerging Legal Issues' (n 17); Hecker (n 17).

rights.[19] Faced with this plurality, the ECtHR could not rely on domestic classifications to determine whether an interest qualified as a possession.[20] Doing so would have led to inconsistent and fragmented application of the Convention. The solution developed by the Court was to adopt an autonomous concept of 'possessions', interpreted in light of the Convention's structure, purposes and values:

> The concept of 'possessions' referred to in the first part of Article 1 of Protocol No. 1 has an autonomous meaning which is not limited to ownership of physical goods and is independent from the formal classification in domestic law: certain other rights and interests constituting assets can also be regarded as 'property rights', and thus as 'possessions' for the purposes of this provision. The issue that needs to be examined in each case is whether the circumstances of the case, considered as a whole, conferred on the applicant title to a substantive interest protected by Article 1 of Protocol No. 1.[21]

This doctrinal move serves three purposes. First, as mentioned, it avoids confining the notion of possession to domestic definitions of ownership and spares the Court from resolving complex disputes about the existence or scope of property rights under national law.[22] Second, it prevents governments from evading their obligations through 'legislative or linguistic trickery'.[23] For instance, classifying interests with a proprietary nature as something else to escape the Convention's scope. Third, it enables the Court to apply a uniform standard across member states regarding the interests that meet specific substantive criteria.

The Court's autonomous concept of possessions is far from being conceptually stable. Sometimes it refers to the incidents traditionally included in the classical 'bundle of rights' associated with the rights to use, possess or dispose of an object.[24] At other times, it denotes the object itself: the land, asset or entitlement over which those rights are exercised. In classical legal doctrine, property is defined in terms

[19] Ronald A Cass, 'Property Rights Systems and the Rule of Law' [2003] Available at SSRN 392783; James W Ely, *The Guardian of Every Other Right: A Constitutional History of Property Rights* (Oxford University Press 2008); George Gretton, 'The Protection of Property Rights' in C Himsworth and A Boyle (eds), *Human Rights and Scots Law: Comparative Perspectives on the Incorporation of the ECHR* (Hart Publishing 2002).

[20] *Anheuser-Busch Inc v Portugal* (GC) ECHR 2007-I (2007) 44 EHRR 42 § 63; *Beyeler v Italy* (GC) ECHR 2000-I; *Béláné Nagy v Hungary* (GC) App no 53080/13 (ECtHR, 2016). In the French official version of this paragraph there is little change of the definition of 'possessions' It does not shed a different light. Indeed, the Court indicates: 'La notion de "bien" évoquée à la première partie de l'article 1 du Protocole no 1 a une portée autonome qui ne se limite pas à la propriété de biens corporels et qui est indépendante par rapport aux qualifications formelles du droit interne: certains autres droits et intérêts constituant des actifs peuvent aussi passer pour des "droits patrimoniaux" et donc des "biens" aux fins de cette disposition. Dans chaque affaire, il importe d'examiner si les circonstances, considérées dans leur ensemble, ont rendu le requérant titulaire d'un intérêt substantiel protégé par l'article 1 du Protocole no 1'.

[21] *Broniowski v Poland* (GC) (2004) ECHR 2004-V; *Anheuser-Busch Inc v Portugal* (n 20) §63; *Beyeler v Italy* (n 20) §100; *Béláné Nagy v Hungary* (n 20)§76.

[22] Maxwell (n 1) 83.

[23] ibid 83.

[24] Honoré (n 5). On a critical regard of Honoré's account, Penner (n 8); James E Penner, *Property Rights: A Re-Examination* (Oxford University Press, USA 2020).

of rights over things, not the things themselves.[25] So, the Court's tendency to alternate between these two meanings without a clear distinction blurs the line between the content of property (the rights) and its object (the asset), raising uncertainty about what exactly is being protected under A1P1. This uncertainty is one of the reasons why it is challenging for individuals and states to determine whether a particular interest falls within A1P1's scope of protection.

One strategy to know whether a given interest falls within A1P1 could be compiling a list of all the interests and objects the Court has treated as possessions. But such a strategy would be doomed to fail. First, because given the volume of cases decided under A1P1, it would seem like an impossible task.[26] More importantly, the Court has consistently refused to reduce the notion of 'possessions' to a fixed catalogue or to extract a general formula from its past judgments. Therefore, the fact that an interest has been recognised as a possession in the past is neither a necessary nor a sufficient condition for its future inclusion.

The Court has insisted on a flexible approach to defining whether something qualifies as a possession as follows: '[W]hether the circumstances of the case, considered as a whole, conferred on the applicant title to a substantive interest protected by Article 1 of Protocol No. 1'.[27]

Institutional innovations, emerging forms of value, and new types of entitlement may give rise to interests that function like property but do not yet fall within traditional categories.[28] Therefore, keeping the definition open allows the Court to preserve its ability to adapt the concept of possessions to changing social and economic conditions. As such, the case-law could respond to novel claims without being bound by rigid classifications.

However, this flexibility comes at a cost. First, it creates legal uncertainty, as neither individuals nor states can predict with absolute certainty whether a particular interest will be protected. The outcome would depend on how the interest is structured, how far it is vested and what expectations the legal framework creates.[29] Second, the open-ended nature of the concept of property can encourage applicants to frame marginal or speculative interests as possessions in the hope of extending the Court's doctrine.[30] This can result in overburdening judicial resources and blurring the line between ordinary economic regulation and genuine interference with property rights. Moreover, the absence of clear boundaries can weaken the coherence of A1P1 and complicate its application.

[25] Penner (n 8); Penner, *Property Rights: A Re-Examination* (n 24); James E Penner, 'The Bundle of Rights Picture of Property' (1995) 43 *UCLA Law Review* 711.

[26] Maxwell (n 1) 80.

[27] *Anheuser-Busch Inc v Portugal* (n 20) [63].

[28] Maxwell (n 1) 81.

[29] This was part of the evolution of the case law of pension entitlements under A1P1 developed in chs 4 and 5.

[30] Jonas Christoffersen and Mikael Rask Madsen, *The European Court of Human Rights between Law and Politics* (Oxford University Press 2011); Joshua L Jackson, 'Broniowski v. Poland: A Recipe for Increased Legitimacy of the European Court of Human Rights as a Supranational Constitutional Court' (2006) 39 *Connecticut Law Review* 759.

Faced with the Court's flexible approach, what follows is identifying the elements that make an interest count as a possession. That is to say, isolating the functional features of previously defined 'possessions' that are recurrent in the case law. While identifying these features does not amount to a formal, comprehensive definition of the term, they nevertheless offer a structure for understanding how the Court distinguishes protected interests from those that fall outside A1P1.

The first and most basic feature is economic value.[31] For an interest to qualify as a possession, it must be capable of being valued in monetary terms.[32] This criterion excludes moral, emotional or symbolic claims from the scope of A1P1.

A second condition is that the interest must be legally grounded in domestic law. An interest's legal ground may be statutory, contractual or administrative. The Court distinguishes between actual economic interests, which are protected, and speculative or uncertain claims, which are not. In other words, the Convention does not create property rights *ex nihilo*. It only protects interests that, although not recognised as property in national legal orders, are nevertheless recognised as legally existing assets or legally enforced claims. The Court holds the following:

> 'Possessions' can be either 'existing possessions' or assets, including claims, in respect of which the applicant can argue that he or she has at least a 'legitimate expectation' of obtaining effective enjoyment of a property right. By way of contrast, the hope of recognition of the survival of an old property right which it has long been impossible to exercise effectively cannot be considered as a 'possession' within the meaning of Article 1 of Protocol No. 1, nor can a conditional claim which lapses as a result of the non-fulfilment of the condition.[33]

Without legal grounding, there is no 'possession' to protect. This feature is what allowed the Court to recognise all types of interests, like business licences, intellectual property, social security payments and debts. Most of them are grounded in either contractual or statutory law. However, when holding that rights *in personam* are 'property', the Court is suggesting that there are no fundamental distinctions between property and contract law rights.[34] In doing so, the Court inserts itself within the most modern approaches to property, which recognise that personal rights can be transferred and hence enjoy a property nature that protects them against interferences.[35]

[31] Ingrid Leijten, 'From Stec to Valkov: Possessions and Margins in the Social Security Case Law of the European Court of Human Rights' (2013) 13 *Human Rights Law Review* 309, 313.

[32] Van Dijk and Van Hoof (n 1) 896–97.

[33] *Kopecký v Slovakia* (GC) ECHR 2004-IX (2005) 41 EHRR 43 §25.

[34] Like in the case of Hohfeldian jural relations. This point is raised by Shane Nicholas Glackin, 'Back to Bundles: Deflating Property Rights, Again' (2014) 20 *Legal Theory* 1.

[35] This ability (whether *inter vivos* or *mortis causa*) is relevant as it was traditionally believed to be a characteristic solely associated with objects of '*in rem*' rights. Ripert, Boulanger and Planiol (n 7) 493. It is precisely that feature which paved the way towards the current agreement that claims themselves can also be considered 'property'. François Terré, Philippe Simler and Yves Lequette, *Droit Civil: Les Obligations* 11th edn (Dalloz 2013) 1181.

A third feature is that the interest must exist and be currently enjoyed by the applicant, or be assimilated to that condition. In some cases, the applicant does not yet hold the object or benefit but claims to have a reasonable expectation of acquiring or retaining it. The Court has recognised that those expectations allow the interest to be enjoyed in the future to be considered a possession under A1P1.

However, not every hope or aspiration to enjoy an interest that would otherwise be qualified as property allows that interest to qualify as a possession. The expectation must be a 'legitimate expectation'. Namely, it must be sufficiently concrete and legally supported, which implies that it must rest on a provision of domestic law, a settled administrative practice or specific conduct by the public authorities that gives rise to a substantive interest. As pension benefits are claims towards the future, this feature is relevant and requires further examination in the following section.

II. The Temporal Scope of Possessions

To engage A1P1 an interest must have economic value, be grounded in law and must exist. The last feature of possessions brings into focus the temporal dimension of the norm. Knowing at what point an interest becomes a possession for the purposes of the Convention is relevant, as some interests may have no current economic value but may acquire one later. A doctoral thesis, for example, may hold only academic worth today but generate income once published. This situation requires the Court to determine whether the individual would be protected under A1P1 and when such protection would begin.

A. Existing Possessions

The expression 'existing possessions' appears frequently in the case law to denote the temporal scope of A1P1.[36] To invoke A1P1's protection, the applicant must show that the interest at stake exists under the law and that they presently enjoy a legal entitlement to it.[37] Since *Marckx v Belgium*, the Court has consistently held that:

> Article (P1-1) does no more than enshrine the right of everyone to the peaceful enjoyment of 'his' possessions, that consequently it applies only to a person's *existing possessions* and that it does not guarantee the right to acquire possessions whether on intestacy or through voluntary dispositions.[38]

[36] *Anheuser-Busch Inc v Portugal* (n 20) 64; *Broniowski v Poland* (n 21); *Beyeler v Italy* (n 20).

[37] This encompasses well with the French version of the paragraph under analysis, as the expression 'existing possessions' is translated as 'biens actuels'.

[38] *Marckx v Belgium* (n 3) 50 (emphasis added).

In this passage, the Court sets two conditions for the application of A1P1. The first condition is straightforward. A1P1 does not protect imaginary or extinguished property. There is no interference with the peaceful enjoyment of an object that no longer exists.

The second condition concerns attribution that defines the personal scope of A1P1. Objects, even valuable ones, do not by themselves define their legal holder. The role of property law is to identify who has a right to exclude others from those objects and who can claim protection from state interference.[39] For A1P1 to apply, the applicant must demonstrate that they enjoy a right to property over the claimed 'possession' when the disputed measure interfered with their peaceful enjoyment.

B. Future Property

The temporal scope of A1P1 is limited to current existing property. Future property has been consistently considered as falling outside the scope of A1P1.[40] This exclusion concerns both future rights and future possessions. That is to say, the rights to use, own or dispose of property that may arise at a later date, like a right to own my parents' land through inheritance in the future. Moreover, the objects of property that do not currently exist but are expected to materialise in the future, like an apartment not yet constructed. The question that follows is how a pension entitlement, which is a claim on future instalments, can fall under A1P1's scope?

The answer to that question requires exploring the conditions under which the Court is willing to engage A1P1 to protect prospective income. Some assets, like intellectual property and licences, derive their value primarily from the ability to generate income over time. To an extent, the value of pensions is similar. The economic value of these entitlements lies in the right to claim future payments.

The issue of the protection of prospective income came before the Court in *Anheuser-Busch Inc v Portugal*.[41] The case concerned a dispute over the trademark 'Budweiser'. Anheuser-Busch, an American beer company, sought to register the trademark in Portugal. The application was challenged by *Budějovický Budvar*, a Czech brewer that had used the name in Europe for decades. The Portuguese Supreme Court ruled in favour of the Czech company, rejecting Anheuser-Busch's application.

Anheuser-Busch brought the case before the ECtHR, claiming that the Court's refusal to allow their registration as a trademark interfered with their right to peaceful enjoyment of possessions under A1P1. The alleged possession was of an

[39] This is a small and, perhaps, rudimentary summary of the notion of 'exclusion' essential to private ownership: Penner, *Property Rights: A Re-Examination* (n 24); Penner, *The Idea of Property In Law* (n 8); Jeremy Waldron, *The Right to Private Property* (Oxford University Press 1990).

[40] Recently, *Valkov and Others v Bulgaria* App nos 2033/04, 19125/04, 19475/04, 19490/04, 19495/04, 19497/04, 24729/04, 171/05 and 2041/05 (ECtHR, 2011)§ 84, the Court, when collecting the principles guiding the application of A1P1, indicated: 'Thus, that provision [A1P1] does not guarantee the right to acquire property'.

[41] *Anheuser-Busch Inc v Portugal* (n 20).

unregistered trademark, whose value arose from the future revenue expected to be derived from its use.

The ECtHR had to address two questions in this case. The first is whether trademarks qualify as 'possessions'. The Court found that it complied with basic requirements of possession, namely having economic value and being grounded in the law. That is why it was answered affirmatively.[42] The second question concerned the scope of A1P1's protection of such an asset. Namely, whether anticipated future revenue, derived from the use of the trademark, was itself protected. The Court indicated the following:

> [F]uture income cannot be considered to constitute [existing] 'possessions' unless it has already been earned or is definitely payable. Further, the hope that a long-extinguished property right may be revived cannot be regarded as a 'possession'; nor can a conditional claim which has lapsed as a result of a failure to fulfil the condition.[43]

The Court's reasoning relies on a distinction between two types of future payments. The first type is income scheduled for a future date for which a legal entitlement exists today, for instance, a painter whose work is completed for which payment is planned for later. Even if the payment is due in the future, the painter currently holds an enforceable legal claim. The second type of future payment involves income scheduled for a future date for which a legal entitlement does not exist today. The very existence of the entitlement is thus conditioned on future events. This second type relates to speculative or conditional revenue. For instance, someone who plans to apply for a loan to invest in a company. From these types of future payments, only the first one is protected under A1P1.

The Court's reasoning was further developed in *Stran Greek Refineries and Stratis Andreadis v Greece*.[44] In examining whether the state's failure to pay a claimed debt constituted an A1P1 violation, that judgment held the following:

> In order to determine whether the applicants had a 'possession' for the purposes of Article 1 of Protocol No. 1 (P1-1), the Court must ascertain whether [a judgment under dispute] ... had given rise *to a debt in their favour that was sufficiently established to be enforceable*.[45]

This rule establishes that A1P1 protects future revenue only when it arises from an indisputably enforceable claim today. The concept of 'indisputable enforceability' requires fulfilling two conditions. First, the law recognises the creditor's legal right to pursue their debt under current legal provisions. That is to say, the existence of the obligation. Second, the right holder is entitled to assert it at the time of the alleged interference. That is to say, the enforceability of the obligation. Only when both conditions are met simultaneously can A1P1 be engaged.

[42] ibid §47, 72.
[43] ibid 64.
[44] *Stran Greek Refineries and Stratis Andreadis v Greece* Series A no 301-B (1994).
[45] ibid 59 (emphasis added).

The enforceability requirement is central to A1P1. First, the Court has repeatedly held that 'the hope that a long-extinguished property right may be revived cannot be regarded as a "possession"'.[46] This limitation prevents A1P1 from being extended to speculative future revenue. Second, it clarified that protection does not extend to 'a conditional claim which has lapsed as a result of a failure to fulfil the condition'.[47] Claims subject to conditions become enforceable only once the condition is fulfilled. Where the condition remains unmet at the time of the alleged interference, the claim is regarded in law as never having arisen.

In *Vasilyev v Russia*, a case concerning pension entitlements, the Court considered the 'indisputable enforceability' requirement as follows: '[A] "claim" – even concerning a pension – can constitute a "possession" within the meaning of Article 1 of Protocol No. 1 if it is sufficiently established to be enforceable'.[48]

The question that follows in the case of pension entitlements is when a claim would be sufficiently established to be enforceable and hence be considered a 'possession'. Is it when someone fulfils the requirements to receive a pension? Is it when the Social Security Administration recognises their pension? Moreover, what future instalments are already covered by A1P1? Are all future instalments due from the moment of retirement? Or is it only the next instalment? All of these questions become critical in systems where pension rights accrue incrementally over time and where present contributions generate future claims.[49]

Some of those questions are partially addressed under the doctrine of 'legitimate expectations', which will be discussed in the following section. At this stage, it is crucial to notice that such a doctrine is conceptually unstable. As Judge Wojtyczek noted, the Court's case law on legitimate expectations is 'difficult to understand, due to lack of precision and inconsistencies'.[50] Nonetheless, examining this doctrine is essential to understanding the boundaries of A1P1 protection for pension benefits.

III. Legitimate Expectations: Expanding the Temporal Scope of A1P1

A. Legal and Doctrinal Background

The concept of 'legitimate expectations' plays a role across several domains. It is central to prudential reasoning, to legal and moral relations between

[46] *Anheuser-Busch Inc v Portugal* (n 20) § 64.

[47] ibid.

[48] *Vasilyev v Russia* App no 66543/01 (ECtHR, 2013) §38.

[49] I discuss these questions in detail in Kevin Hartmann-Cortés, 'On Future Retirees' Legal Standing: Rethinking A1P1 Admissibility in Pension Reform Cases' [2025] *The European Convention on Human Rights Law Review* 340.

[50] Dissenting Opinion of Judge Wojtyczek in *Béláné Nagy v Hungary* (n 20) §2.

individuals, and to the interaction between individuals and public authorities in legal transitions.[51]

In prudential terms, the ability to form expectations about the future enables individuals to plan their lives effectively.[52] Anticipating the behaviour of others as well as the general course of events could enhance an individual's autonomy and agency.[53] For participants in pension schemes, this capacity is essential. Pension entitlements, in their most basic definition, are claims to future output.[54] Pension schemes are therefore structured around promises about the future. They enable today's contributors to make long-term financial decisions based on expectations about their future retirement income.[55]

In private moral and legal relations, expectations arise about the conduct of others when that conduct is normatively constrained.[56] These expectations are grounded in promises or contracts. When one party relies on the behaviour of another in light of a normative commitment, the frustration of those expectations can result in losses. Oftentimes, the law treats some of those losses as actionable by distinguishing between harms that agents must bear and those that give rise to claims.[57]

A similar reasoning applies to public law. Here, expectations concern the behaviour of the state. Legal stability enables individuals to plan on the assumption that rules will remain in place.[58] It is commonly accepted that the law enables individuals to make plans considering the two features of the law: stability and enforceability. Many individual choices are influenced by the degree of validity and stability of legal rules.[59] Therefore, 'changing the law can therefore cause normatively significant losses to those who based their plans on the expectation that the relevant law will continue its current form'.[60]

In the case of pension benefits, it is noticeable how individuals organise their retirement as a function of two variables. First, the existence of a social security

[51] Fergus Green, 'Legal Transitions without Legitimate Expectations' (2020) 28 *Journal of Political Philosophy* 397, 397.

[52] ibid 397.

[53] ibid 397.

[54] Nicholas Barr, *Economics of the Welfare State* (Oxford University Press, USA 2020); Nicholas Barr and Peter Diamond, 'The Economics of Pensions' (2006) 22 *Oxford Review of Economic Policy* 15.

[55] Nicholas Barr, *Economics of the Welfare State* (Oxford University Press, USA 2020); Nicholas Barr and Peter Diamond, 'The Economics of Pensions' (2006) 22 *Oxford Review of Economic Policy* 15. I am aware of the discussion regarding 'myopic bias' of individuals with respect to long-term planning that has been spelled out by some behavioural economists. Richard H Thaler and Cass R Sunstein, *Nudge: The Final Edition* (Yale University Press 2021). However, the existence of such bias does not undermine the ability of an individual to plan ahead, even with those shortcomings.

[56] Green (n 51) 598.

[57] ibid.

[58] Axel Gosseries and Mathias Hungerbühler, 'Rule Change and Intergenerational Justice' in J Tremmel (ed), *Handbook of Intergenerational Justice* (Edward Elgar 2006) 106.

[59] ibid.

[60] Green (n 51) 399.

system with predefined rules that govern the recognition and calculation of their pension benefit entitlement and second, the closeness to fulfilling the requirements set in the legislation to enjoy such a payment.[61] Therefore, changes in the law affecting any of those variables may frustrate plans that individuals had reasonably made in reliance on the previous regime. This raises the question of whether, and when, such frustrated expectations must be protected or compensated. In our case, whether and when such frustrated expectations could be the object of A1P1's protective scope.

In legal scholarship, the doctrine of legitimate expectations is broad and mainly concerns public law matters in both continental and common law legal traditions. In civil law traditions, the idea of legitimate expectations has been tied to intertemporal law and the protection of vested rights. It developed during the era of codification in the nineteenth century, as a response to the legal uncertainty brought by legislative reform.[62] The concept reflects the broader principle that laws should be stable and that individuals should not suffer from sudden or retroactive changes to their legal position.[63]

In common law systems, the doctrine developed separately.[64] In English law, legitimate expectations entered administrative law in the late 1960s in the case *Schmidt v Secretary of State for Home Affairs*.[65] The key idea is that a public authority may create an expectation in a private party through its conduct or prior representations. When this occurs, the authority may be required to respect that expectation, or at least to offer the individual a fair hearing before deviating from it. The doctrine serves both procedural and substantive goals and is rooted in fairness and trust.[66]

As it occurred with the very notion of private property, the ECtHR adopted its own version of legitimate expectations. While the concept is related to these broader traditions, it has a specific and autonomous meaning in the context of A1P1.

[61] Some authors evidence the way in which the old-age savings behaviour of individuals in late Prussia was directly affected after the introduction of the mandatory Bismarckian pension scheme. See Sibylle Lehmann-Hasemeyer and Jochen Streb, 'Does Social Security Crowd out Private Savings? The Case of Bismarck's System of Social Insurance' (2018) 22 *European Review of Economic History* 298.

[62] Most European civil legislations that were organised in codes incorporated such a doctrine within the first articles of the new regulation. As a matter of example, consider Arts 1 and 4 of the Swiss Civil Code, Art 5 of the Austrian Civil Code or Art 2 of the French Civil Code.

[63] Amongst of the other doctrines concerned with issues emerging from intertemporal law we might see, for instance, the theories of *causae finitae, pendentes, futurae and facta praeterita, pendentia, futura*. See Etienne de Szaszy, 'Doctrine Des Droits Acquis En Droit Transitoire Ou Intertemporal, La' (1936) 17 *Revue de Droit International et de Législation Comparée* 406. Moreover, Martin Wolff, *Private International Law* (Clarendon Press 1950) 24.

[64] Christopher F Forsyth, 'The Provenance and Protection of Legitimate Expectations' (1988) 47 *The Cambridge Law Journal* 238.

[65] ibid 238.

[66] ibid.

B. The Court's Use of Legitimate Expectations in A1P1

The ECtHR employs three different conceptions of 'legitimate expectations' depending on the stage of the judgment. First, at the admissibility stage, to determine whether the applicant's interest qualifies as a 'possession'. Second, at the lawfulness stage, where legitimate expectations relate to procedural fairness, which seems to follow the common law conception of the notion. Finally, at the proportionality stage, to assess whether an interference struck a fair balance between individual rights and public interests.[67]

Only the first use is relevant for this chapter. At the admissibility stage, the Court uses the concept of legitimate expectations to extend the scope of A1P1 in cases where an applicant does not yet have full enjoyment of a property right, but has a claim to it. It extends this scope by treating the underlying 'possession' that exists, but is not yet 'indisputably enforceable', as if it were. The rule reads as follows:

> 'Possessions' can be either 'existing possessions' or assets, including claims, in respect of which the applicant can argue that he or she has at least a 'legitimate expectation' of obtaining effective enjoyment of a property right. By way of contrast, the hope of recognition of a property right which it has been impossible to exercise effectively cannot be considered a 'possession' within the meaning of Article 1 of Protocol No. 1, nor can a conditional claim which lapses as a result of the non-fulfilment of the condition.[68]

Here, the Court draws a distinction between two types of beliefs about the future exercise of a right in relation to the underlying 'possession'. On the one hand, a 'hope' that a right will be recognised or revived. On the other hand, an 'expectation' of obtaining effective enjoyment of a property right. While the first category does not bring the claim within the scope of A1P1, the second does. The question that follows is whether there is any substantive difference between hoping and expecting, and what renders one more legitimate than another for the purposes of engaging A1P1.

> The Court considers that there is a difference between a mere hope …, however understandable that hope may be, and a legitimate expectation, which must be of a nature more concrete than a mere hope and be based on a legal provision or a legal act such as a judicial decision.[69]

With this passage, the ECtHR recognises that an expectation is a subtype of a hope, only of a more 'concrete nature'. In other words, the Court recognises that expecting is hoping, but with a particular nature: expecting is more concrete because it is connected to a legal rule or act. This connection is what allows the Court to treat the underlying 'possession' that exists but is not yet 'indisputably enforceable' as a full possession for A1P1.

[67] See ch 6.
[68] *Kopecký v Slovakia* (n 33) [25].
[69] *Gratzinger and Gratzingerova v Czech Republic* (GC) App no 39794/98 (ECtHR, 2002) §72–73.

C. What Makes an Expectation 'Legitimate'?

The Court has developed two cumulative requirements that an expectation must meet to qualify as 'legitimate' under A1P1. First, the expectation must be sufficiently concrete. This condition ensures that speculative hopes are excluded from A1P1's realm, and that only sufficiently established property interests fall within its protection. Second, the expectation must have a legal foundation. This means it must be grounded in a legal provision or a legal act, such as legislation, administrative permission or a judicial decision.

The Court has articulated these requirements across a range of cases. The 'concreteness' requirement was addressed in *Gratzinger and Gratzingerova v the Czech Republic*,[70] where the Court distinguished legitimate expectations from mere hopes. The 'legal foundation' requirement has been developed in several subsequent cases, including *Bata v Czech Republic*,[71] *Pressos Compania Naviera S.A. and Others v Belgium*, *Pine Valley Developments Ltd and Others*[72] and, finally, summarised in *Kopecký v Slovakia*.[73] The following Table 3.1 summarises these cases according to the doctrinal elements they helped develop.

Table 3.1 Unpacking 'Legitimate Expectations'

Requirement	Case
Distinction between expectation and hope	*Gratzinger and Gratzingerova v the Czech Republic* (2002)
Expectation based on legal provision or legal act (General Rule)	*Bata v Czech Republic* (2008)
Expectation based on legal provision	*Pine Valley Developments Ltd and Others* (1991)
Expectation based on a legal act/judicial decision	*Pressos Compania Naviera S.A. and Others v Belgium* (1995) and *Kopecký v Slovakia* (2004)

Source: Own elaboration.

These cases clarify the type of legal support necessary to elevate an individual's claim into a 'legitimate expectation' under A1P1. The following two subsections examine each of these requirements in turn, starting with the notion of concreteness.

[70] *Gratzinger and Gratzingerova v the Czech Republic* (n 69).
[71] *Bata v Czech Republic* App no 43775/05 (ECtHR, 2008).
[72] *Pine Valley Developments Ltd and Others v Ireland* Series A no 222 (1991) 14 EHRR 319.
[73] *Kopecký v Slovakia* (n 33).

i. Concreteness Requirement

The 'concreteness' requirement was first articulated in *Gratzinger and Gratzingerova v the Czech Republic*.[74] The applicants had fled Czechoslovakia in 1982, and as a consequence, their property had been confiscated. After several years, they lost their Czech citizenship. Once democracy was restored, the Supreme Court annulled the confiscations made during the Communist regime, and new legislation opened a restitution process. The applicants claimed what was taken from them, but their claim was rejected due to a lack of Czech nationality.[75]

After exhausting domestic remedies, the applicants brought their case before the ECtHR. They argued that the state's refusal to compensate them violated A1P1, taken together with Article 14 (non-discrimination). While they acknowledged that they were not yet entitled to the confiscated property due to their lack of citizenship, they contended that a pending case before the Constitutional Court challenging the nationality requirement for restitution would likely be decided in their favour and thereby confer such entitlement.

In assessing whether the applicants had a 'legitimate expectation' of a restitution claim, the Court distinguished between two types of expectations. It stated:

> [T]here is a difference between a mere hope of restitution, however understandable that hope may be, and a legitimate expectation, which must be of a nature *more concrete than a mere hope and be based on a legal provision or a legal act such as a judicial decision*.[76]

While the Court did not fully define 'concreteness', its reasoning still offers guidance on what it means. An expectation must be more than a possibility. It must be individually grounded and demonstrably linked to the object of the claim. To illustrate the distinction drawn by the Court, consider two scenarios. In the first, a person bases their claim to property restitution on a pending judicial procedure that has not yet been resolved. In the second, the same person claims restitution based on a speculative event, such as winning a lottery. While both involve future uncertainty, they differ in legal relevance. A pending judicial decision, even if unresolved, belongs to the legal system and could, if favourable, generate enforceable rights. A lottery, by contrast, is unrelated to any legal entitlement to the property in question.

This contrast clarifies the Court's point: a legitimate expectation must rest on more than hope. It must be individualised, meaning specific to the claimant, and legally grounded in a framework that plausibly supports a property right. In addition, the legal grounding must already exist at the time of the alleged interference. The mere possibility that the law might change in the future, even as a result of a court decision, is not sufficient unless that change has already materialised in the claimant's favour.

[74] *Gratzinger and Gratzingerova v the Czech Republic* (n 70).
[75] ibid 6.
[76] ibid 72–73 (emphasis added).

In *Gratzinger*, the applicants' expectation was specific and related to their former property. Still, it failed the 'concreteness' test, because it depended entirely on the outcome of a constitutional case that had not yet been decided. The expectation lacked the legal grounding required under A1P1. With this case, the Court introduced a temporal principle in the doctrine of legitimate expectations. For an expectation to qualify as a possession, it must be justified on present legal circumstances, not in future legal developments.

Having clarified the first requirement, the Court's case law also establishes a second: a legitimate expectation must be grounded in a legal provision or legal act. The following subsection examines this second requirement.

ii. Legal Grounding Requirement

According to the Court's case law, for an expectation to be legitimate, it must be grounded in a legally binding instrument. These include statutes, contracts and judicial decisions. In *Bata v Czech Republic*[77] the Court clarified that political statements and repealed laws do not constitute a legally binding instrument and, therefore, they cannot serve as a basis for legitimate expectations. Only acts that have legal force at the relevant time can meet this requirement.

The *Bata* case concerned a claim for compensation following the nationalisation of a family business. The applicant relied on a pre-Communist statute that granted a right to compensation whenever nationalisation occurred. That statute was repealed under the Communist regime. After the restoration of democracy, the applicant sought to revive his compensation claim, pointing to political statements by public officials that purported to restore the pre-Communist statute. Having exhausted judicial remedies that denied him any compensation, he applied to the ECtHR, arguing that his compensation claim constituted a possession under A1P1 and that the state's refusal to compensate breached that article.

The Court held the application inadmissible *ratione materiae*, finding that while a restitution claim could be considered a 'possession' under A1P1, the claim at stake was insufficiently grounded. According to the Court, neither the repealed law nor the political statements could support a legitimate expectation.[78]

The judgment held that for an expectation to be legitimate, it must rest on a legally binding source at the time of the application. Statements by public officials or repealed laws, however authoritative they may appear, do not meet this threshold. Only instruments that are in force and capable of producing legal effects can provide sufficient legal grounding. These instruments are of two kinds. On the one hand, legal acts such as judgments or administrative decisions. On the other hand, legal provisions such as statutory rules. The following subsections examine how each of these instruments can ground an expectation and render it legitimate.

[77] *Bata v Czech Republic* (n 71).
[78] ibid 77.

a. Legitimate Expectations Based on Legal Acts

The Court has recognised that legal acts can ground legitimate expectations when, as a consequence of their operation, enforceable rights emerge. Examples of legal acts are tort rules, administrative decisions and judicial rulings. The case of *Pressos Compania Naviera S.A. and Others v Belgium* illustrates this principle.[79]

The case arose when some shipping companies challenged a 1988 Belgian law that retroactively abolished the State's liability for damage caused by sea pilots.[80] Under the previous regime, the State could be held liable in tort for such damage.[81] Because the new law applied retroactively, not only did it extinguish future tort claims but also previous pending claims for accidents that had already occurred.[82]

After exhausting domestic remedies, the applicants went to the ECtHR claiming that the retroactivity of the new law constituted a breach of A1P1 for two reasons. First, by exempting the State from liability, the law placed a disproportionate burden on shipowners and their insurers to cover any damages that had occurred or would occur in the future. Second, and more relevant for this chapter, the retroactive effect of the law interfered with existing tort claims for accidents against the state that preceded the new legislation.[83] In response, the government contended that the applicants had no legitimate expectation because the tort claims were pending, and therefore, they had not yet obtained final judgments confirming the existence of liability claims.

The Court ruled in favour of the applicants. In doing so, it illustrated the operation of legal acts in grounding legitimate expectations. The judgment held that: '[t]he rules in question are rules of tort, under which claims for compensation come into existence as soon as the damage occurs'.[84] In other words, the Court recognised that the applicants' claims had arisen *ex lege* at the moment the damage occurred, regardless of judicial recognition. The Court's reasoning was informed by the case law of the Belgian Cour de Cassation, which jurisprudence contends that a tort claim arises automatically once damage occurs and does not depend on judicial recognition to exist as a legal asset. That being said, the ECtHR underscored that '[a] claim of this nature [tort] "constituted an asset"'[85] and therefore amounted to 'a possession within the meaning of the first sentence of Article 1 (P1-1)'.[86] Consequently, the applicants could legitimately expect their claims to be adjudicated under the general law of torts as it stood at the time of the incidents.[87]

[79] *Pressos Compania Naviera SA and Others v Belgium* Series A no 332 (1995).
[80] ibid 7.
[81] ibid 18.
[82] ibid 28.
[83] ibid.
[84] ibid 31.
[85] ibid.
[86] ibid.
[87] ibid.

This judgment demonstrates that legal acts can generate legitimate expectations under A1P1 when they give rise to enforceable rights through their mere operation. In *Pressos*, the applicants' tort claims existed by virtue of the law and were sufficiently concrete to constitute possessions, even in the absence of a final judgment. The retroactive legislation interfered with these established claims and deprived the applicants of compensation they were entitled to seek under the applicable tort rules. Following this precedent, what matters is not whether a court confirmed the claim, but whether it was legally created and enforceable under the prevailing legal framework at the time of the alleged interference.[88]

b. Legitimate Expectations Based on Legal Provisions

Legal provisions such as statutes or administrative permissions can also ground legitimate expectations when they confer rights or benefits that are legally binding and sufficiently precise. The Court has recognised that when an individual relies on a provision to make decisions, and when the provision has not been invalidated or contested at the time of reliance, it may create a legitimate expectation. This type of expectation does not create a new right but extends the scope of an existing property.

This principle was illustrated in *Pine Valley Developments Ltd and Others v Ireland*.[89] The case concerned a land development project in which the applicants, after purchasing land, obtained a planning permission from the Ministry for Local Government. This permission was duly recorded in the public register, and some work had already begun. However, Irish courts later invalidated the provision on which the Ministry of Local Government granted the planning permission, holding that the Minister lacked the competence to grant it. As a result, the land's development potential and market value declined considerably.

The 'possession' at stake here was the land whose value depended on the possibility of developing the applicant's projects according to the originally granted planning permission. The core legal issue was whether an administrative decision, like that of the Ministry of Local Government, even if later revoked, could give rise to a legitimate expectation protected under A1P1.[90]

The Court found that the applicants had relied on the planning permission, which had been duly recorded in a public register and appeared valid at the time of purchase.[91] The permission represented a favourable decision regarding the proposed development and could not be reopened by the planning authority.[92]

[88] In this case there is a further detail. The 'legitimacy of the expectation' to make claims of compensation as a consequence of a harm was based not only on the provisions of the law of tort, but also on two Supreme Court rulings from 1983 and 1985 which held that the Belgian State was liable under the General law of torts.

[89] *Pine Valley Developments Ltd and Others* (n 72).

[90] ibid 51.

[91] ibid.

[92] ibid.

Based on this, the Court concluded that the applicants had at least a legitimate expectation of being able to carry out the project over their land. The Court held the following:

> In these circumstances it would be unduly formalistic to hold that the Supreme Court's decision did not constitute an interference. Until it was rendered, the applicants had at least a legitimate expectation of being able to carry out their proposed development and this has to be regarded, for the purposes of Article 1 of Protocol No. 1 (P1-1), as a component part of the property in question.[93]

This reasoning highlights two elements. First, it was the formal recording of the permission that gave it an official and authoritative character, making it reasonable for the applicants to rely on it. Second, the permission's nature as a definitive administrative act meant it had legal consequences for both the authorities and the beneficiaries. The Court thus treated the expectation as an integral component of the protected possession, even if the underlying administrative decision was later invalidated.

This reasoning underscores a central feature of the Court's legitimate expectations doctrine. The existence of a legitimate expectation does not depend on the finality or immutability of the administrative decision itself, but on whether the applicant's reliance on that decision was justified at the time it was granted. By linking the expectation to the permission formally registered and granted to the applicable legal framework, the Court confirmed that even provisional or revisable administrative decisions can give rise to legitimate expectations, provided they have clear legal effects and are relied upon in good faith.

The following section addresses the final strand of this analysis: legitimate expectations based on judicial decisions. The transition should make clear that while administrative decisions can ground expectations under certain conditions, judicial decisions raise other kinds of issues. The reason is that, in that case, their authority depends on the decision being definitive and the absence of interpretive dispute on how the relevant legal rules apply.

c. Legitimate Expectations Based on Judicial Decisions

Judicial decisions represent a distinct category of legal provisions capable of grounding a legitimate expectation. Unlike administrative acts, whose legal effect can arise from formal registration or reliance, for an expectation to qualify as 'legitimate', the judicial decision must be final and no longer subject to challenge. This raises the question of whether and under what circumstances a non-final or contested judicial decision can give rise to a legitimate expectation. The Court addressed this question most thoroughly in *Kopecký v Slovakia*,[94] which provides the most developed articulation of this doctrine.

[93] ibid.
[94] *Kopecký v Slovakia* (n 33).

The case arose, once again, from a restitution claim. The applicant sought the return of special coins that had been confiscated from his father in 1959. The Judicial Rehabilitation Act of 1990 opened the possibility of restitution, but required applicants to specify the location of confiscated property.[95] A first-instance court ordered the return of the coins. But the decision was later overturned on appeal, because the applicant could not prove where the coins had been deposited.[96]

After exhausting judicial remedies, the applicant brought the case before the ECtHR. He argued that the reversal of the first-instance decision violated A1P1, as he had complied with the statutory conditions for restitution.[97] The Fourth Section of the Court initially agreed. It considered that the first-instance judgment had created a legitimate expectation of restitution. However, the Grand Chamber reversed this view.[98]

The Grand Chamber reiterated that legitimate expectations are not independently protected interests. Instead, they help determine whether a claim that lacks 'indisputable enforceability' can nevertheless qualify as a 'possession' under A1P1. In doing so, it set a clear standard:

> [N]o legitimate expectation can be said to arise where there is a dispute as to the correct interpretation and application of domestic law and the applicant's submissions are subsequently rejected by the national courts.[99]

This rule serves a double function. First, it preserves legal certainty by requiring that the expectation rest on a binding domestic rule. Second, it protects the Court from acting as a final instance on questions of national law. The ECtHR does not resolve internal legal disputes. It only steps in once a rule has been applied in a final, authoritative manner.

Because the first-instance decision in *Kopecký* was later reversed, it failed to establish a settled legal position. The Court held that expectations grounded in judicial decisions must rest on a definitive and uncontested application of domestic law. Where the relevant legal issue remains open to dispute or is subsequently rejected by national courts, no legitimate expectation arises.

Conclusions

This chapter examined how the ECtHR defines and delimits the notion of 'possessions' under A1P1. It began by situating the Court's approach within its broader institutional and interpretive framework, marked by principles such as subsidiarity, proportionality and methods like autonomous interpretation. From this

[95] ibid 12–13.
[96] ibid 17–20.
[97] ibid 26.
[98] ibid 41.
[99] ibid 50.

perspective, the concept of possessions is not determined by national law but by self-contained Convention standards.

The second section showed how the Court developed an autonomous concept of possessions, encompassing not only the usual forms of property but also claims and entitlements with economic value and provided they are legally recognised or 'indisputably enforceable'. Within this framework, the third section focused on the doctrine of legitimate expectations concerning claims recognised as property. This doctrine plays a threshold role in bringing certain future or disputed interests – like pension entitlements – within the material scope of A1P1. The analysis identified two cumulative conditions: the expectation must be concrete, and it must be grounded in a legally binding instrument. Together, these requirements define how the Court extends the Convention's protection to interests that are not yet fully realised but already sufficiently formed in legal terms.

Three findings are especially relevant for the following chapters. First, A1P1 protects legal positions that exist at the time of alleged interference. This temporal condition excludes future entitlements unless the individual already holds an enforceable claim or a recognised expectation grounded in the law. Second, the value of the claim is insufficient to determine its property nature. Legal protection under A1P1 depends on how the entitlement is structured, attributed and supported in domestic law. Third, the doctrine of legitimate expectations plays a relevant role in the admissibility stage. It extends A1P1's reach to cases where the applicant does not yet enjoy the benefit but holds a legal expectation strong enough to count as a possession.

These findings set the analytical parameters for the rest of the book. The following chapters examine how these criteria apply to different types of pension claims. What follows will describe when pension entitlements started falling within the scope of A1P1, how the Court has applied the notion of possessions in pension-related cases, and where the limits of protection lie.

4

The Formalistic Doctrine in Early A1P1 Pension Jurisprudence (1971–1996)

Introduction

In 1971, the European Commission of Human Rights (the Commission) first addressed the question of whether pension entitlements were 'possessions'. For more than two decades, the case law considered that the answer was contingent on formalities like the type of pension scheme from which the entitlement arose. This chapter examines this 'formalistic doctrine' and outlines its key features.

The formalistic doctrine was developed through a series of decisions. In *X v the Netherlands*,[1] the Commission introduced the 'identifiable share' criterion, holding that only entitlements from which the contributor had an 'identifiable' share could be considered as 'possessions'. In *G v Austria*,[2] it drew another distinction between funded schemes allowing 'own coverage' and unfunded systems based on a 'principle of support', privileging protection of rights arising from the former. In *Kleine Staarman v the Netherlands*,[3] it further separated schemes that established a direct contribution–benefit link from those that did not, finding that only the former allowed for rights to fall under A1P1's scope.

These decisions reveal a consistent pattern: only entitlements resembling private contractual arrangements counted as possessions, while solidarity-based, public law benefits were excluded as mere gratuities.[4] The Commission developed a screening method that limited A1P1's scope for pensions, since most European pensions are derived from public schemes. Two factors might explain this stance. Institutionally, A1P1's open-textured compromise left scope and content to Strasbourg, and in its early welfare cases, the Commission, still consolidating

[1] *X v Netherlands* App no 4130/69 (EComHR, 1971) Yearbook of the European Convention on Human Rights 224.

[2] *G v Austria* App no 10094/82 (EComHR, 1984).

[3] *Kleine Staarman v Netherlands* App no 10503/83 (ECtHR, 1985).

[4] This restrictive approach contrasts sharply with Charles Reich's arguments for expanding property protection to encompass public benefits: Charles Reich, 'The New Property' (1964) 73 *Yale Law* 733; Charles A Reich, 'Social Welfare in the Public-Private State' (1965) 114 *University of Pennsylvania Law Review* 487.

authority, proceeded with prudence to avoid pushback from Council of Europe states.[5] Doctrinally, the approach paralleled an ongoing debate, especially in the United States, on whether welfare entitlements are protectable 'property' or non-protectable gratuities given their public law character.[6] However, as Strasbourg's legitimacy consolidated, its conception of possessions widened, and pension entitlements moved within A1P1's protection.[7]

During this period, the Commission also clarified the scope of protection for entitlements that did fall under A1P1. In *Müller v Austria*,[8] it elaborated the content and limits of protection, while *X v Austria*[9] addressed the temporal question of when such protection would begin. These cases provided practical guidance on the extent of property protection in pension cases, guidance that continues to influence the Court's jurisprudence today.

This chapter has two sections. Section I analyses how the Commission established and maintained the funded/unfunded distinction as the central determinant for A1P1 protection. Section II examines how the Commission defined the scope of protection for entitlements that were previously classified as possessions. The conclusion evaluates how this two-step formalism shaped the trajectory of pension rights protection under A1P1.

I. Funded versus Unfunded Entitlements

Between 1971 and 1996, the Commission determined that only pension entitlements arising from funded schemes qualified as 'possessions' under A1P1. This view first emerged in *X v the Netherlands*[10] with the 'identifiable share' doctrine. Later cases used different terminology, speaking of 'own coverage' versus the 'principle of support' and the 'strictness of the relationship between contributions and benefits'. However, they meant the same. For the Commission's early case law, only funded schemes created property rights. This section describes the Commission's reasoning to arrive at that conclusion.

A. The 'Identifiable Share' Criterion

In *X v the Netherlands*[11] the Commission first addressed an application concerning the question of whether pension entitlements could constitute 'possessions'

[5] Douglas Maxwell, *The Human Right to Property: A Practical Approach to Article 1 of Protocol No. 1 to the ECHR* (Bloomsbury Publishing 2022) 76–77.
[6] Reich, 'The New Property' (n 4); Reich, 'Social Welfare in the Public-Private State' (n 4).
[7] See ch 5.
[8] *Müller v Austria* [1975] European Court of Human Rights 5849/72.
[9] *X v Austria* [1976] European Court of Human Rights 7045/75.
[10] *X v the Netherlands* (n 1).
[11] ibid.

under A1P1. The case arose from a challenge to the Dutch state pension system (*Algemene Ouderdomswet* or AOW) by members of the Women's Action Committee for Advanced Old-Age Pension. While their primary claim concerned gender discrimination in pension eligibility ages, they also advanced an innovative argument about property rights: that their compulsory contributions to the pension system had created a 'vested interest' protected by A1P1. This second argument required the Commission to determine, for the first time, whether and when pension contributions could create property rights protectable under A1P1.[12]

The applicants' claim presented two arguments about property rights in pension schemes. The first challenged the compulsory nature of contributions. The argument was that mandatory payments interfered with their existing possessions (their wages) in a discriminatory way, since unmarried women had to contribute for more extended periods than married women.[13] The second argument suggested that once contributions were paid, any subsequent changes to benefit calculations or eligibility rules would interfere with their property rights.[14] The latter forced the Commission to consider whether and how traditional property protection could extend to modern social security entitlements.

The judgment started by describing how the old-age scheme in the Netherlands operated at the time. Since the introduction of AOW in 1957, the Dutch system was a pioneer of what by the end of the 1990s would be conceptualised as a 'multi-pillar' pension system.[15] At the time, the first tier was financed by a mix of payroll contributions and general taxation, the latter being negligible according to the applicants. Such a tier has provided a flat-rate benefit equal to 70 per cent of the minimum wage for residents with a 40-year contribution history by the age of retirement.[16] The second pillar was composed mainly of quasi-mandatory (industry-wide) occupational pension funds, providing a supplementary pension. According to the Commission, the system obliged every Dutch resident to make contributions to the pension system, and guaranteed a retirement benefit roughly proportional to the workers' income.[17]

[12] Moreover: 'they considered it as being discriminatory that, up to the age of 45 years, unmarried and divorced women were also required to make contributions under the Widows' and Orphans' Act, although their chances to marry and to have children, and thus to benefit from the provisions of that Act, consistently decreased', ibid 228–30. The Committee dismissed this allegation swiftly arguing that the difference of treatment was justified 'based on the legislator's appreciation of the general family pattern while making allowances for the generally different situation of a married couple compared to that of a single person', ibid 248.

[13] In the French version of the ruling, the expression 'vested interest' is translated as 'un droit acquis'. *X v the Netherlands* (n 1) 231.

[14] ibid 230.

[15] Richard Hinz, 'The World Bank's Pension Policy Framework and the Dutch Pension System: A Paradigm for the Multi-Pillar Design' in L Bovenberg, C van Ewijk and E Westerhout (eds), *The Future of Multi-Pillar Pensions* (Cambridge University Press 2012) 46.

[16] Marc Gérard, 'Reform Options for Mature Defined Benefit Pension Plans: The Case of the Netherlands' (International Monetary Fund 2019) WP/19/22.

[17] *X v the Netherlands* (n 1) 226–28.

After describing the facts of the case, the Commission addressed each allegation in turn. To address the first allegation, the Commission acknowledged that the Convention does not recognise a right to a pension. Moreover, A1P1 does not require States to organise or establish a social security system in any particular way. Therefore, it was judged that the first argument, which seemed to challenge the way in which a social security system was organised was ill-founded for incompatibility *rationae materiae*.[18]

To address the second allegation, the Commission reframed it in two questions. First, does the compulsory nature of the contribution constitute an interference with the contributor's possessions? Second, is there a protected (vested) interest as a result of compulsory contributions, and, in the affirmative, is it a 'possession' protected under A1P1?[19] As for the first question, the Commission held that:

> In these circumstances the Commission finds that, although compulsory contributions to a pension fund necessarily interfere with a person's possessions such contributions are not, under the above provisions of the Dutch law, disproportionate to the incomes taxed. It follows that the imposing of the obligation to make such contributions to the Dutch national insurance scheme according to the law in force in the Netherlands is clearly within the right of the State 'to secure the payment of taxes or other contributions' within the meaning of the second paragraph of Art. 1 of Protocol No. 1.[20]

This reasoning provides an underlying recognition of wages as 'possessions' because the Commission considers that compulsory contributions 'interfere' with them. If the Commission had conceptualised pensions as 'deferred salaries',[21] by transitivity, they would have also been considered 'possessions'. However, that was not their reasoning. The judgment instead dismissed that there was no breach of A1P1 for two reasons. First, as recognised in the very text of A1P1, states have the right to set these types of compulsory obligations. According to the norm, states may secure the payment of taxes or other contributions through their taxing power. Second, because the Dutch scheme's Contribution rate was set at a proportional and reasonable rate to an individual's income.[22] That being said, neither of those reasons actually discussed whether pensions could be considered 'possessions' under A1P1. That would come later when addressing the second question, whether making compulsory contributions might create

[18] ibid 238.

[19] ibid 240.

[20] ibid.

[21] Guido Van Limberghen, 'In Min of in Meer: Wettelijke En Aanvullende Pensioenen' in Willy Van Eeckhoutte and Marc Rigaux (eds), *T. BOD, Het pensioenbegrip, Zwolle, Tjeenk Willink, 1994, 12* (Mys & Breesch 1996) 579.

[22] Morally speaking, claiming 'property' over gross wages seems to be also misleading, if not false, see Liam Murphy and Thomas Nagel, *The Myth of Ownership: Taxes and Justice* (Oxford University Press 2002).

any rights that could fall within the category of 'possessions' under A1P1. Here, the Commission indicated:

> [W]hile it is clear that no right to a pension is as such included in the Convention, the making of compulsory contributions to a pension fund may, in certain circumstances, create a property right in a portion of such fund and that such right might be affected by the manner in which the fund is distributed.[23]

And continued:

> [T]he legislator has chosen a system under which payments made over a certain year are financed from contributions received in that year. It is therefore clear, both from the manner in which the funds are administered and from the system of distribution adopted, that this branch of the Dutch social insurance legislation is based on the principle of solidarity which reflects the responsibility of the community as a whole to provide a minimum financial basis for its aged members and for survivors … The contributions which the younger members of the community are obliged to make are collected in a revolving fund from which the older or surviving members of the community receive their pension. The distribution of the pension funds considers the economic realities of the period concerned to the extent that persons benefiting from this system receive their pension in accordance with the wage index established for the period in which the pension is paid and not according to that established for the periods in which they made contributions. There is, therefore, no relationship between the contributions made and the pension received in the sense that the amounts paid by the insured person are accumulated with a view to covering the pension benefits accruing to him when reaching pensionable age. Consequently, a person does not have, at any given moment, an identifiable share in the fund claimable by him but he has an expectancy of receiving old-age or survivors pension benefits subject to the conditions envisaged by the Acts concerned.[24]

Here, the Commission drew a line that would shape the following decades of the pension rights' jurisprudence. In this part of the judgment, the Commission

[23] *X v the Netherlands* (n 1) 240–42. The French version indicates '*La Commission estime que, s'il est clair que le droit à une pension n'est pas inclus en tant que tel dans la Convention, le versement de cotisations obligatoires à une Caisse de pensions peut, dans certaines circonstances, créer un droit de propriété sur une partie de ces fonds et que ce droit pourrait être affecté par la manière dont ces fonds sont repartis*', ibid 241.

[24] *X v the Netherlands* (n 1) 244. The French version of the judgment has a similar wording: '*Les cotisations que les membres plus jeunes de la communauté sont tenus de verser constituent un fonds de roulement qui permet aux membres plus âgés de la communauté et à leurs survivants de percevoir des pensions. Dans la répartition des fonds des caisses de pension, il est tenu compte des réalités économiques de la période, dans la mesure où le montant des pensions versées aux personnes qui bénéficient de ce régime est fonction de l'indice des salaires qui a été détermine pour la période au cours de laquelle la pension est versée, et non de celui qui a été détermine pour les périodes au cours desquelles ces personnes ont payé leurs cotisations. Il n'y a donc pas de relation entre le montant des cotisations versées et celui de la pension perçue, en ce sens que les sommes versées par l'assuré seraient accumulées en vue de couvrir le montant des prestations qui lui sont dues lorsqu'il atteint l'âge auquel s'ouvre le droit à pension. Par conséquent, nul ne possède à un moment donné un droit à une fraction identifiable des fonds disponibles, mais chacun peut s'attendre à percevoir des prestations au titre de la pension de vieillesse ou de la pension due aux survivants, sous réserve des conditions prévues par les lois à ce sujet*', ibid 245.

established a crucial distinction in how different pension financing arrangements could create property rights. At its core was the concept that property rights could emerge only where contributions created an 'identifiable share' in a fund's assets. This idea gives great weight to the way in which pensions are structurally arranged to determine the property nature of an entitlement: only systems where contributions were accumulated and preserved in a fund, rather than immediately redistributed, could generate property rights.

The Commission reasoned that when contributions build up an identifiable capital in a fund, they create a legally enforceable claim over a specific portion of those assets. This claim – the right to a quantifiable share of the fund corresponding to one's contributions – is what would constitute a 'possession' that 'might be affected by how the fund is distributed'.

When applying this reasoning to the Dutch state pension system, the Commission found that these qualifying circumstances were absent. The system to which there were compulsory contributions operated on a pay-as-you-go (PAYG) basis, where current workers' contributions directly financed current pensioners' benefits, rather than accumulating contributions in individual accounts. This meant that individual contributors could never point to a specific portion of accumulated capital as 'theirs'. Therefore, contributors hold no claimable stake in any fund, thereby creating no property interest whatsoever.

The Commission's initial response was to sort pension entitlements by legal form and funding structure. Rights that resembled private contracts could count as possessions, while rights grounded in public law and financed on solidarity terms could not. In funded schemes, the benchmark was an asset-backed position: the beneficiary needed an 'identifiable share' of the fund's assets, a direct contribution–benefit link capable of actuarial valuation, and a legally enforceable claim against the managing institution. Where benefits were paid from current revenues and redistributed immediately by the operation of a statute, there was no quantifiable stake in accumulated capital. Therefore, the claimant held a public law expectation that could be revised by legislation, and as such, could not be a complete 'possession'. The result of this reasoning was imposing a screening method that favoured funded designs and sidelined general PAYG pensions at this early stage of the case law.

This early view of the Commission appears to have been shaped by how defined-contribution (DC) schemes are conceived. These schemes most closely resembled traditional private contract arrangements. DC schemes have been typical in occupational pension systems since the early twentieth century. They create clear individual property interests through their financing structure.[25] During the accumulation phase, worker and employer contributions build up identifiable capital in individual accounts, granting each participant a legally enforceable claim

[25] Bruno Palier, *Réformer Les Retraites* (Presses de Sciences Po 2021).

to a specific share of the fund's assets.[26] This feature seems to be the key to conceiving an entitlement as a 'possession'. In PAYG systems, the Commission reasoned, participants never acquired ownership of identifiable assets. Instead, they merely held what the Commission described as 'an expectancy of receiving old-age or survivors' pension benefits subject to the conditions envisaged by the Acts concerned'.[27] In other words, a conditional promise of future benefits dependent on statutory requirements. Unlike a claim over accumulated capital, this expectancy lacked the concrete characteristics of property that A1P1 was designed to protect.[28] This was also the interpretation of Judge Treschel, whose separate opinion in *Müller v Austria* claimed that, in this case:

> According to the Commission's case law, 'the payment of mandatory contributions to a pension fund may, in certain circumstances, create a property right over a portion of these funds, and this right could be affected by the way these funds are distributed' … Continuing its reasoning, the Commission expressed the opinion that such a property right cannot be recognized for the insured person when the pension fund operates under the so-called pay-as-you-go system. It implied that the situation could be different when the pension fund operates under the so-called capitalization system.[29]

The identifiable share criterion, in sum, rests on three grounds. First, in funded systems, contributions result in a legally enforceable 'claim' over a share of the

[26] Nicholas Barr and Peter Diamond, 'The Economics of Pensions' (2006) 22 *Oxford Review of Economic Policy* 15; Nicholas Barr, *Economics of the Welfare State* (Oxford University Press, USA 2020). However, there is some dispute on the exact property content they supposedly entail. Legally speaking, the image of property in those schemes is far from being easy. Richard Nobles, 'Pensions as Property' (1994) 14 *Legal Studies* 345; Paddy Ireland, 'Law and the Neoliberal Vision: Financial Property, Pension Privatisation and the Ownership Society' (2011) 62 *Northern Ireland Legal Quarterly* 1.

[27] *X v the Netherlands* (n 1) 244. The French version of the judgment has a similar wording: '*Les cotisations que les membres plus jeunes de la communauté sont tenus de verser constituent un fonds de roulement qui permet aux membres plus âgés de la communauté et à leurs survivants de percevoir des pensions. Dans la répartition des fonds des caisses de pension, il est tenu compte des réalités économiques de la période, dans la mesure où le montant des pensions versées aux personnes qui bénéficient de ce régime est fonction de l'indice des salaires qui a été détermine pour la période au cours de laquelle la pension est versée, et non de celui qui a été détermine pour les périodes au cours desquelles ces personnes ont payé leurs cotisations. Il n'y a donc pas de relation entre le montant des cotisations versées et celui de la pension perçue, en ce sens que les sommes versées par l'assuré seraient accumulées en vue de couvrir le montant des prestations qui lui sont dues lorsqu'il atteint l'âge auquel s'ouvre le droit à pension. Par conséquent, nul ne possède à un moment donné un droit à une fraction identifiable des fonds disponibles, mais chacun peut s'attendre à percevoir des prestations au titre de la pension de vieillesse ou de la pension due aux survivants, sous réserve des conditions prévues par les lois à ce sujet*', ibid 245.

[28] *X v the Netherlands* (n 1) 248.

[29] This is an own translation from the original French in the ruling that said: '*Selon la jurisprudence de la Commission, le "versement de cotisations obligatoires à une caisse de pensions peut, dans certaines circonstances, créer un droit de propriété sur une partie de ces fonds et de ce droit pourrait être affecté par la manière dont ces fonds sont repartis" … Poursuivant son raisonnement, la Commission a exprimé l'opinion qu'un tel droit de propriété ne saurait être reconnu à l'assuré lorsque la caisse de pensions fonctionne selon le système dit de la répartition. Elle a laissé entendre qu'il saurait en être autrement, lorsque la caisse de pensions fonctionne selon le système dit de la capitalisation*'. Opinion Separée du Juge M. Treschel, *Müller v Austria* (n 8).

fund. Second, this claim creates a corresponding obligation for the fund towards the contributor. Third, this obligation entails making payments at retirement equal to the value of the contributor's share in the fund. Because the contributor owns a fraction of the accumulated capital, the resulting payments constitute a 'possession' protected under A1P1. In contrast, unfunded systems do not confer such ownership, as payments come directly from transfers between the working population and retirees rather than from accumulated capital.

The 'identifiable share' criterion has two key implications for A1P1. First, participants in funded schemes would be able, in principle, to challenge regulations affecting their 'claim' over their share in the fund under A1P1 since their 'possession' arises with their first contribution. In contrast, contributors to unfunded schemes lack such a claim, as their contributions are immediately redistributed rather than saved in an identifiable account. Second, in funded schemes, the entitlement to pension benefits itself qualifies as a 'possession' protected under A1P1, whereas entitlements in unfunded schemes do not enjoy the same status.[30]

B. Principle of Support versus Own Coverage

After establishing the basic framework through the identifiable share criterion, the Commission refined its approach. In *G v Austria*,[31] a widower challenged his denial of a survivor's pension from his deceased wife, who had been employed as a civil servant by the city of Vienna. Under Austrian law male survivors had to demonstrate 'special need' (defined as insufficient income) to qualify for these pensions, while female survivors faced no such requirement. The applicant argued this gender-based distinction violated A1P1 in conjunction with Article 14's prohibition on discrimination.

The applicant's claim rested on three grounds. First, that survivor benefits from civil service pensions constituted protected property rights. Second, that the denial of these benefits constituted a deprivation of property without due process. Third, that the denial based on his gender discriminatory and hence unlawful. The case required the Commission to determine whether civil service pension entitlements could constitute 'possessions' under A1P1 before it could address the discrimination claim.[32]

To address this question, the Commission introduced a new conceptual framework distinguishing between two types of pension arrangements: schemes based

[30] That is also an interpretation suggested by Frankie McCarthy, 'Article One of the First Protocol to the European Convention on Human Rights: The Evolution of a Right in Europe and the United Kingdom' (PhD Thesis, University of Glasgow 2010) 57–60.

[31] *G v Austria* (n 2) on the admissibility of the application.

[32] ibid 84–85.

on the 'principle of support' and those based on 'coverage by own contributions'. The judgment began by acknowledging that:

> [T]he fact that a person has made contributions to a social security system intended to cover the benefits which he will later derive therefrom … prompted the Commission to assimilate the right to such benefits to a property right within the meaning of Article 1 of the Protocol.[33]

This formulation suggests that the crucial factor for determining whether a pension entitlement qualifies as a 'possession' was the relationship between contributions and future benefits. In other words, the degree of actuarial fairness is defined as the relationship between contributions paid and benefits received.[34] However, as it will be clear, the Commission's proper focus instead was also the existence of identifiable accumulated capital serving to pay the pension entitlement.[35]

The Commission continued claiming that civil service schemes are entirely different,[36] noting that 'the contributions which have been paid are not intended to provide full coverage of the benefits'.[37] On this basis, it concluded that 'Article 1 of the First Protocol does not apply to civil servants' pension schemes of the kind which exist in Austria'.[38] This judgment – although expressed in new terms – effectively reinforced the screening between funded and unfunded schemes for the purposes of determining whether an entitlement is a 'possession'.

The distinction becomes clearer in the French version of the judgment, which speaks explicitly of the 'destination' of contributions:

> On voit par-là que la Commission a reconnu la nature différente des régimes de retraite des fonctionnaires, notamment en ce qu'ils se fondent sur le principe du soutien plutôt que sur une couverture assurée par les contributions de l'intéressé lui-même. Cependant, c'est précisément le fait que le retraité du régime de sécurité sociale a versé des contributions destinées à couvrir les prestations dont il devait bénéficier plus tard, qui a incité la Commission à assimiler le droit à de telles prestations à un droit de propriété au

[33] ibid.

[34] The notion of actuarial fairness should be understood as 'the level of benefits in relation to the contributions paid'. Jennifer Alonso-García, María del Carmen Boado-Penas and Pierre Devolder, 'Adequacy, Fairness and Sustainability of Pay-as-You-Go-Pension-Systems: Defined Benefit versus Defined Contribution' (2018) 24 *The European Journal of Finance* 1100, 1101. For a critical note on the notion of Actuarial Fairness, Xavier Landes, 'How Fair Is Actuarial Fairness?' (2015) 128 *Journal of Business Ethics* 519, 519–33.

[35] The French version of this paragraph provides a clearer vision of what was meant by the judgment: '*Par conséquent, nul ne possède à un moment donné un droit à une fraction identifiable des fonds disponibles, mais chacun peut s'attendre à percevoir des prestations au titre de la pension de vieillesse ou de la pension due aux survivants, sous réserve des conditions prévues par les lois à ce sujet*'. *X v the Netherlands* (n 1) 245. The choice of words is important in this case. The Court uses the word 'expectancy' instead of 'expectation', and so much less a 'legitimate expectation', as the latter is used in the case law to qualify those claims with respect to which an applicant might enjoy a property right in the assessment of the alleged possession. See *Kopecký v Slovakia* [2004] European Court of Human Rights 44912/98.

[36] *G v Austria* (n 2) 84–85.

[37] ibid.

[38] ibid.

> sens de l'article 1 du Protocole. Le système appliqué aux fonctionnaires en Autriche est d'une nature entièrement différente, et les contributions versées ne sont pas destinées à assurer une couverture totale des prestations. Dans ces conditions, la Commission considère que l'article 1 n'est pas applicable à des régimes de pensions de fonctionnaires tels que ceux qui existent en Autriche.[39]

The French text reveals the evolution of the 'identifiable share' criterion. The key factor to recognise a property entitlement stemming from a pension scheme remained whether contributions created individually identifiable shares. However, this was now expressed through the concept of contribution's 'destination'. The key distinction lay between contributions '*destinées à couvrir les prestations dont il devait bénéficier plus tard*' (intended to accumulate for the contributor's own future benefits) and those serving immediate redistribution through 'collective support'. Again, a fundamental distinction is made using the methodology of financing of each system, whether funded or unfunded.

The Commission suggests that since the applicant's contributions were 'not intended to provide full coverage of the benefits'[40] but instead operated on the principle of collective support, his claim to a survivor's pension could not constitute a 'possession' under A1P1. While the Commission's terminology evolved from 'identifiable shares' to 'own coverage' versus 'principle of support', its underlying analysis remained consistent: only arrangements that created individually attributable capital could give rise to possessions under A1P1. This doctrine would be further reinforced in *Kleine Staarman v the Netherlands*.

C. Relationship between Contributions and Benefits

In *Kleine Staarman v the Netherlands*[41] the Commission confronted the funded versus unfunded distinction in a new context: disability benefits. While previous cases had focused on retirement and survivors' pensions, this case required examining whether disability insurance contributions could create protected property rights.

The applicant in this case had received disability benefits since 1979 due to bone cancer, but these were terminated upon her marriage under a provision that

[39] ibid 88–89. 'It can be seen from this that the Commission has recognized the distinct nature of civil servants' pension schemes, particularly in that they are based on the principle of support rather than coverage ensured by the contributions of the beneficiary themselves. However, it is precisely the fact that retirees under the social security system have made contributions intended to cover the benefits they were to receive later that led the Commission to equate the right to such benefits with a property right under Article 1 of the Protocol. The system applied to civil servants in Austria is of an entirely different nature, and the contributions made are not intended to provide full coverage of the benefits. Under these conditions, the Commission considers that Article 1 does not apply to civil service pension schemes such as those existing in Austria'.

[40] ibid.

[41] *Kleine Staarman v the Netherlands* (n 3). ECHR On the admissibility of the application.

specifically withdrew benefits from married women.[42] After being denied the reinstatement of her benefits following divorce, the applicant challenged the 1978 law before the European Court of Human Rights (ECtHR). She claimed it violated her right to peaceful enjoyment of possessions and discriminated between women based on marital status.[43] This application required the Commission to determine whether disability benefits could constitute possessions under A1P1, allowing it to develop further its doctrine about the relationship between contributions and property rights.

The Commission's analysis departed from the formalistic framework established in *X v Netherlands* and *G v Austria* to examine the financing structure of the Dutch disability scheme. After finding that this scheme operated on what the Commission named 'the principle of solidarity',[44] it found that: '[N]o direct link exists between the level of contributions and the benefits awarded. Consequently, a person does not have, at any given moment, an identifiable and claimable share in the fund'.[45]

The Commission's framing conveys the same ideas laid out in previous cases: had the applicant's benefits arisen from accumulated contributions creating identifiable shares, changes to eligibility rules that effectively eliminated those shares would have constituted interference with protected property rights. However, in solidarity-based schemes, states retained broader authority to modify eligibility conditions, regardless of how much they could affect he beneficiary. Based on this framing, the Commission concluded that there was no 'possession' at stake, and therefore the application was inadmissible.[46]

D. The Persistent Influence of the Formalistic Approach

Despite its abandonment by the ECtHR's case law in later cases,[47] the formalistic doctrine that underscores the differences between funded and unfunded pension schemes, considering their capacity to create property rights, is still influential today. Such an idea keeps influencing policy debates, legal proceedings and some theoretical understandings of pension rights.

In the international policy debates, the formalistic distinction has maintained its attractiveness, especially amongst economists and policymakers.[48] It found renewed expression in the pension reform campaigns of the 1990s and 2000s after the publication of the World Bank's influential 1994 report 'Averting the Old

[42] ibid 163.
[43] ibid 166.
[44] ibid.
[45] ibid.
[46] ibid.
[47] See ch 5.
[48] Mitchell A Orenstein, *Privatizing Pensions: The Transnational Campaign for Social Security Reform* (Princeton University Press 2008).

Age Crisis'.[49] Such a report, and the ones that followed it, promoted a multi-pillar approach that encouraged partially replacing public pension systems with mandatory funded schemes, preferably of the individual DC type.[50]

The supporters of this model advanced two property-based claims. First, that funded schemes were presented as creating stronger ownership connections that would increase participation[51] and financial discipline.[52] Financial sector stakeholders argued that individual accounts would transform passive beneficiaries into active asset owners,[53] enabling the creation of a robust capital market that could enhance the competitive position of any country.[54] Second, these property rights would supposedly shield retirement savings from political interference,[55] thereby reducing a so-called political risk.[56] These two arguments directly echo the Commission's concern with the precariousness of unfunded entitlements.[57]

[49] World Bank, *Averting the Old Age Crisis: Policies to Protect the Old and Promote Growth. Summary* (The World Bank 1994); Orenstein (n 48) 15.

[50] World Bank (n 49); Robert Holzmann, Richard Paul Hinz and Mark Dorfman, 'Pension Systems and Reform Conceptual Framework' (2008) 824 World Bank Discussion Paper.

[51] Jan B Kuné, 'The Controversy of Funding versus Pay-as-You-Go: What Remains of the Debate?' (2001) 26 *The Geneva Papers on Risk and Insurance-Issues and Practice* 418, 421.

[52] Carmelo Mesa Lago, 'Evaluación de Cuatro Décadas de Privatización de Pensiones En América Latina, 1980–2020. Promesas y Realidades' [2021] *Revista General de Derecho del Trabajo y de la Seguridad Social* 28; Carmelo Mesa Lago, 'La Privatización de Las Pensiones En América Latina. Promesas y Realidades' [2021] *Nueva sociedad* 15; James A Dorn, 'Pension Reform in China: A Question of Property Rights' (2003) 23 *Cato Journal* 433.

[53] Richard Minns, *The Cold War in Welfare: Stock Markets versus Pensions* (Verso 2001); Robin Blackburn, *Banking on Death: Or, Investing in Life: The History and Future of Pensions* (Verso Books 2002); Ireland (n 26); Marek Naczyk, 'Agents of Privatization? Business Groups and the Rise of Pension Funds in Continental Europe' (2013) 11 *Socio-Economic Review* 441.

[54] Marek Naczyk and Bruno Palier, 'Feed the Beast: Finance Capitalism and the Spread of Pension Privatisation in Europe' [2014] Available at SSRN 2551521.

[55] Kuné (n 51) 426.

[56] Interestingly, Diamond argues that unfunded entitlements should, from an economic point of view, enjoy the same property-like protection as funded entitlements. Peter Diamond, 'Insulation of Pensions from Political Risk' in Salvador Valdes-Prieto (ed), *The Economics of Pensions, Principles, Policies and International Experience* (Cambridge University Press 1997). However, such an idea, while interesting in the abstract, does not provide a sufficient legal foundation that could support it accordingly.

[57] Estelle James, Truman Packard and Robert Holzmann, 'Americas: From'Averting the Old-Age Crisis' to'Keeping the Promise of Old-Age Security'and Beyond' [2007] *Lessons from Pension Reform in the Americas* 164, 181; Robert Holzmann and others, 'Comments on Rethinking Pension Reform: Ten Myths about Social Security Systems by Peter Orszag and Joseph Stiglitz' in R Holzmann, and JE Stiglitz (eds), *New Ideas About Old Age Security* (The World Bank, 2001) 81; Lans Bovenberg and Casper Van Ewijk, 'Designing the Pension System: Conceptual Framework' in *The Future of Multi-Pillar Pensions* (Cambridge University Press 2011) 167; Lans Bovenberg and Casper Van Ewijk, 'The Future of Multi-Pillar Pension Systems' in *The Future of Multi-Pillar Pension Systems* (Cambridge University Press 2011) 384. There are also recent advocacy for introducing a similar property-right idea within unfunded PAYG systems as well, advanced exactly by the promoters of funded schemes in the past Salvador Valdes-Prieto, 'Securitization of Taxes Implicit in PAYG Pensions' (2005) 20 *Economic Policy* 216; Assar Lindbeck and Mats Persson, 'The Gains from Pension Reform' (2003) 41 *Journal of Economic Literature* 74.

These property-based arguments shaped a pension privatisation campaign internationally.[58] Between 1988 and 2008, 29 countries implemented structural reforms that partially or fully replaced public systems with mandatory funded pillars or schemes in different ways.[59] Even if the literature tends to focus on the reforms deployed in Latin American[60] and Eastern European countries,[61] the same arguments are recycled in the pension reform debate almost everywhere, including the United States[62] and Western Europe.[63]

Nevertheless, the 2008 financial crisis revealed fundamental tensions in the model based on funding entitlements. Private pension accounts suffered significant losses, and governments faced with severe fiscal constraints could no longer easily afford the transition costs associated with diverting contributions from public to private systems.[64] These pressures led several countries to scale back their funded pillars and reintroduce a large PAYG tier.[65] Moreover, after several decades of their introduction, many countries that had bet on a higher privatised system found that the property-based promises failed to materialise.[66] Despite claims that private accounts would create more secure property rights, leading to higher replacement rates in privatised systems, they fell well below established standards, with many contributors failing to qualify for benefits at all.[67]

In the Council of Europe, various countries reversed their mandatory occupational pillars in the aftermath of the financial crisis, including Slovakia, Lithuania, Latvia, Estonia, Croatia, Romania, Poland and Hungary.[68] As a result, various applications were introduced before the ECtHR.

[58] Orenstein (n 48); Mitchell A Orenstein, 'Pension Privatization in Crisis: Death or Rebirth of a Global Policy Trend?' (2011) 64 *International Social Security Review* 65.

[59] Robert Holzmann, 'Global Pension Systems and Their Reform: Worldwide Drivers, Trends and Challenges' (2013) 66 *International Social Security Review* 1, 2.

[60] Lago (n 52); Mesa Lago (n 52); Isabel Ortiz and others, 'Reversing Pension Privatization: Rebuilding Public Pension Systems in Eastern European and Latin American Countries (2000–18)' [2018] Available at SSRN 3275228.

[61] Leokadia Oręziak, *Pension Fund Capitalism: The Privatization of Pensions in Developed and Developing Countries* (Routledge 2022); Naczyk (n 53); Marek Naczyk and Martin Seeleib-Kaiser, 'Solidarity against All Odds: Trade Unions and the Privatization of Pensions in the Age of Dualization' (2015) 43 *Politics & Society* 361.

[62] Blackburn (n 53) 374–379; Susanne N Beechey, *Social Security and the Politics of Deservingness* (Springer 2016).

[63] Adam D Dixon, 'The Rise of Pension Fund Capitalism in Europe: An Unseen Revolution?' (2008) 13 *New Political Economy* 249.

[64] Jan Drahokoupil and Stefan Domonkos, 'Averting the Funding-Gap Crisis: East European Pension Reforms since 2008' (2012) 12 *Global Social Policy* 283; Marek Naczyk and Stefan Domonkos, 'The Financial Crisis and Varieties of Pension Privatization Reversals in Eastern Europe' (2016) 29 *Governance* 167; Ortiz and others (n 60); Lago (n 52).

[65] Drahokoupil and Domonkos (n 64); Naczyk and Domonkos (n 64); Ortiz and others (n 60).

[66] Mesa Lago (n 52); Lago (n 52).

[67] Lago (n 52).

[68] Ortiz and others (n 60).

One of the most relevant cases for this chapter was *E.B. v Hungary*.[69] Following the privatisation reversal introduced by the government in three different moments, an applicant challenged these measures, claiming that such measures 'expropriated' her accumulated assets. Her claim explicitly invoked the formalistic distinction between entitlements arising from funded/unfunded schemes, arguing that, unlike state pensions, which create only statutory expectations, funded pension schemes reflected individual contributions that constituted protected property under A1P1. Therefore, according to the applicant, the reversal was a direct interference with her rights to a peaceful enjoyment of her private property. The Court rejected this attempted revival of the formalistic distinction, holding that:

> [T]hroughout the entire period of her employment, the contributions which the applicant has made to either the private pension fund or the State fund have conferred on her an entitlement to pension payments in the future.[70]

By emphasising that her entitlement remained intact regardless of the financing mechanism, the Court confirmed that, as it was clear since 2005,[71] the funded/unfunded distinction no longer determined the status of pension entitlements under A1P1. This judgment reinforced the Court's abandonment of the purely formalistic approach to pension rights that had prevailed in earlier decisions.

The reason why the formalistic distinction persists in policy discourse could be found in its connection to normative theories that continue to shape public understanding of pension entitlements. Two theoretical frameworks are particularly relevant in explaining this disconnect between legal evolution and policy discourse.

First, desert-based theories of property rights provide one foundation for the persistence of the formalistic distinction. These theories suggest that individuals deserve benefits corresponding to their specific contributions.[72] This intuition aligns well with funded systems where contributions are visibly accumulated. The corresponding framework suggests that fairness relates to entitlements, which are the result of a direct and strict relationship between what one contributes and what one receives. That is a notion similar to actuarial fairness,[73] which, contrary to the general intuition, could be a feature found in both funded and unfunded systems.[74] However, in general policy discourse, it is generally assumed that it is only funded

[69] *EB v Hungary* [2013] European Court of Human Rights 34929/11.

[70] ibid 6.

[71] See ch 5.

[72] Joel Feinberg, 'Justice and Personal Desert' in M Friedman, L May, K. Parsons and J Stiff (eds), *Rights and Reason: Essays in Honor of Carl Wellman* (Springer 1970); Julian Lamont, 'The Concept of Desert in Distributive Justice' (1994) 44 *The Philosophical Quarterly (1950–)* 45; Jeffrey Moriarty, 'Desert-Based Justice' in *The Oxford Handbook of Distributive Justice* (Oxford University Press 2018) 152.

[73] Landes (n 34); Alonso-García, Boado-Penas and Devolder (n 34).

[74] Pierre Devolder, Susanna Levantesi and Massimiliano Menzietti, 'Automatic Balance Mechanisms for Notional Defined Contribution Pension Systems Guaranteeing Social Adequacy and Financial Sustainability: An Application to the Italian Pension System' (2021) 299 *Annals of Operations Research* 765; Pierre Devolder and Sébastien De Valeriola, 'Pension Design and Risk Sharing: Mixed Solutions Between Defined Benefit and Defined Contribution for Public Pension Schemes' in M Peris-Ortíz, J Álvarez-García, I Domínguez-Fabián and P Devolder (eds), *Economic Challenges of Pension Systems: A Sustainability and International Management Perspective* (Springer 2020) 311.

systems, with their accounts tracking specific contributions and investment returns, that could align more intuitively with this desert-based conception than unfunded systems based on intergenerational transfers.

The second normative track that could explain the persistence of the formalistic distinction in policy discourse relates to the rather influential Lockean property theory in property law.[75] According to Locke's labour theory of property, individuals establish property rights by mixing their labour with resources.[76] The formalistic distinction seems to conceive that only funded pensions can parallel this process: contributions derived from labour create a property-like claim to the accumulated capital, hence seeming more intuitively like 'property' than unfunded systems based on intergenerational transfers.

Nevertheless, the formalistic distinction faces severe limits when applied to modern pension systems. Even the very idea of 'ownership' in funded schemes is legally uncertain.[77] It is not always clear what the protected asset is meant to be or how a property should protect it.[78] It could refer to the underlying fund, the account balance or the promise of a future benefit. Disputes over how surpluses are used, what powers employers have, and how trustees manage the funds all show that legal rules structure ownership.[79] These rules limit control and introduce a level of institutional complexity that weakens any simple claim to individual property. What the participant holds, therefore, is not direct ownership of assets, but a position shaped by multiple layers of regulation and oversight.[80]

Even if one puts aside the definitional issues and accepts that funded schemes offer some degree of property protection, the underlying argument still relies on a fixed idea: that the method of financing determines whether an entitlement qualifies as property. On this view, owning an account balance or a share in a fund creates a protected expectation, whereas PAYG entitlements do not. But this reasoning is inconsistent. Defined Benefit schemes, for instance, are often funded, yet they rarely give individuals any legal claim to the underlying capital before retirement.[81] The entitlement takes the form of a future benefit, not ownership of an asset. This indicates that the presence of funding alone does not establish a legal right. In other words, the distinction based on structures of financing, far from being a coherent legal principle, is rather a selective way of assigning legal protection to some expectations and not to others.

[75] Gregory S Alexander and Eduardo M Peñalver, *An Introduction to Property Theory* (Cambridge University Press 2012); Jeremy Waldron, *The Right to Private Property* (Oxford University Press 1990).

[76] Alexander and Peñalver (n 75).

[77] Nobles (n 26); Ireland (n 26).

[78] Nobles (n 26); Ireland (n 26).

[79] Blackburn (n 53); Nobles (n 26); Ireland (n 26).

[80] Nobles (n 26).

[81] ibid. In the Netherlands there was a debate on whether accruals in funded second pillar plans were property in the context of the new pension reform. Systematically, Dutch Courts have denied such a claim: Erik Lutjens, 'Wet Toekomst Pensioenen: Wet Toekomst Pensioenen: Nieuwe Methode Pensioenopbouw – Een Onzekerder Pensioen En Een Fors Aantal Procedures' [2023] *Nederlands Juristenblad* 3; Erik Lutjens, 'Invaren Pensioen: De Relevantie van Recht Op Eigendom' (2021) 10 *Tijdschrift voor Arbeidsrecht in Context* 3.

It reveals that the distinction based on structures of financing is not a coherent legal principle, but a selective way of assigning legal protection to some expectations and not others. In that sense, it is a political argument dressed in legal form.[82]

The complexity of legal structures underlying pension arrangements explains why the formalistic approach proves weak in legal doctrine. Even courts that do protect pension entitlements through the lens of property have consistently struggled to recognise the relevance of the financing method to provide a privileged protection of funded entitlement as opposed to unfunded ones.[83] That is why they usually tend to protect entitlements independently of their methodology of financing based on a different, more functional approach to the benefit itself, so much like the ECtHR after *Stec and Others v United Kingdom*.[84]

II. Defining the Scope of Property Protection

In this early period, apart from the question of which pension entitlements could constitute 'possessions' under A1P1, the ECtHR had also to define the scope of protection of the norm for those entitlements that fell under its protective scope.

In *Müller v Austria* and *X v Austria* the Commission established two principles. On the one hand, the 'substance of the right' doctrine. Here, the case law defined that A1P1's protection did not entail an entitlement to a specific amount. On the other hand, the temporal scope of A1P1's protection. Anyone claiming to be entitled to a pension benefit that constitutes a 'possession' would only be able to dispute an interference with its peaceful enjoyment once it has fully crystallised. A1P1 protects only current benefit holders as opposed to participants who have not yet met the statutory requirements to claim such a benefit.[85]

A. 'The Essence of the Right'

The Commission first articulated the 'substance of the right' doctrine in *Müller v Austria*.[86] The case arose from a unique situation that would highlight some tensions between different conceptions of pension rights. The applicant was a retiree who had made both compulsory and voluntary contributions to an

[82] Nobles (n 26).

[83] Pál Sonnevend, *Eigentumsschutz Und Sozialversicherung: Eine Rechtsvergleichende Analyse Anhand Der Rechtsprechung Des Bundesverfassungsgerichts Und Des Ungarischen Verfassungsgerichts*, vol 185 (Springer-Verlag 2007).

[84] ibid. Also see chs 5 and 6.

[85] This question is fully addressed in Kevin Hartmann-Cortés, 'On Future Retirees' Legal Standing: Rethinking A1P1 Admissibility in Pension Reform Cases' [2025] *The European Convention on Human Rights Law Review* 340.

[86] *Müller v Austria* (n 8). This judgment is only available in French. The English translation is from the author.

unfunded scheme. However, as a consequence of the retroactive application of an international treaty, his benefit was reduced.

The applicant of the case had contributed for 37 years to the Austrian Workers' Old Age Insurance Scheme. When he later found employment in Liechtenstein, the Austrian law encouraged him to continue making voluntary contributions, promising these would be treated exactly like his previous compulsory contributions for the purposes of calculating the final benefit.[87] However, a subsequent treaty between Austria and Liechtenstein retroactively changed how these voluntary contributions would be counted.[88] The new legislation provided that previous voluntary contributions would no longer be considered in the final estimation of the amount of the pension benefit recognised by the mandatory old-age scheme. Instead, they would be treated separately: as contributions to acquire a complementary pension or *Höherversicherung*, a different scheme.[89] In simpler terms, those contributions would no longer be included in the calculation of the Austrian mandatory old-age insurance scheme's pension replacement rate. Instead, they would be treated as separate payments made to acquire a pension in a different yet complementary scheme.

The applicant learned only upon claiming his pension that the revised rules for counting prior contributions reduced his benefit.[90] He challenged the retroactive effects of the new legislation in the judiciary, although with little success.[91] After exhausting domestic remedies, the applicant went to the ECtHR claiming a potential interference with his property. He argued that voluntary contributions, unlike compulsory ones, created a distinct type of property right that should be protected against retroactive changes. The main argument was that while compulsory contributions could be subject to legislative changes, voluntary payments explicitly made to secure additional benefits deserved stronger protection under A1P1.

This case presented the Commission with a question about the nature of pension rights under A1P1: did different types of contributions (voluntary versus mandatory, which differ from the funded/unfunded cleavage) create different levels of property protection? Moreover, could changes to benefit calculation rules that lower the expected benefit constitute an interference with property rights?

The judgment would avoid answering the first question altogether. However, it established two principles about the scope of A1P1 protection for pension entitlements. These principles remain valid even today. First, it held that while pension entitlements might constitute possessions, this protection did not extend to guaranteeing any specific amount. Second, and more significantly, it introduced what would become known as the 'substance of the right' doctrine. While benefit

[87] ibid 50.
[88] ibid 50–51.
[89] ibid 51.
[90] ibid.
[91] ibid.

reductions are generally permissible, changes that affect the very essence of the pension right could breach A1P1.[92]

The Commission's analysis began by establishing the framework within which it would develop what would become known as the 'substance of the right' doctrine. First, it recalled that A1P1 does not guarantee any right to *acquire* property.[93] Applied to pension entitlements, it means that it does not guarantee any right to acquire a pension.[94]

Then, it acknowledged that this case would be helpful to develop the rule established in *X v the Netherlands*[95] according to which: 'the making of compulsory contributions to a pension fund may, in certain circumstances, create a property right in a portion of such fund and that such right might be affected by how the fund is distributed'.[96] However, as the Court recognised, this application only disputed the fact that some of his voluntary contributions were affected by the retroactive application of the bilateral treaty.[97]

Müller v Austria essentially relates to a classic problem of conflicts of law in time.[98] This problem raises at least three questions. First, what are the interests, values and rights that demand recognition whenever the two laws conflict?[99] Second, how does the conflict of laws affect these interests, values and rights? Finally, is it justified if there is an effect on these interests, values and rights?[100]

Despite being the heart of the problem at stake, the Commission did not acknowledge any of those questions. Judge Treschel, in his separate opinion, was also concerned by the judgment's lack of engagement with these questions. In his

[92] See ch 6 for further discussion on what this means for pensions as property under A1P1.

[93] *Müller v Austria* (n 8) [10].

[94] There is always a question of whether A1P1 imposes a right to a minimum guarantee. The literature suggests that it does not, and that it is unlikely that the case-law would go in that direction any time soon. See Ingrid Leijten, 'The Right to Minimum Subsistence and Property Protection under the ECHR: Never the Twain Shall Meet?' (2019) 21 *European Journal of Social Security* 307.

[95] *Müller v Austria* (n 8) [11].

[96] ibid.

[97] ibid 28.

[98] This is one of the most classic problems in law. For a seminal work, refer to Pierre Roubier, *Le Droit Transitoire (Les Conflits de Lois Dans Le Temps)* 2nd edn (Dalloz 1960) 1.

[99] These questions are grouped within the category of the 'foundation' of intertemporal conflicts of law. JR Trahan, 'Time for a Change: A Call to Reform Louisiana's Intertemporal Conflicts Law (Law of Retroactivity of Laws)' (1998) 59 *Loyola Law Review* 661, 668.

[100] One way to frame and solve some problems relative to intertemporal conflicts of the law is by using the idea of a transition loss. Transition losses may be defined as those 'losses in the expected return on effective investment'. Axel Gosseries and Mathias Hungerbühler, 'Rule Change and Intergenerational Justice' in J Tremmel (ed), Handbook of Intergenerational Justice (Edward Elgar 2006) 106, 110. The applicant made a voluntary investment (his voluntary contributions) based on a regulation that would significantly accrue his pension benefit entitlement. Had he known that these contributions no longer accrue his benefit at the same rate, he would not have paid them. For these cases, one can imagine a measure of compensation. For instance, exempting the applicant from the rule change after the treaty's ratification. In other words, to keep applying the old-law. This phenomenon is called in the Italian and Latin-American legal traditions as 'ultra-activity' of the law, to the extent that it keeps producing effects after it had been changed. In the French tradition is called 'postactivity' or 'survival of the law'. In the American tradition, it is called 'grandfathering'. See Trahan (n 99) 706.

view, addressing that question would have implied a different outcome.[101] Instead, what it did was frame the case as involving two unrelated questions, but which would help develop its case law on pensions as property under A1P1. The first one was, what exactly was the 'possession' at stake? This was not immediately clear, as the case concerned rules about how contributions would affect benefit calculations rather than a straightforward property claim. Second, what level of protection should A1P1 provide to such possessions?

The Commission approached these questions by examining whether pension entitlements could create different types of property rights:

> Assuming that the payment of contributions to an old-age insurance scheme gives rise to a right protected under Article 1 of the Additional Protocol, the question arises as to whether this right merely entails benefiting from payments made by the fund while remaining a beneficiary of the social insurance system or whether it grants entitlement to the payment of a specific sum, calculated, for example, according to actuarial rules. The Commission considers that, at most, only the first of these solutions follows from the interpretation of Article 1 of the Additional Protocol. While it is conceivable that the right to be a beneficiary of an old-age insurance scheme to which one has contributed falls within the guarantee of property rights as ensured by Article 1 of the Additional Protocol, the same does not necessarily apply to the exact amount of the pension. Indeed, the Commission considers that even if one were to accept that Article 1 of the Additional Protocol guarantees those who have paid contributions to a social insurance system the right to benefit from it, it cannot, however, be interpreted as granting entitlement to a pension of a specific amount.[102]

This was a crucial analytical move. To establish the scope of protection under A1P1, the Commission first assumes the existence of an entitlement protected under A1P1. It then distinguished between two possible interpretations of what A1P1 might protect: either the basic right to receive benefits as a scheme participant,

[101] '[T]he present case has the particularity that the applicant made voluntary contributions to obtain additional benefits. This leads me to conclude that he has acquired a property right, within the meaning of Article 1 of the Additional Protocol, over a specific sum, which must be calculated according to actuarial rules'. In the original French '*[L]a présente affaire offre cette particularité que le requérant a versé des cotisations volontaires pour obtenir des prestations supplémentaires. Ce fait m'amène à conclure qu'il a acquis un droit de propriété, au sens de l'article 1 du Protocole additionnel, portant sur une somme déterminée, qui doit être calculée selon les règles actuarielles*'. Opinion Separée du Juge M Treschel, *Müller v Austria* (n 8).

[102] ibid 29–30. The French version reads: '*A supposer que le versement de cotisations à un régime d'assurance-vieillesse donne naissance à un droit protégé par l'article 1 du Protocole additionnel, la question se pose de savoir si ce droit se rapporte simplement au fait de profiter des versements de la caisse en restant bénéficiaire du système d'assurance sociale, ou s'il ouvre le droit au versement d'une somme détermine, calculée, par exemple, d'après les règles actuarielles. La Commission estime que c'est tout au plus a la première de ces solutions qui découle de l'interprétation de l'article 1 du Protocole additionnel. Or, alors qu'il est concevable que le droit d'être bénéficiaire d'un système d'assurance-vieillesse auquel on a contribué relève de la garantie du droit de propriété telle qu'elle est assurée par l'article 1 du Protocole additionnel, il n'en va pas nécessairement de même pour ce qui concerne le montant exact de la rente. En effet, la Commission estime que, même si l'on admettait que l'article 1 du Protocole additionnel garantit à ceux qui ont payé des contributions à un système d'assurance sociale le droit de tirer un bénéfice de ce système, il ne peut cependant être interprète comme donnant droit à une rente d'un montant déterminé*'.

or a right to a specific calculated amount. In choosing the former interpretation, the Commission established a fundamental principle: while A1P1 could protect pension rights as possessions, its scope does not guarantee any particular amount.

> The operation of a social security system cannot be equated with the management of a private life insurance company. Given its public significance, it must take political considerations into account, particularly financial policy. It is conceivable, for example, that a deflationary trend might compel a state to reduce the nominal amount of pension benefits. Such fluctuations could not fall within the guarantee of property as a human right. In the present case, it was the harmonisation of social security systems at a bilateral or even European level that led to a similar outcome for the applicant.[103]

In this case, the Commission creates a distinction between entitlements supposedly arising from private insurance contracts, where specific amounts are guaranteed, and social insurance schemes, which must remain flexible to respond to broader policy needs. The property protection for social security entitlements would differ substantially from that of private insurance entitlements in the sense that they are not (and ought not to be) contractually fixed. Therefore, it would not be possible to equate the legal entitlement emerging from social insurance participation with the legal entitlement emerging from a contractual insurance relation. Such a difference, according to this judgment, is relevant to determining precisely the scope of protection provided by A1P1.

This rule on the scope of A1P1 raised a new question: considering that states have a broad competence to modify benefits, what type of meaningful protection does A1P1 provide for pension entitlements? The judgment addressed this by introducing what would be known as the 'essence of the right' doctrine: 'It is true that, in certain cases, a substantial reduction in the amount of the pension could be considered as affecting the very essence of the right to remain a beneficiary of the old-age insurance system'.[104]

This reasoning has been repeated several times in the case law in cases related to pension entitlements under A1P1.[105] While states could generally modify benefit amounts, they must do so reasonably and proportionally. Changes so substantial that they would undermine the very *essence* of being a scheme beneficiary would breach A1P1. The debate on what this 'essence' is in the case of pension benefits will be discussed in chapter six. At this stage, it suffices to explain that the reduction in this case was about 3 per cent of the otherwise expected pension, which, according to the Court, does not imply a 'substantial' reduction. Therefore, the Commission considered that there was no breach of A1P1.

[103] ibid 31.

[104] ibid 32. The French version reads: 'Il est vrai que, dans certains cas, une réduction substantielle du montant de la rente pourrait être considérée comme affectant la substance même du droit de rester bénéficiaire du système d'assurance-vieillesse'.

[105] *Kjartan Ásmundsson v Iceland* [2004] European Court of Human Rights 60669/00; *Rasmussen v Poland* [2009] European Court of Human Rights 38886/05; *Maggio and Others v Italy* [2011] European Court of Human Rights (46286/09, 52851/08, 54486/08 and 56001/08).

B. The Temporal Scope of A1P1 to Pension Entitlements

The question of when a pension entitlement becomes a 'possession' protected under A1P1 was addressed in *X v Austria*.[106] This case built upon previous jurisprudence regarding the distinction between funded and unfunded schemes relevant for A1P1's protection. In this case, the Court would set a rule that is still also relevant today: A1P1's scope of protection only starts when a pension claim is payable to the beneficiary. That implies a limited coverage for retirees only.[107]

The applicant lodged a claim alleging discrimination regarding the reduction of his pension benefit. Having made contributions to the old-age scheme both as an employee in the private sector and as a self-employed tradesman, he eventually retired. His pension was granted by the Old Age Pension Fund for Tradesmen. In an effort to increase his income, he took on additional employment. After informing the authorities of his new position, they diminished his pension benefit. The justification for this reduction was the perceived incompatibility between the pension received from the Tradesmen Pension Fund and the applicant's new job. The applicant contended that such a reduction was unfair, particularly considering that retirees from the public servants' old-age scheme were exempted from such reductions under the law.

The judgment holds that the applicant's argument centred around the idea that 'by paying contributions to the Old-Age Pension Scheme during 43 years, he has acquired an irrevocable legal title to being paid the corresponding pension'.[108] Furthermore: 'the decision of the Social Insurance Fund for Tradesmen to reduce his pension was an infringement of vested rights which were possessions within the meaning of Article 1, paragraph 1 of the protocol'.[109]

Quoting *Müller v Austria*, the Commission suggested that a reduction in the old-age pension could interfere with the peaceful enjoyment of someone's right. However, it might be acceptable because A1P1 did not include the protection of a specific amount.[110] At this point, the temporal aspect emerged: 'The legal regulations providing for a reduced pension claim in these circumstances were already in force when the applicant paid his contributions, and he could therefore never expect to get a full pension under these conditions'.[111]

The Commission's interpretation here distinguishes between enforcing pre-existing rules and changing rules through subsequent legislation. This raises the question: when does a claim to a pension benefit 'exist' for A1P1? Is it after making compulsory contributions, as suggested in *X v the Netherlands*? Alternatively, does the claim come into existence when meeting all statutory requirements to receive

[106] *X v Austria* (n 9).
[107] I discuss at length this rule and the implications for future retirees in Hartmann-Cortés (n 85).
[108] *X v Austria* (n 9) 103.
[109] ibid.
[110] ibid.
[111] ibid 105.

a pension benefit? In that scenario, any changes affecting the potential expected pension would not raise issues under A1P1, considering that social insurance systems are governed by different rules than private insurance contracts. The Commission held that:

> In the present case, there is therefore no question of the reduction of existent claims by supervening legislation, but a pre-existent limitation of the claim which the applicant would have had if he had met certain additional conditions. The Commission considers that the limitation of the applicant's claim is not a deprivation of possessions within the meaning of Article 1, paragraph 1 of the Protocol.[112]

With this decision, it became clear that pension entitlements could become protected possessions only when the statutory conditions for receiving benefits are met. What matters for A1P1 protection is whether changes to pension entitlements occur through subsequent legislation after the claim has formed.

The judgment also examined another allegation: whether the Austrian legislation was discriminatory between retirees based on the type of scheme from which they received their pension benefit. The judgment stated that: '[t]he distinction and different treatment of two groups of social security pensioners does not … in itself amount to discrimination concerning their property rights'.[113] Moreover, it provided an analysis that would be referenced in subsequent case law:

> It is true that pension claims of civil servants and other State-employed persons assimilated to their status are under no circumstances subject to reduction on account of an additional working income, and that those persons are in this respect treated differently in comparison to social security pensioners.[114]

The Commission then explained why this difference in treatment might be justified:

> The Commission considers, however, that there is a basic difference between the legal situation of civil servants and that of self-employed tradesmen and private employees which can justify, under Article 14 of the Convention, that the system adopted by the legislation for retirement pensions of civil servants is not based on the same principles as the social insurance schemes for tradesmen and employees. In Austria, the system of civil servants' retirement pensions is governed by the principle of support and the question whether the civil servant concerned has reached full coverage of his pension by his own contributions i.e. the situation in which the pensions of tradesmen and private employees are subject to reduction-therefore does not arise.[115]

The Commission's reasoning in this case reveals a contradiction in its approach to pension rights under A1P1. In *X v the Netherlands* and other early cases, the

[112] ibid.
[113] ibid 105–06.
[114] ibid 106.
[115] ibid.

Commission had established that funded schemes (where contributions create 'identifiable shares') generated stronger property rights deserving A1P1 protection. In contrast, unfunded solidarity-based schemes created weaker claims that might not qualify as possessions. Yet in this case, the Commission reversed this logic.

By accepting that civil servants' pensions based on 'the principle of support' should not be reduced upon re-employment, while allowing reductions to pensions where retirees had 'reached full coverage by their own contributions', the Commission would have effectively granted stronger practical protection to the supposedly 'weaker' property right. A more analytical critique would go further by suggesting that even if assuming that the financing methodology of pension systems may be a valid justification for differing treatment of benefit entitlements between different types of schemes, it does not explain why a reduction would be less problematic for one retiree compared to another. This aspect will be revisited in the next chapter.

This inconsistency revealed how the Commission's approach to pension rights under A1P1 was still evolving during this period, with underlying tensions between different rationales for protection. On one hand, the Commission maintained its formal doctrine that pension entitlements resembling private property (through funding mechanisms) deserved stronger A1P1 protection. On the other hand, when confronted with practical questions about benefit reductions, it sometimes reached conclusions that contradicted this formal approach. Despite this apparent contradiction, the Commission's position that funded schemes created stronger property rights than unfunded ones remained the dominant interpretation for decades, until *Stec and Others v the United Kingdom*.[116] In that judgment, the Court finally harmonised protection across different types of social security benefits.[117]

The temporal dimension of A1P1 in pensions established in this case has remained unchallenged. Ever since, the Court would only engage A1P1 for cases that relate to already payable pension entitlements. By determining that protection under A1P1 begins only when statutory requirements are fulfilled, the Commission created a demarcation between those entitled to pension benefits and those in their contributory phase. This distinction shields current retirees from pension reforms while leaving future retirees without recourse to challenge measures that may reduce their expected benefits.[118] The asymmetry in A1P1's protection creates an incentive for lawmakers to design reforms that preserve benefits for current retirees – who can challenge reductions through A1P1 – while concentrating cuts on future benefits claimed by individuals who would lack standing.[119]

[116] *Stec and Others v the United Kingdom* [2006] European Court of Human Rights 65731/01 and 65900/01.

[117] See ch 5.

[118] Hartmann-Cortés (n 85).

[119] ibid.

Conclusions

This chapter traced the European Commission of Human Rights' early approach to pension rights under A1P1. Between 1971 and 1996, the jurisprudence centred on two main questions: which pension entitlements could constitute possessions, and once recognised as such, what type of protection did they deserve. The Commission addressed those questions with a narrow conception of A1P1's reach. Only pension benefits arising from funded schemes could be considered property. Such a position reduced the scope of A1P1's engagement in the pension field, considering that the majority of states in the Council of Europe had established unfunded schemes.

The institutional distinction between funded and unfunded schemes, as well as its relevance, was expressed through a series of terms that shifted over time but preserved the same structure of reasoning. The Commission initially referred to an 'identifiable share', then to 'own coverage' and later emphasised a strict link between contributions and benefits. Each formulation reinforced the idea that funding determined the property nature of the entitlement. In other words, the method of financing defined whether A1P1 was applicable.

This early case law also defined limits to the protection of pensions under the property clause, which still have validity today. The 'substance of the right' doctrine established that while A1P1 protected the general status of being a beneficiary, it did not guarantee any particular payment level. The judgments further emphasised that social security systems must remain adaptable to changing political and economic circumstances, distinguishing them from private insurance contracts. Within this logic, only changes that affected the core of the entitlement could amount to a violation of A1P1. States, therefore, retain a broad margin to review benefit levels, provided the legal status of the beneficiary was preserved.

The temporal scope of protection further limited A1P1's protective reach, establishing that claims became possessions only when statutory requirements were fully met. This created a sharp divide in standing possibilities between current retirees, who could challenge reforms affecting their benefits, and future retirees, who remained unprotected regardless of their proximity to retirement. This distinction gave states a clear incentive to focus adjustments on future claims. It also confined A1P1's protective function to a narrow phase of the pension lifecycle.

Finally, the formalistic doctrine of the Court still has some relevance today. By equating property with funding, it reinforced the view that only funded schemes could generate secure and legitimate entitlements. This view entered policy discourse in the 1990s and 2000s, particularly through the influence of multilateral institutions promoting pension reforms. Funded pensions were portrayed as individual property, immune from political interference. Unfunded schemes were seen as politically fragile and economically unstable. This framing supported a wave of structural reforms, especially in Latin America and Eastern Europe, where public systems were partially replaced with funded, defined-contribution schemes. Although courts would later reject the formalistic test, its categories remained powerful in shaping the language of reform. Legal doctrine had moved on, but policy narratives continued to rely on distinctions the Commission had drawn. The next chapter examines how the Court replaced this framework with a more functional understanding of possessions under A1P1.

5

The Functional Doctrine in A1P1 Pension Jurisprudence (1996–Today)

Introduction

In 1996, the European Court of Human Rights (ECtHR) took its first step away from the formalistic approach that had previously governed its interpretation of pension entitlements under Article 1 of Protocol No 1 (A1P1). In *Gaygusuz v Austria*,[1] the Court recognised that a non-contributory benefit could be a 'possession'. This case marked the beginning of a broader revaluation of what kinds of welfare rights fell under the realm of the property clause, and what could justify such protection.

At the time, the Court faced both external and internal pressures. Externally, domestic constitutional courts in Germany and Hungary had already recognised pension entitlements as property rights, irrespective of their funding mechanism.[2] These courts viewed pension benefits as performing a 'freedom-securing function' traditionally associated with private ownership.[3] Internally, the ECtHR's case law – discussed in chapter four – was expanding the reach of A1P1 and was uncertain about how to apply the clause on different types of pension claims.

For nearly a decade after *Gaygusuz*, the Court started to grant A1P1 protection to a broader range of welfare entitlements. These judgments appeared purely *ad hoc* because they lacked a clear and sufficiently developed reasoning for why A1P1 was now applied to those entitlements. This doctrinal ambiguity reopened the tension regarding the scope of the property clause. Applicants would rely on the Court's *ad hoc* decisions that granted admissibility to pension cases under A1P1. At the same time, governments and dissenting judges continued to invoke the older, formalistic framework to oppose their admissibility.

The ambiguity was finally resolved in *Stec and Others v the United Kingdom*.[4] That case consolidated the shift from the formalistic to the functionalist doctrine. In that judgment, the Court provided the long-awaited justification on how, why

[1] *Gaygusuz v Austria* (GC) ECHR 1996-IV (1997) 23 EHRR 364.
[2] Pál Sonnevend, *Eigentumsschutz Und Sozialversicherung: Eine Rechtsvergleichende Analyse Anhand Der Rechtsprechung Des Bundesverfassungsgerichts Und Des Ungarischen Verfassungsgerichts*, vol 185 (Springer-Verlag 2007).
[3] ibid.
[4] *Stec and Others v United Kingdom* (GC) ECHR 2006-VI (2006) 43 EHRR 47.

and to what extent A1P1 applies to all pension benefits. The judgment is a truly landmark case, because it redefined the meaning of 'possessions' in the context of welfare entitlements, including pensions. This doctrinal turn raised two main questions, which structure this chapter. First, how did the Court justify extending property protection to pension entitlements not previously covered by A1P1? Second, how did this redefinition affect the concept of 'possessions' in the context of the modern welfare state?

The chapter is organised in five parts, including this introduction. Section I reviews the transitional case law between 1996 and 2005, beginning with *Gaygusuz* and tracing the interpretive tensions that followed. Section II analyses how *Stec* resolved these tensions and established a new doctrinal foundation. Section III describes the normative and conceptual underpinnings of this shift, situating it within broader debates on property and welfare. The chapter concludes by evaluating the scope and limits of the Court's new functionalist approach, setting the stage for chapter six, which examines its operation in the context of pension reform.

I. The Transitional Period: From Formalism to Functionalism (1996–2005)

Chapter four examined the formalistic doctrine developed by the Commission between 1972 and 1996. During this period, case law held that the financing structure of a pension scheme was central to determining whether the resulting entitlements qualified as 'possessions' under A1P1. Only entitlements from funded schemes were protected, while entitlements from unfunded schemes, grounded in the 'principle of support', fell outside the scope of A1P1. The case law also defined the substantive and temporal boundaries of A1P1's protection in this context.

In 1996, the Court began to move away from this approach. Rather than focusing on the system's technical features to determine A1P1's applicability, it reflected on the broader role that the welfare entitlements play in modern states. This shift culminated in the enlargement of A1P1's scope to include all statutory pension entitlements, regardless of their design or financing structure. The transformation began with *Gaygusuz v Austria*.

A. *Gaygusuz v Austria*: Extending A1P1's Scope

Gaugusuz v Austria[5] marked the beginning of a transformation in the Court's approach to pension entitlements under A1P1. After decades of distinguishing

[5] *Gaygusuz v Austria* (n 1).

between funded and unfunded schemes, the Court began to reconsider whether welfare benefits (pensions or assistance entitlements) should be entitled to property protection regardless of their funding mechanism.

The applicant, a Turkish national, had worked in Austria for several years and paid contributions to the Austrian social security system. After losing his job, he started to receive unemployment benefits. When exhausting those benefits, he applied for an emergency allowance (*Notstandshilfe*), a form of assistance available to individuals who had depleted their unemployment entitlements. According to the law, to receive those benefits, an applicant needed to have paid previous contributions to the unemployment insurance fund and be an Austrian citizen. His application was rejected because he did not hold Austrian citizenship.[6]

The applicant challenged this decision before the ECtHR, arguing that denying him the emergency allowance based on nationality constituted discrimination contrary to Article 14 of the Convention in conjunction with A1P1. Article 14 prohibits discrimination in the enjoyment of the rights and freedoms outlined in the Convention, but can only be invoked with another Convention right. This meant that his discrimination claim required the Court first to determine whether the emergency allowance qualified as a 'possession' protected under A1P1.

The Austrian government contested the applicability of A1P1, arguing that the emergency allowance was not linked to the payments to the unemployment fund, but constituted 'an emergency payment granted by the State to people in need'.[7] On this view, the applicant's previous contributions were irrelevant to his entitlement. Thus, the benefit fell outside the scope of A1P1's scope of protection.

The Court rejected the government's characterisation. It found that while the emergency allowance did not directly correspond to the amount of prior contributions, eligibility was nevertheless conditional on having made prior contributions to the unemployment insurance system. This link to previous contributions played a central role in the Court's reasoning, as it established a relationship between the applicant's financial input and his entitlement to receive benefits. That relationship resembled the property-like connection the Court had held in its early jurisprudence in cases involving funded pension schemes.

The Court's assessment of whether the emergency allowance constituted a 'possession' under A1P1 appeared in two paragraphs that would later be regarded as doctrinally inconsistent. In paragraph 39, the Court stated:

> Entitlement to this social benefit [welfare benefit, namely the emergency allowance] is therefore linked to the payment of contributions to the unemployment insurance fund, which is a precondition for the payment of unemployment benefit. It follows that

[6] ibid §33.
[7] Ibid §38.

> there is no entitlement to emergency assistance where such contributions have not been made.[8]

This reasoning suggested that the contributory nature of the benefit was decisive in classifying it as a possession. It appeared to reaffirm the Court's earlier case law, which treated the payment of contributions as the basis for recognising a property-like interest in social security benefits. However, in paragraph 41, the Court offered a broader formulation:

> The Court considers that the right to emergency assistance – in so far as provided for in the applicable legislation – is a pecuniary right for the purposes of Article 1 of Protocol No. 1 (P1-1). That provision (P1-1) is therefore applicable without it being necessary to rely solely on the link between entitlement to emergency assistance and the obligation to pay 'taxes or other contributions'.[9]

This statement indicated a shift in emphasis. It implied that statutory entitlements could qualify as possessions under A1P1 even in the absence of a direct contributory link. The Court's language opened the possibility that non-contributory welfare benefits might also fall within the protective scope of A1P1.

Having decided that the emergency allowance constituted a possession, the Court then examined whether the nationality requirement imposed by Austrian law constituted unjustified discrimination. It held that denying to the applicant the benefit solely based on his nationality violated Article 14, read in conjunction with A1P1. The Court found no reasonable or objective justification for treating non-Austrian nationals differently, particularly given that the applicant had lawfully lived and worked in Austria, paid taxes and contributed to the unemployment system on the same terms as Austrian citizens.

While the outcome of the case was clear, the basis for recognising the emergency allowance as a 'possession' left room for interpretation. It was unclear whether the Court was rejecting its earlier formalistic approach, which focused on funded versus unfunded entitlements, and outlining a new distinction based on the contributory nature of the benefit.

Part of this ambiguity arises from the doctrinal flexibility that the Court appears to adopt when applying Article 14 in conjunction with A1P1. In such cases, the Court does not always require a fully vested entitlement to establish that a 'possession' exists. Instead, the relevant question becomes whether, but for the allegedly discriminatory criterion, the applicant would have received the benefit.[10] In *Gaygusuz*, this approach allowed the Court to focus on the unequal treatment of a person who had otherwise satisfied the contributory conditions, rather than on a strict analysis of property rights under A1P1.[11]

[8] ibid § 39. Words in brackets are mine.

[9] ibid §41.

[10] Lieneke Slingenberg and Ingrid Leijten, 'Social Security in the Case Law of the European Court of Human Rights' in F Pennings and G Vonk (eds), *Research Handbook on European Social Security Law* (Edward Elgar Publishing 2023) 41–43.

[11] ibid.

This mode of reasoning, while effective in addressing the discrimination claim, left the scope of A1P1 unclear. It became the source of interpretive division in subsequent case law. Some applicants and governments read *Gaygusuz* as confirming that only contributory benefits deserved property protection. Others interpreted it as extending A1P1 to all statutory welfare entitlements, regardless of their financing structure. As will be seen in the next section, this uncertainty persisted in cases such as *Wessels-Bergervoet v the Netherlands* and *Koua Poirrez v France*.[12]

B. Interpretive Drift and Doctrinal Uncertainty

The tension between paragraphs 39 and 41 of *Gaygusuz* produced a transition period in the Court's jurisprudence. Later judgments extended A1P1 protection to all categories of welfare benefits, whether contributory or not. The Court never explained why it abandoned its earlier formalism, nor did it formulate an alternative doctrine. Instead, it allowed its reasoning to evolve gradually, refining its reasoning on a case-by-case basis.

Over time, the Court's emphasis on the relevant factor that triggered A1P1's protection shifted away from the funding mechanism and toward the statutory conditions for entitlement. What mattered was whether the applicant had met the legal requirements established by domestic law to receive a benefit, rather than whether the entitlement arose from a funded or unfunded scheme. This doctrinal turn was reinforced by a broader recognition of the role of welfare benefits, including pensions, in securing economic stability. By framing these interests as forms of property under A1P1, the Court laid the groundwork for a functional approach that would later be articulated in *Stec*.

i. Wessels-Bergervoet v the Netherlands*: Extending A1P1 to Non-Contributory Pensions*

Wessels-Bergervoet v the Netherlands[13] confirmed the Court's evolving approach to pension rights during this transitional period. The case concerned a reduction in the applicant's pension of about 38 per cent of her retirement pension under the non-contributory statutory scheme AOW (*Algemene Ouderdomswet*, General Old Age Pensions Act). The applicant's pension was initially calculated on her late husband's insurance record. After his death, the social security institution recalculated it based on her own record, which was significantly shorter. The applicant argued that, after her husband's death, she was entitled to the full benefit and that the reduction imposed amounted to discrimination based on sex.

[12] *Wessels-Bergervoet v the Netherlands* ECHR 2002-IV; *Koua Poirrez v France* ECHR 2003-X (2004) 40 EHRR 2.

[13] *Wessels-Bergervoet v the Netherlands* (n 12).

The Dutch government contested the applicability of A1P1, relying on the formalistic distinction developed in earlier case law. They argued that:

> [B]enefits under social-insurance schemes characterized by the principle of social solidarity could not be regarded as 'possessions' within the meaning of Article 1 of Protocol No.1 in that, unlike systems under which the level of benefit was linked to contributions paid, a system based on social solidarity distributed the available resources equally among all claimants.[14]

The government expanded on this position by emphasising the non-contributory structure of the AOW scheme:

> Persons who had reached the age of 65 or who had little or no income did not contribute to the scheme. Entitlement to a pension under the Act did not depend on whether or not contributions had been paid. Therefore, the group of contributors was different from the group of beneficiaries. Given the absence of a connection between contribution and entitlement under the scheme, the Government considered that a pension under the Act could not, therefore, be regarded as falling within the scope of Article 1 of Protocol No. 1.[15]

The government's argument drew on paragraph 41 of *Gaygusuz*, hence reiterating the formalistic view that only contributory arrangements could generate protectable interests under A1P1. By highlighting the absence of a direct link between contributions and entitlements, the government maintained that pensions under the AOW scheme fell outside the scope of property protection.

The Court's reasoning in *Wessels-Bergervoet* reflected a shift in focus. Rather than directly addressing the government's argument that the non-contributory structure of the AOW scheme excluded it from A1P1 protection, the Court stated:

> [I]nsofar as Article 1 of Protocol No. 1 includes the right to derive benefits from a social security system, the person concerned must, in order to establish that right, satisfy the conditions set by domestic law ... Turning to the facts of the instant case, the Court notes that ... that the applicant's right to a pension under the AOW can be regarded as a 'possession' within the meaning of Article 1 of Protocol No. 1 and that, consequently, Article 14 of the Convention is applicable.[16]

This passage marked a conceptual shift in the Court's reasoning. By framing the protected interest as 'the right to derive benefits' from a social security system, the Court shifted its focus away from assessing how a scheme was funded. Instead, it focused on whether the applicant had satisfied the statutory conditions for receiving the benefit. The key question was no longer whether contributions created

[14] ibid §39.
[15] ibid §40.
[16] ibid. This quote comes from the Final Decision of the First Section on the Admissibility of the Case, which was referenced by the Second Section in the final Judgment in §43.

identifiable shares, but whether domestic law conferred a legal entitlement that could qualify as a possession under A1P1.[17]

Having recognised the applicant's pension as falling within A1P1's ambit, the Court concluded that the reduction based on her husband's insurance record amounted to unjustified discrimination on the ground of sex, in violation of Article 14 taken together with A1P1. However, some doctrinal questions remained. While the outcome suggested a departure from the Court's earlier formalism, the reasoning relied heavily on the logic of non-discrimination rather than on an explicit redefinition of what constitutes a 'possession'. As a result, *Wessels-Bergervoet* was unable to solve the interpretive tension between the Court's evolving application of A1P1 and the unresolved legacy of its earlier case law.

ii. Koua Poirrez v France: *Rejecting the Contributory Requirement*

Koua Poirrez v France[18] presented a more direct test of the Court's evolving approach to non-contributory benefits. Unlike the emergency allowance in *Gaygusuz*, which had at least some connection to prior contributions, or the AOW pension in *Wessels-Bergervoet*, which operated within a broader social security system, the disability allowance in *Koua Poirrez* was entirely non-contributory. It had no link to any history of employment or individual contributions.

The applicant was an Ivorian national whom a French citizen had adopted. Suffering from a severe disability, he applied for a disability allowance provided under French law. The benefit was funded entirely through general taxation, and eligibility depended solely on disability status rather than employment or contribution history. However, the French authorities denied his application solely on the ground that he was neither a French national nor a national of a country with which France had a reciprocal social security agreement. Therefore, the applicant claimed a breach of A1P1 in conjunction with Article 14.

The response of the French government directly challenged the applicability of A1P1, invoking the formalistic distinction between contributory and non-contributory benefits. It relied on paragraph 39 of *Gaygusuz*, arguing that the Court had affirmed a limiting principle: 'the Court had expressly pointed out that entitlement to a social benefit [welfare benefit] was linked to the payment of contributions'.[19] Therefore, the government claimed that 'Article 1 of Protocol No. 1 did not include non-contributory benefits'.[20] This reasoning sought to reduce the strength of *Gaygusuz* by framing it as a judgment that responded to

[17] It is notable that, in both the partial and final admissibility decisions in *Wessels-Bergervoet* the Court placed particular emphasis on the fact that the pension entitlement constituted the applicant's means of subsistence. This framing the benefit as essential to material survival would become central in *Stec*, where the Court used it to justify extending A1P1 protection to all statutory benefit entitlements.

[18] *Koua Poirrez v France* (n 12).

[19] ibid §33.

[20] ibid.

an exceptional factual context. In doing so, the strategy aimed at reinstating the Court's early formalistic approach.

In this judgment, the Court marked a more explicit departure from the formalistic distinction between contributory and non-contributory benefits. It began by referencing paragraph 41 of *Gaygusuz*, reaffirming that A1P1 applies 'without it being necessary to rely solely on the link between entitlement to emergency assistance and the obligation to pay "taxes or other contributions"'.[21] Afterwards, the Court addressed the government's attempt to exclude non-contributory benefits from A1P1 protection as follows:

> In that connection, the Court considers that the fact that, in that case, the applicant had paid contributions and was thus entitled to emergency assistance ... does not mean, by converse implication, that a non-contributory social benefit such as the AAH does not also give rise to a pecuniary right for the purposes of Article 1 of Protocol No. 1.[22]

This paragraph constituted the most explicit rejection of the view that only contributory benefits could constitute possessions. It clarified that the applicant's prior contributions in *Gaygusuz* were not decisive. What mattered was that domestic law conferred a legally enforceable pecuniary right, regardless of whether the benefit was funded by individual contributions or general taxation.

In this case, once the Court determined that the disability allowance qualified as a possession, it judged that denying such a claim to the applicant solely based on his nationality violated Article 14 in conjunction with A1P1. It found no reasonable and objective justification for excluding non-French nationals from access to the benefit.

Despite the clarity of the majority's position, Judge Mularoni issued a dissenting opinion that directly challenged the Court's interpretation as follows:

> According to the Commission's case law, 'the payment of mandatory contributions to a pension fund may, in certain circumstances, create a property right over a portion of these funds, and this right could be affected by the way these funds are distributed' ... Continuing its reasoning, the Commission expressed the opinion that such a property right cannot be recognised for the insured person when the pension fund operates under the so-called pay-as-you-go system. It implied that the situation could be different when the pension fund operates under the so-called capitalization system ... To my mind, however, there is an essential difference between the two cases, namely the payment of contributions. In Gaygusuz the Court followed the Commission's reasoning and concluded that Article 14, taken in conjunction with Article 1 of Protocol No. 1, was applicable (and had been violated), after finding that '[e]ntitlement to the social benefit is therefore linked to the payment of contributions to the unemployment insurance fund, which is a precondition for the payment of unemployment benefit ... It follows that there is no entitlement to emergency assistance where such contributions have not been made'.[23]

[21] ibid § 37.
[22] ibid.
[23] See Dissenting Opinion of Judge Mularoni in ibid § 73.

The dissenting opinion underscored the ongoing disagreement within the Court regarding the reasons for extending property protection under A1P1 to non-contributory benefits. Judge Mularoni advocated for a return to the formalistic distinction, asserting that it is the payment of contributions that gives a benefit its property character. The fact that a member of the Court could still sustain this position demonstrated that the move toward a more functional approach remained incomplete and doctrinally unsettled. A more comprehensive articulation was required to explain why A1P1 should be extended. This would eventually be addressed in *Stec and Others v the United Kingdom*.

II. Turning Point: The Emergence of the Functionalist Doctrine

After nearly a decade of uncertainty following *Gaygusuz*, the Court addressed the doctrinal ambiguity surrounding welfare benefits under A1P1 in *Stec and Others v the United Kingdom*.[24] This landmark judgment provided the first comprehensive justification for extending property protection to all statutory welfare entitlements, irrespective of their funding structure or contributory basis. In doing so, the Court finally articulated a comprehensive reasoning on the concept of property protection in the case of pension benefits, moving decisively away from the formalistic approach that had characterised its earlier case law. This section examines the facts of *Stec*, analyses the Court's reasoning, and considers the implications of its functional approach for understanding pension entitlements as possessions under A1P1.

A. *Stec and Others v the United Kingdom*: Resolving the Tension

Stec and Others v the United Kingdom concerned the UK's Reduced Earnings Allowance (REA), a non-contributory benefit funded through general taxation. The REA was part of the statutory occupational accident and disease scheme, intended to compensate for reduced earning capacity resulting from work-related injuries. Five applicants – Anna Stec, Regina Hepple, Patrick Lunn, Sybil Spencer and Oliver Kimble – challenged regulations that reduced or replaced their REA upon reaching pensionable age. The pensionable age was set at 65 for men and 60 for women.

The applicants had all suffered workplace injuries or diseases that affected their ability to earn a living. They initially received REA, but upon reaching pensionable

[24] *Stec and Others v the United Kingdom* (n 4).

age, their benefits were either frozen or replaced with Retirement Allowance (RA), which was paid at a lower rate. This reduction occurred earlier for female applicants than for male applicants due to the different pensionable ages.[25]

Before reaching the ECtHR, the cases were referred to the European Court of Justice (ECJ) by the UK's Social Security Commissioner.[26] The ECJ ruled that the differential treatment regarding pensionable age fell within an exception under Article 7 of Council Directive 79/7/EEC.[27] When the case returned to the national level, the Commissioner followed the ECJ's ruling and dismissed the applications.

The applicants brought their case before the ECtHR, arguing that the government's decision to reduce their benefits violated A1P1 in conjunction with Article 14. They claimed that the entitlement to a REA benefit constituted a possession, even though it was derived from a non-contributory scheme. In their submissions, the applicants acknowledged the Court's previous distinction between contribution-based systems and non-contributory social assistance schemes. However, they challenged this distinction as arbitrary, 'and without any sensible policy objective'.[28] The core of their argument was that '[t]here was no principled reason for drawing a distinction'.[29] In their view, there was no legitimate basis for treating entitlements financed through compulsory contributions, which 'undoubtedly fell within the scope of Article 1 of Protocol No. 1'[30] differently from those funded through general taxation, such as the REA or RA schemes.[31]

The UK government directly challenged the applicability of A1P1 to non-contributory benefits such as REA. It argued that 'non-contributory benefits, like REA and RA, could not be considered to fall within the scope of Article 1 of Protocol No. 1'.[32] Furthermore, it held that 'did not confer a right to receive benefits from the State. It was a matter for the State's discretion what provision to make, since there was no right under the Convention to acquire possessions',[33] and that

> [t]he applicants were seeking to widen the concept of a "possession" to include claims which had no basis in domestic law, to bring a general complaint of discrimination of the type which would be covered by the new Protocol No. 12 but not by Article 14.[34]

The government also advanced a broader argument about the nature of the Convention itself. It contended that the Court should not forget that the Convention concerned Civil and Political rather than Social and Economic Rights,

[25] ibid. Decision on admissibility §§16–20.
[26] ibid §23.
[27] ibid §24.
[28] ibid §37.
[29] ibid §38.
[30] ibid.
[31] ibid.
[32] ibid §34.
[33] ibid.
[34] ibid.

and that '[t]o treat a claim to a non-contributory social security benefit as property within the scope of Article 1 of Protocol No. 1 would conflict with the purpose and effect of the 1961 European Social Charter'.[35] In fact, the government argued: 'to conclude that Article 1 of Protocol No. 1 applied to non-contributory benefits would be to expand the scope of that provision beyond what had been recognised in the Court's jurisprudence'.[36]

This case presented the Court with an ideal opportunity to resolve the interpretive uncertainty that had persisted since the *Gaygusuz* decision. The ECtHR had to determine conclusively whether the formalistic doctrine remained relevant for A1P1 protection and, if not, provide a comprehensive justification for extending property protection to all welfare benefits.

B. The Court's Reasoning: Consistency, Dependency and Vulnerability

The central question in *Stec* was whether non-contributory benefits could qualify as 'possessions' under A1P1.[37] This judgment sought to settle the issue decisively. To do so, the Court devoted a substantial part of the judgment to developing the reasoning behind extending A1P1 to protect all benefit entitlements.

The Court's reasoning relied on two arguments. First, the relevance of preserving internal consistency across the Convention. Since non-contributory benefits were already treated as 'pecuniary rights' under Article 6, they should receive the same treatment under A1P1.[38] Second, and more importantly, extending A1P1 protection must be done on the basis of the functional role of such entitlements, which enables the attainment of values like autonomy in a modern welfare state. Each argument will be addressed in turn.

i. *The Internal Consistency Argument*

The Court's first argument appealed to the need to preserve the internal consistency in the Convention's interpretation. Consistency ensures that similar interests are interpreted alike regardless of which Convention right is at stake. If all welfare benefits are treated as economically valuable under one article, there seems to be no good reason to exclude that feature under another without undermining legal

[35] ibid.

[36] ibid §35.

[37] ibid §41. By 'interests' the Court means the claims of retirees to their payments. In the French version, it is more explicit by speaking about *créances*: 'Dans ces conditions, il convient d'examiner à nouveau la question de savoir si *une créance* portant sur une prestation sociale non contributive doit entraîner la protection de l'article 1 du Protocole no 1'.

[38] ibid §49.

certainty. In the case law of Article 6 § 1,[39] the Court had already recognised all welfare benefits as being pecuniary rights as follows:

> It is noteworthy in this respect that, in its case-law on the applicability of Article 6 § 1, the Court originally held that claims regarding only welfare benefits which formed part of contributory schemes were, because of the similarity to private insurance schemes, sufficiently personal and economic to constitute the subject matter of disputes for 'the determination of civil rights' ... Article 6 § 1 was held also to apply to a dispute over entitlement to a non-contributory welfare benefit, the Court emphasising that the applicant had an assertable right, of an individual and economic nature, to social [welfare] benefits.[40]

The Court observed that its early case law under Article 6 had limited the notion of 'civil rights' to claims involving contributory benefits. In *Deumeland v Germany*,[41] a widower sought a survivor's pension under a supplementary pension scheme, but the domestic courts rejected her claim following protracted proceedings. The key question before the ECtHR was whether this type of social security benefit constituted a 'civil right' within the meaning of Article 6 § 1. The Court held that it did, identifying three relevant characteristics: (i) the right concerned the applicant personally; (ii) it had clear economic implications; and (iii) it was derived from specific legal rules rather than administrative discretion.

The Court acknowledged that the scheme combined both public and private features but emphasised that the latter predominated. It reasoned that the pension could be viewed as 'an extension of the salary payable under the contract, the civil character of this salary being beyond doubt'.[42] This approach reflected a preference for entitlements grounded in private law relationships. The underlying logic was closely aligned with the formalistic framework that had long shaped the interpretation of A1P1, as discussed in chapter four.

The ECtHR departed from this approach in *Salesi v Italy*.[43] *Salesi* concerned a claim to a disability allowance granted under a non-contributory scheme. The applicant complained of excessive delays in the proceedings to determine her eligibility for the benefit. The Italian government argued that such allowances lacked the private law characteristics necessary to fall within the scope of Article 6 § 1. The Court rejected this argument, stating: 'Article 6 para. 1 does apply in the field of social insurance, including even welfare assistance'.[44]

[39] That Article reads as follows: 'In the determination of his civil rights and obligations or of any criminal charge against him, everyone is entitled to a fair and public hearing within a reasonable time by an independent and impartial tribunal established by law. Judgment shall be pronounced publicly but the press and public may be excluded from all or part of the trial in the interests of morals, public order or national security in a democratic society, where the interests of juveniles or the protection of the private life of the parties so require, or to the extent strictly necessary in the opinion of the court in special circumstances where publicity would prejudice the interests of justice'.

[40] *Stec and Others v the United Kingdom* (n 4) §48.

[41] *Deumeland v Germany* Series A no 100 (1986) 8 EHRR 448.

[42] ibid §71.

[43] *Salesi v Italy* App no 13023/87 (ECtHR, 1993).

[44] ibid §19.

The Court held that, despite institutional differences between social assistance and social insurance schemes, 'they cannot be regarded as fundamental at the present stage of development of social security law'.[45] The decisive point was that the applicant:

> [D]espite the public law features pointed out by the Government, Mrs Salesi was not affected in her relations with the administrative authorities as such, acting in the exercise of discretionary powers; she suffered an interference with her means of subsistence and was claiming an individual, economic right flowing from specific rules laid down in a statute giving effect to the Constitution.[46]

The judgment in *Salesi* clarified that claims to non-contributory benefits could fall within the scope of Article 6 § 1, provided they met the core criteria: they must involve an individual, economic right established by statute and enforceable through legal proceedings. The Court concluded: '[The] Court sees no convincing reason to distinguish between Mrs. Salesi's right to welfare benefits and the rights to social insurance benefits asserted by [others]'.[47]

This shift in the case law of Article 6 § 1 laid the groundwork for the functional turn adopted in *Stec*. In that case, the Court explicitly invoked *Salesi* to align the interpretation of 'possessions' under A1P1 with the concept of 'pecuniary rights' under Article 6:

> It is in the interests of the coherence of the Convention as a whole that the autonomous concept of 'possessions' in Article 1 of Protocol No. 1 should be interpreted in a way which is consistent with the concept of pecuniary rights under Article 6 § 1 of the Convention. It is moreover important to adopt an interpretation of Article 1 of Protocol No. 1 which avoids inequalities of treatment based on distinctions which, nowadays, appear illogical or unsustainable.[48]

By framing welfare entitlements as pecuniary rights under Article 6 § 1, the Court established both a doctrinal and conceptual basis for treating them as possessions under A1P1. It is no longer accepted that the applicability of property protection depended on a scheme's funding structure or its resemblance to private-law arrangements. What became decisive was the existence of an enforceable, individual, economic entitlement grounded in domestic law.

This reasoning opened the door for revisiting property protection under A1P1 in the case of pension benefits. Just as Article 6 § 1 had evolved to protect all statutory benefit claims that met these criteria, so too could A1P1 move beyond the formalistic approach. The next subsection describes the second line of reasoning offered by the Court that completed the normative turn in the Court's evolution.

[45] ibid.
[46] ibid.
[47] ibid.
[48] ibid §§47–49.

ii. The Functional Argument

The Court's second argument for extending A1P1 protection to all welfare benefits rests on a shift in how it conceives these entitlements: what they are, what role they play in modern societies, and what A1P1 must do to secure them. It states:

> In the modern, democratic state, many individuals are, for all or part of their lives, completely dependent for survival on social security and welfare benefits. Many domestic legal systems recognise that such individuals require a degree of certainty and security, and provide for benefits to be paid – subject to the fulfilment of the conditions of eligibility – as of right.[49]

This statement marks a decisive turn. By emphasising individuals' 'complete dependence' on welfare benefits, the Court acknowledged that such entitlements are often the only means by which vulnerable individuals can participate meaningfully in economic and social life. For the ECtHR, pension benefits provide a degree of certainty and security that mirrors the traditional role of property in safeguarding autonomy. In this respect, they perform the same stabilising function that capital or assets play for those who possess them. As a result, A1P1 must extend protection not only to accumulated wealth but also to legal entitlements on which those without capital rely.

The Court thus adopts a functional understanding of property protection. What defines property in this context is not its form, but its function: it provides autonomy and economic security. If a welfare benefit – regardless of whether it is contributory, non-contributory, funded or unfunded – fulfils that function, it should be treated as a 'possession' under A1P1.[50]

This approach completes the doctrinal shift from formalism to functionalism in the field of social security. Protection is now justified by the role the entitlement plays in the individual's life, rather than by the institutional features of the scheme. Where a person satisfies the statutory conditions for a benefit, and that benefit enables autonomy or independence, it must be recognised as a protected possession.

The idea that welfare benefits serve a 'freedom-securing function' was not novel in European legal and constitutional thought. It had already been recognised by the German and Hungarian Constitutional Courts, which held that public-law entitlements such as social security benefits could fall within the constitutional guarantee of property. Both courts grounded their reasoning in the traditional view that property protects individual autonomy.

The German Constitutional Court explained the purpose of constitutional property protection as follows: '[T]o secure the bearer of the fundamental right a space of freedom in the area of property law, and thus to enable him or her to shape life in a self-responsible manner'.[51]

[49] *Stec and Others v the United Kingdom* (n 4) § 51.

[50] See ch 2 for the normative approaches to property and property protection.

[51] Federal Constitutional Court of Germany (BVerfGE) 24, 367; 389 'Article 14, Paragraph 1, Sentence 1 of the Basic Law guarantees private property both as a legal institution and in its specific

The Hungarian Constitutional Court, similarly, stated:

> The Constitution grants fundamental rights protection to property rights as the traditional material basis of individual autonomy of action. Constitutional protection must follow the change in the social role of property in such a way that it can perform the same protective task. Therefore, when it comes to the protection of individual autonomy, fundamental property protection extends to property rights that have taken over the former role of property, as well as rights based on public law (for example, social security claims).[52]

The Court's approach in *Stec* tracks these developments. It ties the protection of welfare entitlements not to their contractual basis or the presence of prior contributions, but to their role in securing individual freedom. For those who rely entirely on social benefits, such entitlements do not merely support autonomy: they make it possible. In this light, traditional distinctions between public and private law, insurance and assistance or contributory and non-contributory schemes, become irrelevant in determining whether a benefit falls within the scope of A1P1. What matters is the function the entitlement performs in the individual's life and whether it gives rise to a legally protected interest under the Convention.

In *Stec*, the Court expressly rejected the formalistic logic that had previously governed access to property protection under A1P1. As discussed in chapter four, earlier case law had limited such protection to benefits tied to identifiable contributions or resembling private-law entitlements. *Stec* departed from that approach, affirming instead that what matters is the existence of a legally enforceable claim. Once an individual satisfies the statutory eligibility criteria, the benefit constitutes a possession, regardless of its funding structure.

This shift in reasoning required the Court to clarify and restate the criteria for what qualifies as a 'possession' under A1P1:

> Article 1 of Protocol No. 1, … places no restriction on the Contracting State's freedom to decide whether or not to have in place any form of social security scheme, or to choose the type or amount of benefits to provide under any such scheme. If … a Contracting State has in force legislation providing for the payment as of right of a welfare benefit – whether conditional or not on the prior payment of contributions – that

form in the hands of the individual owner. Property is an elementary fundamental right that is intrinsically linked to the guarantee of personal freedom. In the overall structure of fundamental rights, it has the task of ensuring the bearer of the fundamental right a space of freedom in the area of property law and thus enabling him to shape his life independently. The guarantee of property as a legal institution serves to secure this fundamental right'. (Own translation from German through Deepl).

[52] Hungarian Constitutional Court Decision 64/1993 (XII.22) A.B. ABM 1993 (Own translation from Hungarian through Google Translate). Moreover, in that decision, the Hungarian Constitutional Court claims to be aligned with the conception of property as advanced by the ECtHR as follows: 'The Constitutional Court's understanding of property protection is in line with the European Convention on Human Rights and the judgment of the Human Rights Court'. (Own translation from Hungarian through Google Translate). However, as mentioned, it was only a couple of years later that the Court recognised social security entitlements as covered by A1P1.

> legislation must be regarded as generating a proprietary interest falling within the ambit of Article 1 of Protocol No. 1 for persons satisfying its requirements.[53]

The Court then removed any remaining ambiguity as follows:

> [I]f any distinction can still be said to exist in the case-law between contributory and non-contributory benefits for the purposes of the applicability of Article 1 of Protocol No. 1, there is no ground to justify the continued drawing of such a distinction.[54]

Following this reasoning, the Court's position became settled: all claims to social security benefits, including social assistance, can qualify as 'possessions' capable of engaging A1P1. The distinction between contributory and non-contributory schemes no longer determines the scope of protection. What matters is whether the claimant satisfies the statutory eligibility criteria. If so, they hold a possession and are entitled to the peaceful enjoyment of it. As Leijten observed: '[T]he rule laid out in *Stec* unsurprisingly inspired new social security-related applications: ever since the decision, applicants invoke *Stec* as the main argument for why their complaints deserve to be reviewed under the Convention.'[55]

By adopting this functional view, the Court articulated a robust justification for extending A1P1 protection to all statutory welfare entitlements. The goal was not to freeze existing distributions or treat all claims equally, but to ensure that individuals who depend on these benefits are not arbitrarily deprived of them. As will become clear in chapter six, and contrary to popular assumptions about the neutrality of property rights, A1P1 does not protect pension entitlements equally or in a distributive-blind manner. Its protective function is shaped by the claimant's level of dependency on the entitlement in question. The jurisprudence suggests that the Convention prioritises protection where the interference affects individuals in more vulnerable or precarious positions.[56] In this sense, vulnerability operates as a normative filter for determining when property protection under A1P1 is necessary.

However, vulnerability is not the only factor considered by the Court in cases concerning pension entitlements. The level of protection also depends on the institutional structure of the benefit. In contributory systems, the Court examines whether the reform in question maintains a reasonable balance between the contributions made and the benefits received. Where a reform

[53] *Stec and Others v the United Kingdom* (n 4) §54. The Court also claimed that such a scheme must render benefits compatible with the non-discriminatory clause.

[54] ibid §53.

[55] Ingrid Leijten, 'From Stec to Valkov: Possessions and Margins in the Social Security Case Law of the European Court of Human Rights' (2013) 13 *Human Rights Law Review* 309, 321. This will be later confirmed in Slingenberg and Leijten (n 10).

[56] In the case at stake, having established that the REA and the RA constituted possessions, the Court proceeded to assess whether the difference in pensionable age violated Article 14. It found no violation, as the differential treatment was objectively justified as part of a phased transition toward equal retirement ages. The degree to which and how A1P1 applies in practice is the object of ch 6.

disrupts this balance in a way that is excessive or arbitrary, it may trigger a violation of A1P1.[57]

III. Theoretical and Normative Foundations of the Functionalist Approach

The Court's evolving approach to welfare entitlements under A1P1 reflects a rejection of the implicit hierarchies that once governed which claims qualified for property protection. Earlier case law drew a sharp distinction between entitlements deserving protection based on formal characteristics, for example, whether the entitlement derived from a funded scheme or resembled a contractual claim. This approach excluded statutory welfare rights from A1P1's protective scope. By adopting a functional perspective, the Court dismantled such a hierarchy. What now matters is no longer the legal form of an entitlement, but the role it plays in securing the individual's autonomy and material security. In this way, all welfare benefit entitlements, including pensions, may fall within the protective scope of A1P1.

The functional turn did not only emerge from an internal, ad hoc evolution of the Court's case law. Instead, it reflects a broader normative and intellectual shift in the conception of property and its justification. Essentially, the ECtHR's functionalist turn rests on an instrumental view of property. As explained in chapter two, instrumental views justify property as a means to realise broader social values. These may be monistic, reducing property to a single value such as freedom, or pluralistic, recognising that property serves multiple functions, including autonomy, stability and security.[58] In *Stec*, the Court acknowledged that in modern welfare states, wealth is no longer confined to traditional property forms like land or capital, through which such values were historically secured. Instead, statutory entitlements such as welfare benefits have become the primary means through which individuals access those same values.

This recognition aligns with the fact that many individuals depend entirely on social security for their subsistence. Because welfare entitlements now provide their main source of material stability and personal autonomy, they perform the same function that traditional property once did. Extending A1P1's protection to these benefits, therefore, serves to protect the same underlying values. This reasoning echoes Kantian theory, which treats property rights as essential for external freedom. In simple terms, the ability to pursue goals without depending on others' choices.[59]

This functional view finds an early formulation in Charles Reich's theory of the New Property. This theory offers a framework for thinking about

[57] See ch 6.
[58] See ch 2.
[59] ibid.

property protection in light of the changing economic structures of post-war welfare states.[60] The New Property theory is an instrumental account of private property.[61] It views property as a means to ensure individual autonomy, independence and economic security. On this view, legal protection should not be confined to classical forms of property such as land and capital, but should expand to include state-conferred benefits such as licences, welfare payments and pensions.[62] The justification is evolutionary. Before the expansion of the welfare state, classical forms of property, such as land, were the principal sources of individual wealth and how people achieved the values associated with property ownership. As societies industrialised and later transitioned into service economies, however, the traditional foundations of wealth shifted. Economic security came to rest increasingly on state-administered benefits. These new entitlements, Reich argued, had come to perform the same functional role that traditional property once played.[63]

This shift in the sources of individual wealth and economic dependence was not unique to Reich's account. It would later be confirmed by scholarship on the historical development of property rights. Scholars like CB Macpherson described how the evolution of capitalism changed the understanding of the institution of private property.[64] In precapitalistic systems, property was understood as a right to revenue or benefit from the use of property, whether privately or communally.[65] With capitalism, the idea of property became synonymous with exclusive, alienable rights in material things. However, Macpherson noted a twentieth-century reversion to earlier ideas: property would be seen again as a right to a revenue, which would be a right to access the productive capacity of the community.[66] The rise of the welfare state created new forms of wealth that became rights to revenue, such as welfare benefits, including old-age pensions. For many individuals, pension entitlements represented their primary form of wealth: their claim on society's productive resources that enable future consumption and security.[67]

[60] Charles Reich, 'The New Property' (1964) 73 *Yale Law* 733.

[61] For the normative discussion about different visions of property, refer to ch 2.

[62] Reich, 'The New Property' (n 58); Charles A Reich, 'Social Welfare in the Public-Private State' (1965) 114 *University of Pennsylvania Law Review* 487.

[63] Reich, 'The New Property' (n 58).

[64] Crawford Brough Macpherson, 'Capitalism and the Changing Concept of Property' in Eugene Kamenka and Ronald Stanley Neale (eds), *Feudalism, Capitalism and Beyond* (Australian National University Press 1975).

[65] ibid.

[66] ibid 116.

[67] It is interesting to note that there are conceptions of retirement pensions that characterize them as claims to future output. In this view, the financial structure supporting the entitlement (whether funded or pay-as-you-go) is equalised and therefore irrelevant to consider the nature of what is at stake when discussing a pension reform. See Nicholas Barr, *Economics of the Welfare State* (Oxford University Press, USA 2020); Nicholas Barr and Peter Diamond, 'The Economics of Pensions' (2006) 22 *Oxford Review of Economic Policy* 15; Nicholas Barr and Peter Diamond, *Reforming Pensions: Principles and Policy Choices* (Oxford University Press 2008).

However, statutory entitlements were legally conceptualised as the by-product of state regulation and financed by governmental 'largess', which ultimately transformed them into mere gratuities.[68] Gratuities, as opposed to property, lacked procedural guarantees and are vulnerable to sudden revocation by administrative discretion.[69]

Considering this, the New Property theory directly challenged the traditional distinction between public and private entitlements. Reich argued that what mattered was the entitlement's *function*: in particular, the extent to which individuals relied upon it.[70] The central concern behind his account was precisely the protection of individuals whose autonomy and social participation increasingly depended on statutory benefits, such as social security or disability payments. Reich emphasised that beneficiaries' reliance on these state-conferred benefits mirrored the dependence individuals previously had on classical forms of property, such as land or capital.[71] Therefore, if statutory benefits served as a person's principal means of securing autonomy and economic security, their legal protection should be equivalent in degree and principle to traditional forms of property.[72]

There are some critiques of this approach. Ronald Sackville, for example, questioned whether welfare benefits should be subsumed into the concept of property at all.[73] He suggested that the phrase 'New Property' functioned more as a political slogan than an analytical category, warning that excessive expansion of property risked diminishing its explanatory power.[74] Instead, Sackville proposed developing a different theory of entitlement: one that acknowledged the normative weight of state-conferred benefits without redefining property itself.[75] Still, he shared Reich's fundamental concern: that individuals who depended on these benefits deserved legal protection against administrative discretion.

Despite these reservations, the 'New Property' legacy endured. In the United States, the Supreme Court explicitly adopted Reich's reasoning in *Goldberg v Kelly*, holding that the termination of welfare benefits required procedural safeguards

[68] Reich, 'Social Welfare in the Public-Private State' (n 60).

[69] Reich, 'The New Property' (n 58); Charles A Reich, 'Individual Rights and Social Welfare: The Emerging Legal Issues' in P Robson (ed), *Welfare Law* (Routledge 2020).

[70] This came to be also explicitly stated in later work Reich, 'Social Welfare in the Public-Private State' (n 60); Reich, 'Individual Rights and Social Welfare: The Emerging Legal Issues' (n 68).

[71] Reich, 'The New Property' (n 58).

[72] ibid. This position was not new. Years before, Walter Jones had already argued that the welfare state was a big source of new rights, and he put as the example of those rights 'the expectations created by a comprehensive system of social insurance'. He questioned the idea that terms like 'rights' or 'property' should be constrained only to traditional private law interests, such as ownership of land or goods and not to these new other expectations or interests created by the welfare state. Harry W Jones, 'The Rule of Law and the Welfare State' (1958) 58 *Columbia Law Review* 143, 154.

[73] Ronald Sackville, 'Property, Rights and Social Security' (1977) 2 *UNSW Law Journal* 246.

[74] ibid.

[75] ibid.

under the Due Process Clause.[76] This position was later reaffirmed in *Atkins v Parker*, which confirmed that statutory entitlements, even if public in origin, could not be withdrawn arbitrarily once granted.[77] These decisions transformed Reich's theory into an enforceable constitutional doctrine.

More recently, both conservative and progressive literature have also challenged Reich's framework, although from different angles. On the conservative side, legal scholars have rejected the idea that social security entitlements constitute property, returning to a vision of public benefits as gratuities rooted in state benevolence rather than legal obligation.[78] According to this view, welfare payments are not grounded in enforceable rights but in political discretion, and should not attract the protections normally associated with property.[79]

Progressive critics, by contrast, have expressed concern about the internal contradictions of Reich's theory.[80] These accounts argue that the strong individualist and libertarian tone of Reich's writings sits uneasily with the communitarian values needed to support a substantive right to welfare.[81] His concept of 'new property' offered a powerful critique of bureaucratic discretion and helped shape procedural protections, but it lacked a clear normative foundation for redistributive justice. While Reich acknowledged the sacrifices and contributions of the poor, his theory ultimately rested on rights-as-immunities and failed to articulate a convincing rationale for positive welfare obligations. In doing so, it risked reproducing the very atomisation it sought to resist.[82]

That being said, in *Stec and Others v the United Kingdom* the Court adopted a functional approach to A1P1 that closely mirrors Reich's reasoning. It recognised that in modern welfare states, social benefits have become one of the main sources of material security and personal autonomy. The Court's shift was explicitly framed as a structural response to contemporary forms of dependence and vulnerability. While avoiding some of Reich's more problematic assumptions, the ECtHR built on his insight that legal protection must reflect the evolving conditions under which individual freedom is exercised. Such a reconfiguration of welfare entitlements as functionally equivalent to traditional property provides the normative foundation for the analysis developed in the next section and ties closely with the themes examined in chapter six.

[76] *Goldberg v Kelly* 397 US 254 (1970). For commentaries of this case, see Albert H Meyerhoff and Jeffrey A Mishkin, 'Application of Goldberg v. Kelly Hearing Requirements to Termination of Social Security Benefits' (1973) 26 *Stanford Law Review* 549; Lucie E White, 'Goldberg v. Kelly on the Paradox of Lawyering for the Poor' (1990) 56 *Brooklyn Law Review* 861.

[77] Atkins v Parker 472 US 115 (1985).

[78] Rick J Hecker, 'On the Subject of Property and Social Security: A Traditional Analysis' (2012) 7 *Liberty University Law Review* 143.

[79] ibid 165.

[80] Elizabeth Bussiere, 'The "New Property" Theory of Welfare Rights: Promises and Pitfalls' (2004) 13 *The Good Society* 1.

[81] ibid.

[82] Harold A McDougall, 'The New Property vs. the New Community' (1989) 24 *University of San Francisco Law Review* 399.

Conclusions

This chapter has completed the jurisprudential genealogy of pension entitlements under A1P1. From early case law grounded in a formalistic reading that excluded entitlements on technical grounds, the ECtHR gradually moved toward a more inclusive, functional interpretation. This evolution fundamentally redefined what constitutes a 'possession' in the context of the modern welfare state. The Court now unequivocally recognises that all pension entitlements qualify for protection once an individual meets the legal conditions for eligibility.

The core of this transformation lies in a shift in the Court's approach to A1P1's protection. Rather than focusing on whether a pension structurally resembles a contractual claim, it turned to whether denying protection would undermine the freedom and security function that private property aims to realise, and which A1P1 is called to protect. This functional turn rejects earlier hierarchies between types of pension schemes and aligns A1P1 with contemporary understandings of property. In welfare states, legally guaranteed entitlements are now recognised as a central form of wealth as they secure individuals' autonomy and material independence.

This reconfiguration reflects the Court's will to reassess and adapt its interpretation of property rights. A1P1 now serves as a space that deals with the tensions between individual legal security and the collective imperatives of welfare state adaptation. This is particularly relevant for pension systems that seek to adapt themselves to the urgent demographic and fiscal pressures.

This shift, however, is not neutral. While dissolving earlier hierarchies between types of entitlements (e.g. contributory/non-contributory, funded/unfunded), it also transforms A1P1 from a rule that protects acquired wealth into a principle mediating between state commitments and individual dependency. This transformation introduces new points of tension: between present and future beneficiaries, between national discretion and supranational standards, and between the formal legal structure of a benefit and its practical function in securing subsistence.

What emerges at this stage is no longer the question of whether A1P1 applies to disputes over pension reform, but rather how its operation defines the boundaries of legitimate state intervention. Chapter six addresses this challenge by examining how the functional understanding of property developed here shapes the threshold, intensity and orientation of the proportionality analysis when pension entitlements are reduced or significantly affected.

6

Pensions as Property: Fair Balance in Pension Reform

Introduction

Since the mid-2000s, the European Court of Human Rights (ECtHR; the Court) has accepted that welfare benefits can constitute 'possessions' protected by Article 1 of Protocol No 1 (A1P1). This chapter examines the implications of that protection. It asks two questions: (i) how does the ECtHR protect pension entitlements under A1P1? (ii) What does the Court's approach reveal about the normative orientation and internal logic of that protection?

To address the first question, the chapter follows the structure of the acceptability test.[1] This test is the procedure followed by the Court when assessing property-related applications. It involves five steps. First, verifying whether the applicant has a protected possession.[2] Second, classifying the nature of the interference with that possession. Third, examining the lawfulness of the measure. Fourth, consider whether the measure pursues a legitimate public interest. Fifth, evaluating whether the measure strikes a fair balance between the individual's rights and the broader interests of society.[3]

This framework weighs the applicant's property interest against the extent of state interference. Whether the Court upholds the individual's claim or accepts the state's justification depends on the specific circumstances of the case. In the context of social and economic policy, however, the Court is generally more inclined to defer to the state's assessment. This deference is reflected in the doctrine of the

[1] Camilo Basilio Schutte, *The European Fundamental Right of Property: Article 1 of Protocol No. 1 to the European Convention on Human Rights: Its Origins, Its Working, and Its Impact on National Legal Orders* (Kluwer 2004).

[2] This was discussed at length in ch 3.

[3] However, it could be argued that the procedure is not a five-step but a two-step one. This was the position held by Judge Gerald Fitzmaurice in his dissenting opinion in *Marckx v Belgium* Series A no 31 (1979) 2 EHRR 330. He described this test as consisting in two steps: first, deciding upon whether the provision invoked is applicable and second, deciding on whether there was a breach of the provision invoked. He argues that: 'Only if it is both applicable, and also has been infringed, can the defendant party be held responsible and (as regards the Convention on Human Rights) a Convention-breaker'. And continues by saying: 'The foregoing are elementary, standard propositions which should not need stating because they are such as everyone would assent to in principle, – but principle is easily lost sight of when eagerness for specific results – however meritorious they may be in themselves – overreaches the still, small voice of the juridical conscience'.

'margin of appreciation', which tends to be broader where complex legislative choices are involved.[4] This approach has produced a 'paradox of protection'. While the Court has progressively broadened the recognition of pension entitlements as possessions, thereby extending procedural access to a greater number of individuals, the substantive safeguards remain limited.[5] As a result, even as formal access has expanded, the likelihood of a successful outcome on the merits remains low.

However, the margin is not unlimited. The state's discretion to reform must not extend to measures that undermine the 'essence' of the individual's rights.[6] This means that there are boundaries to acceptable governmental action, even where broad deference is granted.

The second question is addressed both analytically and doctrinally. Analytically, the chapter argues that the ECtHR applies a dual logic in A1P1 cases. It adopts a liberal and formal approach when defining possessions and interferences, while its proportionality analysis is contextual and impact-sensitive. This tension shapes the protection of pension entitlements. Doctrinally, the Court does not apply a uniform standard of review. It adjusts the breadth of the margin of appreciation in light of the interaction of three factors: the scale of the measure, the scheme's design and the vulnerability of the applicant. Those most severely affected, especially claimants who rely on pensions for basic subsistence, receive stronger protection. This pattern reflects a prioritarian[7] logic in the Court's adjudication and helps specify what the 'essence' of the right is for pension entitlements protected under A1P1.

The chapter proceeds in three sections. Section I sets out the five-step A1P1 review, clarifying interference categories and the limits of procedural safeguards. Section II examines leading judgments to show how the Court's proportionality analysis shifts with the level of harm and claimant vulnerability, revealing an implicit prioritarian logic. Section III considers the implications of making this logic explicit. It argues that acknowledging the Court's distributive reasoning would improve the clarity, consistency and normative coherence of A1P1 adjudication and offer more principled guidance for policymakers designing pension reforms.

[4] Douglas Maxwell, *The Human Right to Property: A Practical Approach to Article 1 of Protocol No. 1 to the ECHR* (Bloomsbury Publishing 2022) 215–18.

[5] Ingrid Leijten, 'From Stec to Valkov: Possessions and Margins in the Social Security Case Law of the European Court of Human Rights' (2013) 13 *Human Rights Law Review* 309, 343.

[6] Sébastien Van Drooghenbroeck and Cecilia Rizcallah, 'The ECHR and the Essence of Fundamental Rights: Searching for Sugar in Hot Milk?' (2019) 20 *German Law Journal* 904; Oddný Mjöll Arnardóttir, 'Res Interpretata, Erga Omnes Effect and the Role of the Margin of Appreciation in Giving Domestic Effect to the Judgments of the European Court of Human Rights' (2017) 28 *European Journal of International Law* 819; Jan Kratochvíl, 'The Inflation of the Margin of Appreciation by the European Court of Human Rights' (2011) 29 *Netherlands Quarterly of Human Rights* 324; Steven C Greer, *The Margin of Appreciation: Interpretation and Discretion under the European Convention on Human Rights*, vol 17 (Council of Europe 2000); Kristina Trykhlib and Vasyl Lemak, 'Autonomous Interpretation by the European Court of Human Rights and Margin of Appreciation' (2022) 22 *International and Comparative Law Review* 135; Maxwell (n 4).

[7] Richard J Arneson, *Prioritarianism* (Cambridge University Press 2022).

I. The Acceptability Test

Chapters three to five discussed what a 'possession' is and the conditions under which the Court accepts social security entitlements to fall under that category. Defining whether an interest at stake falls within the realm of A1P1 is the first step to determine whether the Convention could be engaged and the application could be admitted for substantive judgment. Once that threshold is reached, the Court must classify the type of interference that seems to be occurring to the peaceful enjoyment of someone's possessions. That is the second step of the acceptability test. The third step consists in assessing whether the measure is lawful and compatible with the rule of law, as it is a principle not only drawn from the Convention, but specifically in A1P1's text whenever it holds that the measures must be 'provided by law'. Following that, the Court evaluates whether the impugned measure pursued legitimate 'public interest' reasons to assess its legitimacy and adequacy. Finally, it discusses whether the measure strikes a 'fair balance' between general interests pursued by the measure and the applicant's interests, essentially determining the measure's proportionality and compatibility with the Convention. This chapter will develop these steps accordingly.[8]

A. Instances of 'Interference'

There are various ways in which a government can interfere with the peaceful enjoyment of someone's 'possessions'. These interferences are grouped under the overall label 'governmental measures'. They encompass a wide range of potential actions by the state, including unilateral actions by public administrations (referred to as '*l'acte administratif*' in continental law traditions), legislative changes and even domestic Court judgments.

Pension reforms are usually legislated. The types of legislation affecting pension benefit entitlements are manifold. For instance, during austerity, legislators of many European states established *ad hoc* reductions in the value of pension benefit entitlements. That was the decision of Greek, Portuguese and Italian legislators.[9] Regardless of the type, the various forms of interfering with someone's property are referred to by the Court as 'instances of interference'.

A1P1 includes three broad instances of interference:

> [T]he Court analysed Article 1 (P1-1) as comprising 'three distinct rules': the first rule, set out in the first sentence of the first paragraph, is of a general nature and enunciates the principle of the peaceful enjoyment of property; the second rule, contained in the

[8] These steps are developed for the cases of pensions and A1P1, for a more general view of these steps, see Maxwell (n 4).

[9] Theodoros Papadopoulos and Antonios Roumpakis, 'Rattling Europe's Ordoliberal "Iron Cage": The Contestation of Austerity in Southern Europe' (2018) *38 Critical Social Policy* 505.

> second sentence of the first paragraph, covers deprivation of possessions and subjects it to certain conditions; the third rule, stated in the second paragraph, recognises that the Contracting States are entitled, amongst other things, to control the use of property in accordance with the general interest.[10]

The first instance is total deprivation, which is outlined in the 'second rule'. The second instance is the control of property use, indicated in the 'third rule'. Lastly, the third instance pertains to the general principle of the peaceful enjoyment of possessions, identified in the 'first rule'.

The first instance of interference is also referred to as 'takings', drawing its name from the 'takings clause' in the United States Federal Constitution.[11] A classic example is expropriation, which represents the strongest form of governmental interference with an individual's property. Expropriation entails the formal extinguishment of an individual's ownership, typically for public interest reasons. For such a measure to comply with A1P1, the state must ensure compensation for the deprivation. That compensation must be timely and must satisfy standards of reasonableness and proportionality, taking into account both the market value of the property and the broader public aims pursued.[12]

The second instance of interference is 'control of the use of property'. This clause acknowledges the 'social function of property', which requires states to regulate its use in line with the broader public interest.[13] The role of private property here is not viewed as an absolute or insulated right, but rather as one that carries obligations toward the community. Accordingly, states are entitled to impose limitations that ensure property serves socially legitimate objectives, such as promoting housing access, protecting the environment or facilitating urban development. Measures like planning restrictions, the withdrawal of licences or the imposition of rent controls typically fall within this category.

The third instance of interference describes the broad principle of the peaceful enjoyment of property in a 'broader sense'.[14] It functions as an open clause or catch-all category, intended to capture measures that affect the enjoyment of possessions but do not qualify as either deprivations or 'controls of use'.[15] Examples include unresolved cases of 'takings' that occurred under totalitarian regimes, such

[10] *James and Others v United Kingdom* Series A no 98 (1986) 8 EHRR 123 §37.

[11] Michael B Kent Jr, 'Public Pension Reform and the Takings Clause' (2017) 4 *Belmont Law Review* 1.

[12] Marta Nunes highlights that this rule covers expropriation both in the economic (de facto) expropriation as well as legal expropriation, even though the former has been scarce, in Marta Nunes Vicente, 'Property Rights and Legitimate Expectations under United States Constitutional Law and the European Convention on Human Rights: Some Comparative Remarks' (2020) 26 *Comparative Law Review* 51, 71. Moreover, there is an ongoing debate around the fair compensation, whether it should be market based or otherwise: Maxwell (n 4); Tom Allen, 'Liberalism, Social Democracy and the Value of Property under the European Convention on Human Rights' (2010) 59 *International & Comparative Law Quarterly* 1055.

[13] Maria Luisa Padelletti, *La Tutela Della Proprietà Nella Convenzione Europea Dei Diritti Dell'uomo* (Giuffrè 2003) 13.

[14] *Marckx v Belgium* (n 3).

[15] Vicente (n 12) 70.

as those in former Soviet satellite states in Eastern Europe. For this book, it is worth noting that pension benefit reductions and their discontinuance have been understood to fall within this general category of interference.[16]

B. Lawfulness

The principle of lawfulness comes from the literal expression 'subject to the conditions provided for by law' in A1P1. Any interference with someone's possessions must be lawful.[17] The ECtHR interprets the term 'law' to include not only formal domestic statutes but also administrative action as well as case law.[18]

The lawfulness requirement reflects a commitment to the rule of law, which serves as a safeguard against arbitrariness.[19] A general account of what the Court means by the rule of law is beyond the scope of this chapter.[20] Still, some clarification is necessary. The rule of law 'concerns the manner in which we ideally want to organise our society through law'.[21] It is a concept of great normative power, often invoked when assessing governmental measures that affect individual rights.[22] However, it remains an essentially contested concept, with competing views on its content and implications.[23]

Two broad conceptions dominate the conceptual debate on the rule of law.[24] A procedural account focuses on formal safeguards against arbitrariness: legal certainty, foreseeability, equal treatment before the law and the right to a fair trial. It sees law as a tool to protect individual autonomy by constraining public power.[25] A substantive account, by contrast, holds that these procedural guarantees are insufficient. For law to conform with the rule of law, it must also pursue or reflect

[16] *Fábián v Hungary* (GC) App no 78117/13 (ECtHR, 2017) §60 'The Court has previously held that the modification or discontinuance of supplementary retirement benefits constituted "neither an expropriation nor a measure to control the use of property" and that the reduction of a pension by way of forfeiture was "neither a control of use nor a deprivation of property"'.

[17] *Špaček, s.r.o. v Czech Republic* App no 26449/95 (ECtHR, 1999) §54–57. The same is repeated in social security cases like *Beyeler v Italy* (GC) ECHR 2000-I §109. By 'substantive' or material use of law, it means that the concept of law used by the Court could differ from conceptions of what the law is in domestic legislations. See Geranne Lautenbach, *The Concept of the Rule of Law and the European Court of Human Rights* (Oxford University Press 2013) 95.

[18] Maxwell (n 4).

[19] *East/West Alliance Limited v Ukraine* App no 19336/04 (ECtHR, 2014) §167. Also, Lautenbach (n 17) 73–79. The author argues that the different ways in which the Convention appeals to the rule of law or the principle of lawfulness means to capture the same idea. Namely that of the rule of law.

[20] For a comprehensive study of the rule of law not only in the ECtHR but also in England, Germany and France, see Lautenbach (n 17).

[21] ibid 2.

[22] Jeremy Waldron, 'The Concept and the Rule of Law' (2008) 43 *Georgia Law Review* 1, 5.

[23] Jeremy Waldron, 'Is the Rule of Law an Essentially Contested Concept (in Florida)?' (2002) 21(2) *Law and Philosophy* 137.

[24] Lautenbach (n 17) 2.

[25] LA Sicilianos, 'The Rule of Law and the European Court of Human Rights: The Independence of the Judiciary' [2020] Montenegrin Academy of Sciences and Arts.

values like social justice. From that perspective, it is not enough that a measure follows domestic standards: it must also be normatively acceptable.[26]

The ECtHR has generally preferred the procedural conception of the rule of law. This reflects the Court's cautious posture due to institutional limits and concern over potential backlash.[27] Constraining itself to review whether legislation has a domestic legal basis, is accessible and is sufficiently precise aligns with the principle of subsidiarity.[28] Additionally, the Court often verifies whether the individual had an opportunity to challenge the application or interpretation of the law.[29] In most cases, lawfulness is presumed rather than discovered.[30] Only occasionally has the Court found an interference incompatible with A1P1 based on lawfulness alone.[31]

This cautious approach is particularly salient when the interference arises from legislation itself, such as pension reforms. In such cases, the lawmaker is not applying but changing the rules that govern entitlements. Verifying compliance with the Rule of Law seems more complex. Legislators, unlike administrators, are empowered to redefine legal relationships. The question about legislative constraints is central to constitutional theory, and the tension between democracy and legality.[32] There are significant disagreements on how to solve such a tension. Some views that legislatures act only following substantive notions of democracy. Others argue that legislative discretion must be bounded, mainly when it affects vested rights or creates retrospective changes.[33]

[26] Committee of Ministers, 'Recommendation of the Committee of Ministers to Member States on the Right to the Satisfaction of Basic Material Needs of Persons in Situations of Extreme Hardship' (Strasbourg: Council of Europe, 2000). Moreover, Henry Shue's account connects substantially the very definition of the rule of law to the compliance of the state with a set of 'basic rights'. Henry Shue, *Basic Rights: Subsistence, Affluence, and US Foreign Policy* (Princeton University Press 2020).

[27] On the legitimacy of the ECtHR's review, see Andreas Follesdal, 'The Legitimacy of International Human Rights Review: The Case of the European Court of Human Rights' (2009) 40 *Journal of Social Philosophy* 595.

[28] *Broniowski v Poland* (GC) (2004) ECHR 2004-V §147; Lautenbach (n 17) 87. In that chapter, the author unpacks what the Court means for all of those requirements. Foreseeability implies for the individual to know about the way in which the law is applied. If the law is applied in a way that was not foreseeable by individuals, then there might be a problem with 'lawfulness'.

[29] *Jokela v Finland* App no 28856/95 (ECtHR, 2002) §45; *Lekić v Slovenia* App no 36480/07 (ECtHR, 2017) §95.

[30] Maxwell (n 4) 177. Maxwell even shows how the Court assumes lawfulness in cases where a domestic Court judged that the government actually breached some instances of the rule of law.

[31] ibid 177–82.

[32] Jeremy Waldron, 'Legislation and the Rule of Law' (2007) 1 *Legisprudence* 91; Jeremy Waldron, *The Dignity of Legislation* (Cambridge University Press 1999).

[33] Some of the seminal pieces for this debate are: by Ronald Dworkin, *Law's Empire* (Hart Publishing 1998) 345–48; Waldron, 'Legislation and the Rule of Law' (n 32); Waldron, *The Dignity of Legislation* (n 32); Richard H Fallon Jr, 'The Core of an Uneasy Case for Judicial Review' (2007) 121 *Harvard Law Review* 1693; Jeremy Waldron, 'The Core of the Case Against Judicial Review' (2006) 6 *The Yale Law Journal* 1346; Scott M Noveck, 'Is Judicial Review Compatible with Democracy?' (2007) 6 Cardozo Public Law, Policy & Ethics Journal 401; Roberto Gargarella, *El Derecho Como Una Conversación Entre Iguales: Qué Hacer Para Que Las Democracias Contemporáneas Se Abran–Por Final Diálogo Ciudadano* (Siglo XXI Editores 2021).

When reviewing the lawfulness of a measure of interference of the type of legislation, the Court seems to reflect a thin (and even 'weak'[34]) procedural review of legislative measures, consistent with its subsidiary role.[35] The Court does not articulate a checklist of substantive qualities that laws must possess to satisfy the criterion of lawfulness. On the contrary, it only checks whether legislation complies with some features by means of which the Convention rights are realised.[36] For instance, that legislation must be general, roughly stable, intelligible, consistent, practicable, public and non-retroactive.[37] But it is a thin scrutiny. The Court has accepted retroactive legislation altering pension entitlements as compatible with A1P1, despite its tension with the principle of legal certainty.[38] In *Maggio and Others v Italy*, the Court stated:

> The Court has repeatedly ruled that … the legislature is not prevented from regulating, through new retrospective provisions, rights derived from the laws in force [for instance, a welfare benefit entitlement].[39]

This confirms that retroactivity is not *per se* unlawful under the Convention. While some accounts see the temporal direction of legal norms as central to lawfulness, the Court instead shifts the issue to the proportionality analysis.[40] There, the focus is not on time as such, but on burden distribution. In other words, it determines whether the retrospective change unfairly affects the individual's position relative to others.[41]

In many cases, the ECtHR does not assess the lawfulness of legislative pension reforms in detail. It assumes that the measure meets basic legal standards. Especially in the field of social benefits, the Court avoids confronting states on the lawfulness of their legislative processes. Some scholars attribute this to strategic deference: questioning the rule of law of a Convention state may trigger institutional backlash and risk the Court's authority.[42]

[34] Robert Arnold, 'European Constitutionalism after the Second World War' in Susana Galera (ed), *Judicial Review, a Comparative Analysis inside the European Legal System* (Council of Europe 2010) 39. We shall remember the distinction between the 'diffuse' versus concentrated control of constitutionality. To see a critical approach of the latter in the Colombian case, refer to Kevin Hartmann-Cortés, Juan Felipe Herrera and Gabriel Hernando Angarita, 'La "Privatización" de La Acción Pública de Inconstitucionalidad' [2021] *Revista Derecho del Estado* 203.

[35] Ed Bates, *The Evolution of the European Convention on Human Rights: From Its Inception to the Creation of a Permanent Court of Human Rights* (Oxford University Press 2010) 154–58 and 354–56.

[36] For a great overview of these types of principles see Jeremy Waldron, 'Principles of Legislation' in Richard W Bauman and Tsvi Kahana (eds), *The Least Examined Branch: The Role of Legislatures in the Constitutional State* (Cambridge University Press 2006) ch 1. What follows in the same paragraph is largely based on Waldron's reflections on this topic.

[37] This is the account by Leo Fuller, *The Morality of Law* (Revised, Yale University Press 1969) 33–38.

[38] On an excellent recent discussion of what retroactivity or *ex postfacto* law means for different accounts of the rule of law, see Neil Duxbury, 'Ex Post Facto Law' (2013) 58 *The American Journal of Jurisprudence* 135, 135–61.

[39] See *Maggio and Others v Italy* App nos 46286/09, 52851/08, 54486/08 and 56001/08 (ECtHR, 2011) §43.

[40] Maxwell (n 4) 192.

[41] Lautenbach (n 17) 74–76.

[42] These backlashes could include taking measures to undermine the jurisdiction of the Court, reducing its budget or proposing deep reforms to constraint its competences. On how these

C. Public Interest

A1P1 allows significant interferences with possessions only when they are justified by 'the public interest'. The Convention states: '[n]o one shall be deprived of his possessions except in the public interest'.

In legal and political theory, the notion of 'public interest' is contested.[43] Some scholars reject it as too vague to be operational.[44] Others offer competing accounts based on differing views of what counts as 'public' and as an 'interest'.[45] The ECtHR avoids any substantive definition. Instead, it adopts a procedural approach.[46] The content of the public interest is equated with the outcome of national decision-making processes.[47] As the Court repeatedly states:

> [T]he national authorities, because of their direct knowledge of their society and its needs, are in principle better placed than the international judge to decide what is "in the public interest". Under the Convention system, it is thus for those authorities to make the initial assessment as to the existence of a problem of public concern warranting measures interfering with the peaceful enjoyment of possessions.[48]

This deference is stronger in welfare and social security cases. According to the Court:

> [T]he notion of 'public interest' is necessarily extensive. In particular, the decision to enact laws concerning pensions or welfare benefits involves consideration of various economic and social issues. The margin of appreciation available to the legislature in implementing such policies should therefore be a wide one, and its judgment as to what is 'in the public interest' should be respected unless that judgment is manifestly without reasonable foundation.[49]

In practice, measures framed as responses to fiscal crises are treated as being inherently within the public interest.[50] For example, the Court readily accepted

backlashes operate against international and domestic Courts who have clashed directly with legislatures, see Katharine G Young, *The Future of Economic and Social Rights* (Cambridge University Press 2019).

[43] Eric R Boot, 'Public Interest', in *Oxford Research Encyclopedia of Politics* (Oxford University Press 2022) 1–29.

[44] The lack of definition of such notion has made some authors to claim that it is one of those concepts in which a scholar can project whatever he feels according to his or her preferred theory of values. Therefore, being invalid. This is the position held by Frank J Sorauf, 'The Public Interest Reconsidered' (1957) 19 *The Journal of Politics* 616. Aileen McHarg, 'Reconciling Human Rights and the Public Interest: Conceptual Problems and Doctrinal Uncertainty in the Jurisprudence of the European Court of Human Rights' (1999) 62 *Modern Law Review* 671.

[45] Boot (n 41) conceives a fourfold classification of the different accounts as follows: (i) 'aggregative', (ii) 'procedural', (iii) 'unitary' and (iv) 'civic'.

[46] This is classified under the 'procedural label'. See Eric R Boot, 'The Public Interest: Clarifying a Legal Concept' (2024) 37 *Ratio Juris* 110, 116–17.

[47] ibid 116–17.

[48] *Valkov and Others v Bulgaria* App nos 2033/04, 19125/04, 19475/04, 19490/04, 19495/04, 19497/04, 24729/04, 171/05 and 2041/05 (ECtHR, 2011) §91. This has been consolidated in posterior case law such as *Béláné Nagy v Hungary* (GC) App no 53080/13 (ECtHR, 2016) §113.

[49] *Béláné Nagy v Hungary* (n 48) §113.

[50] See, amongst others, *Maria Alfredina da Silva Carvalho Rico v Portugal* App no 13341/14 (ECtHR, 2015) §40; *Kjartan Ásmundsson v Iceland* ECHR 2004-IX §41 and §10.

a government's claim that a reform aimed to 're-establish an equilibrium in the pension system' was in the public interest.[51] But notions like 'equilibrium' or 'sustainability' are normatively loaded. They allow for different interpretations and policy choices.

One definition, endorsed by the European Commission, defines sustainability in narrow fiscal terms: as the balance between revenues and liabilities in a pension scheme.[52] However, other conceptions exist and expand the notion to include values such as intergenerational equity in resource allocation.[53] More recently, others have also included a political dimension to sustainability, meaning the ability to preserve consensus around a pension model.[54] Each definition carries different distributive outcomes and may justify different levels of interference.

These variations show that invoking sustainability requires a prior normative stance. What qualifies as a legitimate public interest depends on how sustainability is defined and over what horizon. A measure that restores short-term liquidity may differ radically from one pursuing long-term adequacy or consensus. Yet the Court does not engage with these distinctions. It treats such claims as presumptively valid.

This approach raises two concerns. First, it weakens the justificatory force of the public interest requirement. If national authorities both interfere with property and define the public interest behind that interference, the test becomes circular. Second, it shifts all meaningful reviews to the proportionality stage. In effect, the public interest test functions only as a threshold filter. This is why this step has been described as a 'paper tiger':[55] formally present, but substantively hollow.

Unsurprisingly, challenges under A1P1 rarely succeed at this stage.[56] In pension reform cases, no interference has been found unjustified on public interest grounds.[57] A claimant seeking to contest such a measure must therefore focus on disproportionality.

[51] See *Maggio and Others v Italy* (n 39) [49]; *Stefanetti and Others v Italy* App nos 21838/10, 21849/10, 21852/10, 21855/10, 21860/10, 21863/10, 21869/10 and 21870/10 (ECtHR, 2014) §43.

[52] European Commission, 'European Semester Thematic Factsheet: Adequacy and Sustainability of Pensions'.

[53] Asghar Zaidi, Katrin Gasior and Alexandre Sidorenko, 'Intergenerational Solidarity: Policy Challenges and Societal Responses' [2010] Policy Brief, European Centre Vienna.

[54] Ville-Pekka Sorsa and Natascha van der Zwan, 'Sustaining the Unsustainable? The Political Sustainability of Pensions in Finland and the Netherlands' (2022) 32 *Journal of European Social Policy* 91, 92.

[55] Maxwell (n 4) 208.

[56] The examples that could be traced are *SA Dangeville v France* App no 36677/97 (ECtHR, 2002) §53–58. Here, the Court found out that the interference was not a result of an intervention by the legislator, but it was produced due to a lack of it. In that sense, the argument of the government could not be seen to be found on the public interest. Another case is *Rosenzweig and Bonded Warehouses Ltd v Poland* App no 51728/99 (ECtHR, 2005) §56–64. In this case, the Court not only did not find a public interest argument to justify the measure. It went further and claimed that even assuming there was an explanation, it was disproportional and unreasonable, as there were less harsh ways to interfere with the property of the applicant. In that case, the reasonability test seems to be mixed with the proportionality test.

[57] However, from a judicial perspective, one of the consequences when repeatedly abusing the margin of appreciation figure is distorting its rationale and undermining it is the underlying logic. Kratochvíl (n 6) 343.

D. Fair Balance

Once it is established that an interference pursues a legitimate aim, A1P1 requires that it strike a 'fair balance' between the general interest and the individual's rights. This requirement is not expressly stated in the text, but has been judicially inferred from the structure of the provision.[58] In *Sporrong and Lönnroth v Sweden*, the Court considered this balancing requirement as intrinsic to the logic of the Convention:

> For the purposes of the latter provision [Article 1, Protocol 1], the Court must determine whether a fair balance was struck between the demands of the general interest of the community and the requirements of the protection of the individual's fundamental rights ... The search for this balance is inherent in the whole of the Convention and is also reflected in the structure of Article 1.[59]

At this stage, the Court moves beyond the formal legitimacy of the interference and focuses on its effects, asking whether there is 'a reasonable relationship of proportionality between the means employed and the aim sought to be realised'.[60] This is known as the 'fair balance' test, the most substantive component of the acceptability analysis under A1P1.

The literature agrees on how obscure the 'fair balance' test is[61] considering that it does not provide much guidance on how a state should weigh the different interests at stake in a given policy.[62] Despite this doctrinal vagueness, this is the step where A1P1 most 'bites'.[63] At this stage, the ECtHR defines what takes priority under a set of facts: whether the property protection established under A1P1, or the general interest pursued by the disputed measure that interferes with it.[64]

The fair balance test, as applied under A1P1, rests on the idea that Convention rights are not formulated as rigid legal rules but as principles.[65] In Robert Alexy's terms, principles are 'optimisation commands'[66] that must be fulfilled to the

[58] Alastair Mowbray, 'A Study of the Principle of Fair Balance in the Jurisprudence of the European Court of Human Rights' (2010) 10 *Human Rights Law Review* 289.

[59] *Sporrong and Lönnroth v Sweden* Series A no 52 (1983) 5 EHRR 35 [35].

[60] *Beyeler v Italy* (n 17) §114; *Jahn and Others v Germany* (GC) ECHR 2005-VI, 72203/01 and 72552/01 §93. Proportionality has been defined in the constitutional law literature as 'the set of rules determining the necessary and sufficient conditions for a limitation of a constitutionally protected right by a law to be constitutionally permissible'. Aharon Barak, *Proportionality: Constitutional Rights and Their Limitations* (Cambridge University Press 2012) 3.

[61] Leijten, 'From Stec to Valkov: Possessions and Margins in the Social Security Case Law of the European Court of Human Rights' (n 5); Van Drooghenbroeck and Rizcallah (n 6).

[62] Leijten, 'From Stec to Valkov: Possessions and Margins in the Social Security Case Law of the European Court of Human Rights' (n 5); Ingrid Leijten, *Core Socio-Economic Rights and the European Court of Human Rights* (Cambridge University Press 2018); Van Drooghenbroeck and Rizcallah (n 6).

[63] Maxwell (n 4) 297.

[64] In other words, whether the limitation or interference to the right is justifiable Julian Rivers, 'Proportionality and Variable Intensity of Review' (2006) 65 *The Cambridge Law Journal* 174, 174.

[65] I follow Leijten in Ingrid Leijten, 'The Right to Minimum Subsistence and Property Protection under the ECHR: Never the Twain Shall Meet?' (2019) 21 *European Journal of Social Security* 307.

[66] See Robert Alexy, 'On the Structure of Legal Principles' (2000) 13 *Ratio Juris* 294.

greatest extent possible within legal and factual constraints.[67] Because they are optimisation requirements, rights are never absolute in application.[68] When they collide with other principles, complete satisfaction of both is impossible.[69] The role of the Court then becomes one of determining the extent to which each can be realised under the concrete circumstances of the case.

There are two types of conflicts arising from the Convention. The first is between two Convention rights.[70] For instance, between the right to respect for private and family life (article 8) and the right to freedom of expression (article 10).[71] In this setting, the focus is on defining the meaning and limits of each right under the Convention.[72] Here, the Court's task is to define more precisely the scope of each right so that they can co-exist.[73] However, there is not a single universally accepted method to successfully undertake this task.[74] What seems to occur here is that the Court is deploying an interpretive effort to give greater precision to vague norms, to acknowledge their precise scope, rather than balancing them between each other.[75]

The second type of conflict is far more relevant for cases involving pension entitlements under A1P1.[76] It involves a collision between a Convention right, like A1P1, and a collective goal or 'public interest', like sustainability or macroeconomic stability.[77] In this setting, the meaning of the right itself is generally uncontested. The central question is whether, in the specific circumstances, the right may be overridden in pursuit of the public interest.[78] The method to approach this conflict is 'structured balancing'.[79] In this context, the Court's task is to determine if national authorities, when issuing the disputed measure, have observed the Convention's principles.[80] In other words, to balance and evaluate the conflicting

[67] ibid 295.

[68] Alexy, 'On the Structure of Legal Principles' (n 66).

[69] Steven Greer, '"Balancing" and the European Court of Human Rights: A Contribution to the Habermas-Alexy Debate' (2004) 63 *The Cambridge Law Journal* 412.

[70] Eva Brems, 'Conflicting Human Rights: An Exploration in the Context of the Right to a Fair Trial in the European Convention for the Protection of Human Rights and Fundamental Freedoms' (2005) 27 *Human Rights Quarterly* 294; Stijn Smet, 'Freedom of Expression and the Right to Reputation: Human Rights in Conflict' (2010) 26 American University International Law Review 183.

[71] For a good overview of how the Court has solved the tension between those rights, see Smet (n 70).

[72] Greer (n 69).

[73] ibid.

[74] ibid.

[75] ibid.

[76] A development of each of the following steps in the overall A1P1 jurisprudence appears in Maxwell (n 4) 222–54.

[77] Greer (n 69).

[78] ibid.

[79] ibid 418. This method differs from the one that resolves the tension between rights of the same category. Greer shows how reconciling conflicts between two Convention rights (eg, freedom of expression vs freedom of religion) is a more demanding task. In 'rights v rights' conflicts, the primary task for the ECtHR is to determine the meaning and scope of vague rights, which involves judicial discretion but is not typically referred to as 'balancing' in the same way as rights against competing collective interests.

[80] Greer (n 69).

interests of the state and the individual by assessing whether the interference is rationally justified.[81]

Balancing between individual rights and collective goals is highly contextual. It does not have a high degree of (mathematical) precision, and that is one of its most contested features.[82] However, some subprinciples can guide the structured balancing method:[83] 'suitability', 'necessity' and 'proportionality in the narrow sense'.[84] Suitability asks whether the measure is factually capable of achieving its proposed aim.[85] Necessity requires that, among the measures capable of achieving the aim, the one that least interferes with the right be chosen.[86] Finally, proportionality in the narrow sense demands that the extent of the interference be justified by the importance of satisfying the collective goal.[87] In practice, this requires a correlation between the severity of the burden imposed and the quality and strength of the evidence that the measure will indeed achieve the claimed collective goal or public interest.[88]

A priori, these three subprinciples could be applied in a strict, sequential fashion:[89] first, excluding unsuitable measures, then discarding unnecessary ones and finally balancing the competing interests within the strict proportionality standard. This 'vertical' model of proportionality[90] emphasises adherence to each

[81] Maxwell (n 4) 209.

[82] ibid 239; Barak (n 60); Francisco J Urbina, 'Is It Really That Easy? A Critique of Proportionality and "Balancing as Reasoning"' (2014) 27 *Canadian Journal of Law & Jurisprudence* 167.

[83] This is taken from Alexy's approach to balancing in Robert Alexy, 'On Balancing and Subsumption. A Structural Comparison' (2003) 16 *Ratio Juris* 433; Robert Alexy, *A Theory of Constitutional Rights* (Oxford University Press 2010).

[84] Alexy, *A Theory of Constitutional Rights* (n 83) 44–110; Alexy, 'On Balancing and Subsumption. A Structural Comparison' (n 83).

[85] Alexy, 'On Balancing and Subsumption. A Structural Comparison' (n 83); Alexy, *A Theory of Constitutional Rights* (n 83).

[86] Alexy, 'On Balancing and Subsumption. A Structural Comparison' (n 83); Alexy, *A Theory of Constitutional Rights* (n 83).

[87] Alexy, 'On Balancing and Subsumption. A Structural Comparison' (n 83); Alexy, *A Theory of Constitutional Rights* (n 83).

[88] Greer (n 69).

[89] It must be noticed how Alexy's theory is the object of enormous discussion in the constitutional and comparative constitutional law literature. On a great discussion of this principle, see three excellent pieces by Francisco Urbina. Urbina, 'Is It Really That Easy? A Critique of Proportionality and "Balancing as Reasoning"' (n 82); Francisco J Urbina, 'A Critique of Proportionality' (2012) 57 *American Journal of Jurisprudence* 49; Francisco J Urbina, *A Critique of Proportionality and Balancing* (Cambridge University Press 2017).

[90] That is also the position of Jonas Christoffersen, *Fair Balance: Proportionality, Subsidiarity and Primarity in the European Convention on Human Rights*, vol 99 (Brill 2009) 65. However, Brems and Lavrysen hold that even if the Court's approach is 'all things considered', it has nevertheless an important room for discretion to consider whether to include or not a criterion of adequacy, appropriateness and necessity. Eva Brems and Laurens Lavrysen, '"Don't Use a Sledgehammer to Crack a Nut": Less Restrictive Means in the Case Law of the European Court of Human Rights' (2015) 15 *Human Rights Law Review* 139, 141. For a fairly critical approach of the adoption of proportionality in the ECtHR, see Stavros Tsakyrakis, 'Proportionality: An Assault on Human Rights?' (2009) 7 *International Journal of Constitutional Law* 468, 468.

procedural step in turn.[91] The ECtHR, however, does not follow this sequence explicitly. In A1P1 cases, the steps often overlap, and the Court tends to address them collectively within the final 'strict proportionality' stage.[92] In practice, this amounts to an 'all-things-considered' approach that weighs competing interests in context without a fixed order.[93] This approach is commonly described as the 'horizontal' model of proportionality.[94]

Ultimately, the decisive factor in the 'horizontal model of proportionality' often becomes who must prove what, and to what standard. In other words, the method ultimately turns on the allocation of argumentative burdens, which determines whether the state's justification for a measure will prevail over the individual's right. This allocation operates as follows: applicants bear the 'evidential burden' of presenting a prima facie case that a governmental action has breached their rights, meaning they must provide sufficient evidence of the alleged interference in their application.[95]

Once this *prima facie* case is established, the burden shifts to the respondent state, which carries the 'persuasive burden' of demonstrating that the interference pursues a legitimate aim and satisfies the proportionality requirements of the fair balance test.[96] The strength of this justification is tested against the 'intermediate standard' of proof, which is higher than 'proof on a balance of probabilities' but less than 'proof beyond a reasonable doubt'.[97] The Court has, on some occasions, referred to this standard with phrases such as 'convincing and compelling' evidence.[98] The underlying rationale is that the more severe the interference with the right, the stronger and more reliable the state's evidence must be that the measure will realise the collective aim or public interest.[99]

This allocation of burdens and the applicable standard of proof play a decisive role in how the Court approaches A1P1 disputes in practice. In the specific context of pension reform, certain patterns emerge. Governments typically justify their reforms on grounds such as fiscal sustainability, distributive equity or macroeconomic stability.[100] Against these justifications, the Court assesses the nature and strength of the applicant's entitlement and the extent of the interference. It

[91] This approach is also called the 'structured' approach. Michael Fordham and Thomas De La Mare, 'Identifying the Principles of Proportionality' (2001) 27 *Understanding Human Rights Principles* 50.

[92] Maxwell (n 4) 282.

[93] Sarah Nield, 'Proportionality and the Vindication of Property Rights' in Heather Conway and Robin Hickey (eds), *Modern Studies in Property Law*, vol 9 (Hart Publishing 2017) 44. This approach is also labelled as 'non-structured'. Fordham and De La Mare (n 91) 51.

[94] Christoffersen (n 90).

[95] Greer (n 69).

[96] ibid.

[97] Greer argues that phrases like 'clear, strong and cogent' (from US jurisprudence) or 'convincing and compelling' (used by the Court itself on some occasions) fit this requirement. ibid.

[98] ibid.

[99] ibid.

[100] Leijten, *Core Socio-Economic Rights and the European Court of Human Rights* (n 62) 279.

also examines whether any mitigating or compensation measures were adopted to soften the impact.[101] If the burden on the applicant is deemed excessive in light of these factors, the interference will be found incompatible with A1P1.[102]

In theory, the structured balancing method should provide individuals with substantive protection against arbitrary or excessively harsh legislative changes in pension or welfare matters as a matter of A1P1. In practice, however, its effectiveness is severely limited[103] by two concepts that will be discussed in the next section: the 'Margin of Appreciation' doctrine and the 'essence' of the correct standard.

II. Margin of Appreciation and the 'Essence' of the Right

The fair balance requirement, as developed in the previous section, incorporates a proportionality analysis into the structure of A1P1. Proportionality requires two things from governments. First, to provide adequate justification for their measures of interference. Second, to ensure that such measures do not impose disproportionate burdens on individuals. The question that follows is, what is the framework against which to assess these demands? In the Court's case law, two key concepts are central in this regard: the margin of appreciation doctrine and the 'essence' of the right.

A. The Margin of Appreciation Doctrine

As discussed in chapter one, the Margin of Appreciation Doctrine embodies a form of judicial restraint in the Court's interpretive method.[104] Yet, it is an elusive concept because there are no fixed criteria governing its scope.[105] It seems to

[101] These measures might be manifold and depend to the intensity of the interference. For a deeper discussion on the extent to which, in A1P1 cases, compensation measures ought to be above or equal to market value, see Maxwell (n 4) 255–66.

[102] Mowbray (n 58).

[103] Kratochvíl (n 6); Greer (n 6); Oddný Mjöll Arnardóttir, 'Res Interpretata, Erga Omnes Effect and the Role of the Margin of Appreciation in Giving Domestic Effect to the Judgments of the European Court of Human Rights' (2017) 28 *European Journal of International Law* 819; Jeffrey A Brauch, 'The Margin of Appreciation and the Jurisprudence of the European Court of Human Rights: Threat to the Rule of Law' (2004) 11 *Columbia Journal of European Law* 113.

[104] Greer (n 6); Arnardóttir (n 6); Eva Brems, 'Positive Subsidiarity and Its Implications for the Margin of Appreciation Doctrine' (2019) 37 *Netherlands Quarterly of Human Rights* 210; Greer (n 6); Kratochvíl (n 6); Lorenza Mola, 'The Margin of Appreciation Accorded to States in Times of Economic Crisis. An Analysis of the Decisions by the European Committee of Social Rights and by the European Court of Human Rights on National Austerity Measures' (2015) 5 *Lex Social* 174; James A Sweeney, 'A Margin of Appreciation in the Internal Market: Lessons from the European Court of Human Rights' (2007) 34 *Legal Issues of Economic Integration* 27; Trykhlib and Lemak (n 6); George Letsas, *A Theory of Interpretation of the European Convention on Human Rights* (Oxford University Press 2007).

[105] Letsas (n 104) 80–81.

operate mainly as a flexible reference to the discretion left to national authorities in specific cases.[106] This discretion is most visible in disputes concerning social and economic policy:[107]

> [T]he decision to enact laws concerning pensions or welfare benefits involves consideration of various economic and social issues. The margin of appreciation available to the legislature in implementing such policies should therefore be a wide one, and its judgment as to what is 'in the public interest' should be respected unless that judgment is manifestly without reasonable foundation.[108]

The 'Margin of Appreciation' reflects the assumption that domestic institutions are better positioned than international courts to weigh socio-economic policy considerations such as fiscal constraints, demographic shifts and distributive trade-offs. It underscores the ECtHR's subsidiarity to domestic authority in formulating social policy.[109]

The margin serves two functions. First, it reduces the argumentative burden on governments when justifying interferences with property arising from social policy: the wider the margin, the less justification is required.[110] Second, it delineates the limits of permissible governmental action under the Convention.[111] Although the margin is wide, it is not absolute. The margin's boundary is the boundary of the 'essence' of the individual's right.[112] As will become clear in the following subsection, the broader the margin, the more narrowly the essence is defined, and vice versa.[113]

The margin of appreciation is broader in areas like taxation, socio-economic policy and environmental protection.[114] In those cases, regulation is prima facie accepted, for instance, when amending social-security legislation in response to societal changes:

> [T]he Court has accepted the possibility of amendments to social-security legislation which may be adopted in response to societal changes and evolving views on the categories of persons who need social assistance, and also to the evolution of individual situations.[115]

[106] Greer (n 6) 32.
[107] Brauch (n 103).
[108] *Béláné Nagy v Hungary* (n 48) §113.
[109] This has been the common understanding of the literature on the subject. Kratochvíl (n 6) 57.
[110] Arnardóttir (n 103). Evidences that the Court widens or reduces the margin granted to governments as a function of the extent to which they include the Court's considerations within their reasoning to take a given measure.
[111] See the substantive account of the Margin of Appreciation Doctrine by George Letsas, 'Two Concepts of the Margin of Appreciation' (2006) 26 *Oxford Journal of Legal Studies* 705, 706.
[112] At least that is the vision of the 'absolutist' account of the 'essence' doctrine. See the following subsections and Van Drooghenbroeck and Rizcallah (n 6).
[113] ibid.
[114] Maxwell (n 4) 215.
[115] *Béláné Nagy v Hungary* (n 48) [88]. A similar idea was already conveyed in *Müller v Austria* App no 5849/72 (ECtHR, 1975) §31.

The Court has made clear that A1P1 cannot be interpreted as freezing the content of welfare legislation. It does not prevent governments from reducing or recalibrating pension benefits, or from altering the rules governing the social-security system. States remain free to legislate in this field, provided that the measures pursue a legitimate aim and are not manifestly disproportionate.[116] An applicant's success, therefore, depends on demonstrating that the burden imposed was excessive, in particular by showing how it affected the 'essence' of their right.

Given the breadth of the margin of appreciation in this area, the evidentiary and argumentative threshold for establishing such an excessive burden is particularly high, and very few claims can meet such a standard. As a result, disputes arising from public-policy choices – especially those concerning the allocation of public expenditure – are only rarely decided in the applicant's favour.[117]

As demonstrated in chapters four and five, the Court has progressively expanded A1P1's scope to encompass the full spectrum of welfare entitlements, making pension disputes almost automatically admissible under the provision. When this broad threshold is considered alongside the Court's wide margin of appreciation in pension-related cases, a paradox seems to emerge. The expansion of the article's scope suggests that the Court views pension entitlements as deserving robust human rights protection.[118] Yet at the proportionality stage, the Court often denies such protection, dismissing claims through the margin of appreciation. This dual approach results in a substantial number of admissible applications but only a small fraction of favourable outcomes for applicants, thereby creating a paradoxical framework that appears procedurally robust but proves substantively weak.

The apparent paradox dissolves when understanding the Court's dual framework as the Court's pragmatic way to deal with the ambiguity of A1P1's text as a result of the ideological compromise between its drafters.[119] The Court's approach reflects a coherent judicial strategy that draws on competing liberal and social-democratic conceptions of property at different stages of review. The liberal view treats property as a set of pre-existing individual entitlements threatened by state regulation.[120]

In contrast, the social-democratic view regards property as socially constructed and legitimately subject to collective purposes.[121] A1P1's drafting left this tension

[116] Leijten, 'From Stec to Valkov: Possessions and Margins in the Social Security Case Law of the European Court of Human Rights' (n 5).

[117] Maxwell (n 4) 232.

[118] This was pointed out also by Leijten, not as a paradox, but as a tension regarding the broad or narrow way to define a fundamental right concerning the limitations or margin of appreciation used by a Constitutional Court. See Leijten, 'From Stec to Valkov: Possessions and Margins in the Social Security Case Law of the European Court of Human Rights' (n 5) 343.

[119] Allen (n 12).

[120] ibid 1056.

[121] ibid 1058.

unresolved, and the Court has chosen to use each conception at a different stage of analysis. At the admissibility stage, it adopts the liberal framework to recognise pension entitlements as 'possessions' and signal their importance to A1P1's purposes. At the proportionality stage, it shifts to a social-democratic perspective, treating pensions not as inviolable entitlements but as components of broader collective goals, such as solidarity, social justice and fiscal sustainability. These broader goals, on which the state has a wide margin of appreciation, serve as the benchmark against which the Court must balance the individual's possession. In this light, A1P1's role of protection is not to preserve benefits unchanged but to ensure that any modification remains fair, predictable and non-arbitrary.

B. The 'Essence' of the Right

The previous section examined the dual structure of the ECtHR's approach when it comes to protecting pension benefits under A1P1. The Court's framework creates a wide gate but a narrow path: many pension reforms are admissible, but only a few are found to breach the Convention. Still, the fact that few cases succeed does not mean that success is impossible. Even if limited, a set of judgments shows that the Court is willing to find a violation of A1P1 when legislative measures are disproportionate or impose an 'excessive burden'. The questions that follow are: under what conditions can someone successfully claim that there was a breach of their property right as a result of a pension reform? What are the boundaries of the margin of appreciation in social security cases? What follows for pension policy?

As noted earlier, the margin of appreciation granted to domestic institutions is not absolute: it cannot be exercised in a way that undermines the 'essence' content of someone's rights. In other words, there is an interaction between the 'margin of appreciation' and the 'essence' of the right. In principle, these concepts serve different functions: the former identifies an absolute limit on restrictions, while the latter determines the intensity of the Court's scrutiny.[122] In practice, however, they often operate in tandem, with the margin of appreciation effectively neutralising the protection theoretically offered by the essence doctrine.[123] This is particularly evident in social security cases, where the Court typically grants states a wide margin of appreciation, making it exceedingly difficult to establish that a pension reform violates the essence of A1P1 rights.[124]

The doctrine of the 'essence' or 'substance' of fundamental rights emerged in the European Convention on Human Rights system in the 1968 'Belgian Linguistic case'. This case concerned Article 2 of Protocol 1, on the right to education. In that judgment, the Commission argued for the first time that

[122] Kratochvíl (n 6) 347–49.
[123] Van Drooghenbroeck and Rizcallah (n 6).
[124] See ch 5.

the government's regulation must never 'injure the substance of [a Convention Right], the right to education'.[125] Despite its frequent invocation, the essence doctrine remains conceptually ambiguous. Some authors claim that it is like 'sugar in hot milk'.[126]

The doctrine has at least two competing approaches in the literature. On the one hand, an 'absolutist' view that protects some core-objective aspects of Convention rights that cannot be limited under any circumstances. On the other hand, a 'relativist' perspective holds that the 'essence' is not an objectively set of core values for each right ex ante. Instead, it appears as an outcome of a proportionality test under the specific circumstances of each case.[127] The ECtHR's jurisprudence oscillates between these approaches, sometimes suggesting that violations of the essence are per se unjustifiable. At the same time, in other cases, it conducts proportionality analysis despite having identified interference with the essence.[128]

A further distinction exists between 'institutional' and 'subjective' approaches to the essence doctrine. The institutional perspective holds that a right's essence is violated only when the right loses meaning 'for all or nearly all individuals and not just a particular individual'.[129] The subjective approach, by contrast, focuses on the individual and considers that the essence may be violated when a right becomes meaningless for a specific person, even if the general institution remains intact.[130] This distinction has particular relevance for pension rights, as changes to pension systems typically affect individuals differently based on their age, contribution history and personal circumstances.

From a practical point of view, there is a major difficulty in addressing the 'essence' of the right in the ECtHR's jurisprudence. There are two main reasons. First, because the Court has never clearly defined what that 'essence' actually entails, nor for A1P1,[131] nor for most of its rights.[132] Second, because of the methodological inconsistencies of the Court when using the essence concept.[133] Nevertheless, the literature has described the Court's three main purposes when appealing to such a concept. First, to set an absolute limit of the right which is immune from proportionality review.[134] That is to say, to establish what parts of a convention right should never be limited by governmental interference.[135] Second, to act as a vehicle for expanding the Convention's sphere of protection by developing standards linked to specific rights, thereby ensuring that they

[125] *Belgian Linguistic Case ('Relating to Certain Aspects of the Laws on the Use of Languages in Education in Belgium' v Belgium)* Series A no 6 (1968).
[126] Van Drooghenbroeck and Rizcallah (n 6) 904.
[127] ibid 911.
[128] Van Drooghenbroeck and Rizcallah (n 6); Kratochvíl (n 6).
[129] Van Drooghenbroeck and Rizcallah (n 6) 912.
[130] ibid.
[131] Maxwell (n 4).
[132] Van Drooghenbroeck and Rizcallah (n 6).
[133] ibid.
[134] That is the classical understanding of the essence as used by earlier case law which is in turn taken from German constitutional law. See ibid 905.
[135] That is the classical understanding of the essence as used by earlier case law which is in turn taken from German constitutional law. See ibid.

remain practical and effective.[136] Third, to serve as a tool within the fair balance review, where a finding that the essence is strongly engaged prompts the Court to tilt the balance towards the right-holder by imposing higher procedural requirements or narrowing the margin of appreciation.[137] In this third function, the essence does not operate as an untouchable threshold. Instead, once engaged, it shifts the presumption of deference away from the state and towards the individual.[138]

The multiple purposes of the 'essence' concept used by the Court have contributed to an 'overwork'[139] and an 'inflation'[140] of the term, which, in turn, has contributed to diminishing its clarity, coherence and normative strength.[141] In this context, attempting to offer a single, abstract definition of the 'essence' of pension rights under A1P1 would be unproductive. It is more useful to identify recurring patterns in the Court's reasoning in cases concerning these entitlements, to map some practical boundaries that the ECtHR has set for pension reforms under A1P1.

When it comes to the 'essence' of the right in debates concerning pension entitlements and A1P1, the Court has never clearly defined what constitutes a 'substantial' reduction.[142] The relationship between property rights and the essence doctrine in pension cases is particularly challenging given the unique characteristics of pension systems. Unlike traditional property, pension entitlements exist within complex welfare schemes that must balance multiple competing interests: the rights of current beneficiaries, the sustainability of the system for future generations, broader economic policy considerations and the state's fiscal constraints.

However, this chapter seeks to uncover the boundaries and ambiguities surrounding the 'essence' discussion in the pension case law. To do so, this subsection adopts an inductive approach. It examines key pension-related judgments in which the 'essence' played a central role, including both those finding a violation and those rejecting the applicant's claim. Table 6.1 organises the selected judgments along two dimensions: the type of interference, ranging from total deprivation to partial reduction of benefits; and the Court's assessment of whether the measure constituted a breach. This classification reflects a key variable in the Court's reasoning, as the severity of the interference often shapes the intensity of its review.

[136] ibid 905. The authors put as an example the development of the 'flagrant denial of justice' standard under Article 6 to extend procedural guarantees in extradition cases.

[137] ibid 905.

[138] Van Drooghenbroeck and Rizcallah (n 6).

[139] ibid.

[140] Kratochvíl (n 6).

[141] Van Drooghenbroeck and Rizcallah (n 6). In response, Drooghenbroeck and Rizcallah have called for a rationalisation of its use and for its application to be confined to clearly defined functions within the case law.

[142] Leijten, 'From Stec to Valkov: Possessions and Margins in the Social Security Case Law of the European Court of Human Rights' (n 5) 328.

Table 6.1 Pension cases under A1P1

	Total deprivation	**Partial reduction**
No breach of A1P1	*Fábián v Hungary*	*Stefanetti and Others v Italy*
Breach of A1P1	*Ásmundsson v Iceland*	*Maggio and Others v Italy*

Source: Own elaboration.

The examination starts by grouping the case law analysis following the dimensions of Table 6.1. On the one hand, there are cases concerning total deprivation of benefits, and on the other hand, those that deal with partial reductions. For each category, the analysis unfolds in two steps. The first step describes the facts of each case and examines the legal reasoning of the Court to arrive at each decision. Mapping these elements shows how the Court calibrates its review when the 'essence' of the right is alleged to be undermined. The second step distils the argumentative patterns that emerge across these judgments. They reveal how and when the Court shifts from deferential to more demanding scrutiny and what type of thresholds trigger that shift. These patterns involve examining several factors that surround the interference. As it will be clear, the elements governing that behaviour are the scale and permanence of the reduction, the contributory or non-contributory nature of the benefit, and the applicant's degree of vulnerability. Identifying these elements allows us to outline the practical limits of permissible pension reform under A1P1. This provides both legal scholars and policymakers with a framework for understanding the boundaries that the Convention imposes on pension reforms.

i. Total Deprivation of Benefits

Total deprivation of benefits represents one of the clearest and most intrusive forms of interference with pension entitlements under A1P1. In theory, such measures should trigger the Court's highest scrutiny, as they come closest to undermining the 'essence' of the right. Ultimately, the total deprivation of benefits is equated to an expropriation of someone's ownership. But triggering the highest scrutiny does not lead to an automatic violation of A1P1. Such a judgment depends on contextual factors like the distribution of the burden, the presence of alternative means, or the individual's reliance on the benefit. This subsection examines two leading judgments concerning total deprivation of pension benefits with radically different outcomes: *Ásmundsson v Iceland*,[143] where the Court found a violation of A1P1; and *Fábián v Hungary*,[144] where the Court did not. Comparing the reasoning in

[143] *Kjartan Ásmundsson v Iceland* (n 50).
[144] *Fábián v Hungary* (n 16).

each decision makes it possible to isolate the arguments that define the result of the proportionality assessment.

a. *Ásmundsson v Iceland*

Ásmundsson v Iceland concerned the permanent withdrawal of a disability pension that the applicant had received for nearly two decades. As part of a reform aimed at addressing the pension fund's financial deficit, the Icelandic legislature permanently discontinued payments for a narrowly defined subgroup of beneficiaries. The applicant belonged to one of just 54 disability pensioners affected, while the overwhelming majority – 689 pensioners – continued receiving benefits in full.[145]

The Court began by confirming that the pension constituted a 'possession' and that the reform amounted to interference with its peaceful enjoyment. It further recognised that the measure pursued a sufficiently grounded public interest, as it aimed to restore the fund's financial balance. The Court also acknowledged that in socio-economic policy, states enjoy a wide margin of appreciation, though it stressed that this margin is not absolute.[146]

In the balancing procedure, the Court's analysis centred on whether the burden of reform was fairly distributed. The Court found that the selective nature of the deprivation, which fell entirely on a small minority while sparing the majority, amounted to a disproportionate impact on the applicant's rights. This distributional inequity also formed the basis for a violation of Article 14, which the Court considered 'must carry great weight' in the proportionality analysis under A1P1:

> [T]he Court is struck by the fact that the applicant belonged to a small group of 54 disability pensioners (some 15% of the 336 persons mentioned above) whose pensions, unlike those of any other group, were discontinued altogether on 1 July 1997. The above-mentioned legitimate concerns about the need to resolve the Fund's financial difficulties seem hard to reconcile with the fact that after 1 July 1997 the vast majority of the 689 disability pensioners continued to receive disability benefits at the same level as before the adoption of the new rules, whereas only a small minority of disability pensioners had to bear the most drastic measure of all, namely the total loss of their pension entitlements. In the Court's view, although changes made to pension entitlements may legitimately take into account the pension holders' needs, the above differential treatment in itself suggests that the impugned measure was unjustified for the purposes of Article 14 of the Convention, which consideration must carry great weight in the assessment of the proportionality issue under Article 1 of Protocol No. 1.[147]

The Court further emphasised the severity of the measure on the applicant.[148] The applicant lost his entire benefit, despite having reasonably relied on its

[145] *Kjartan Ásmundsson v Iceland* (n 50).
[146] ibid.
[147] ibid 43.
[148] ibid 44.

continuation, especially since the previous system explicitly allowed disability pensioners to engage in alternative employment. The Court stated:

> In the Court's view, the applicant could validly plead an individual legitimate expectation that his disability would continue to be assessed on the basis of his incapacity to perform his previous job. Regard should be had to the fact that, under the former rules, gainful employment was not incompatible with a Fund member's receipt of a full disability pension, provided that that pension did not exceed the member's loss of income. Understandably, after becoming unfit for work as a seaman, and encouraged by the pension system to which he had contributed over a number of years, the applicant, like many other disability pensioners, had pursued alternative employment whilst at the same time receiving a disability pension.[149]

The judgment highlights how the abrupt termination of the applicant's entitlement exacerbated the disproportionality of the measure and undermined the essence of the applicant's property right under A1P1. This emphasis on the applicant's legitimate expectations illustrates a recurring feature in the Court's approach: when long-standing entitlements, fostered by a stable legal framework, are abruptly withdrawn without transitional measures, the interference is more likely to be seen as striking at the essence of the right. In such cases, the margin of appreciation narrows, and the proportionality assessment shifts in favour of the claimant.

Finally, the Court noted that the state had not considered less intrusive alternatives. A reasonable and proportionate reduction could have achieved the same fiscal objectives. The absence of such consideration reinforced the conclusion that the applicant had been made to bear an 'excessive and disproportionate burden', in breach of A1P1.[150]

b. *Fábián v Hungary*

Fábián v Hungary concerned a legislative reform suspending the payment of early retirement pensions to individuals employed in the public sector. The applicant, a former police officer, had been drawing an early retirement pension when he accepted a job in the public administration. Under the new rules, pensioners who took up or continued public sector employment would have their pension payments suspended for the duration of their employment. The applicant challenged this measure, arguing that it constituted a disproportionate and discriminatory deprivation of his property rights.

The Court accepted that the applicant's pension constituted a 'possession' under A1P1 and that suspending its payment while he remained in public employment amounted to an interference with its peaceful enjoyment. However, it characterised the measure not as a permanent deprivation, but as a temporary suspension

[149] ibid 44.
[150] ibid 45.

contingent on the applicant's choice to remain in public service. This distinction placed the case closer to a regulatory measure than to the total expropriation, which was the interference at stake in *Ásmundsson*. The classification was important, as it framed the proportionality review within the context of social-security policy, where states enjoy a wide margin of appreciation.[151]

The Hungarian government justified the suspension as part of a broader reform aimed at promoting the efficient use of public funds and addressing perceived inequities in allowing individuals to receive both a public salary and a public pension simultaneously. The Court recognised such a justification as being in the public interest and as within the wide margin of appreciation afforded to states in shaping social and economic policy.[152]

In the fair balance step, the Court reiterated that the margin of appreciation involves the fact that the interference with an individual's rights is reasonable and proportional. To assess the degree of proportionality, the Court identified three factors as being relevant:

> In examining whether the national authorities acted within their margin of appreciation in the instant case, the Court will have particular regard to the following factors which, from an analysis of its case-law in cases relating to the reduction, suspension or discontinuance of social-security pensions, may be identified as being of relevance, namely the extent of the loss of benefits, whether there was an element of choice, and the extent of the loss of means of subsistence.[153]

The extent of the loss of benefits appears to be a significant factor for the Court. That factor determines the degree of scrutiny under A1P1. However, the Court asserts that this factor alone is not decisive. It is merely another variable to consider in the overall assessment of the interference.[154] In this case, unlike *Ásmundsson*, where the deprivation was permanent and absolute, the suspension of the benefit applied only as long as the applicant remained in public-sector employment. His pension rights were not extinguished but deferred, and could be reinstated in full upon leaving his job.

The second factor is whether an element of choice was involved. This factor examines whether the applicant had any options or opportunities to avoid or prevent the suspension of their welfare entitlement. In the present case, the Court reasonably determined that the applicant could not have known what changes the government would make to his entitlement when he accepted the public sector job.[155] Also, it would be absurd ('disingenuous', says the Court) to hold that the applicant had an element of choice because he could not have taken the public sector job.[156] Instead, the relevant factor is whether, after the new law was enacted,

[151] *Fábián v Hungary* (n 16) [65].
[152] *Fábián v Hungary* (n 16).
[153] ibid 73.
[154] ibid 75.
[155] ibid 76.
[156] ibid.

the applicant was allowed to choose between having his pension or keeping his salary, knowing already the consequences of each decision. In the summary of the facts, it is clear that the applicant understood the implications of accepting this new job.[157]

The last factor is the extent of the loss of means of subsistence. This factor assesses the degree to which the measure's outcome impacts the applicant's ability to sustain their livelihood. The greater the impact on their means of living, the greater the incompatibility with A1P1.[158] If the benefit constitutes the sole source of income to an individual, then a total deprivation of the benefit without much alternative would be disproportionate. This factor did not arise in the present case, considering that the applicant would receive a salary which would meet his living expenses.

These considerations led the Court to conclude that the interference was proportionate to the aims pursued, and therefore, there was no breach of A1P1.[159]

The Court's reasoning in *Ásmundsson* and *Fábián* illustrates that the ECtHR does not automatically declare a breach of A1P1 solely because an entitlement is entirely withdrawn. Total and permanent deprivation increases the intensity of review, but compatibility with A1P1 depends on how the measure interacts with five factors. First, the temporality of the measure: permanent withdrawals trigger higher scrutiny of the state's reasons than temporary suspensions. Second, the magnitude of the interference: *Ásmundsson* shows that 'reasonable and commensurate reductions' act as a benchmark of compatibility, and departures from that threshold without justification increase the risk of a violation. Third, the distributional effects: targeting a narrowly defined group can render a measure discriminatory or disproportionate. Fourth, the claimant's ability to secure a basic livelihood after the reform: measures that leave individuals without means of subsistence are more likely to breach A1P1. Finally, the timing of the reform: sudden or retroactive changes intensify the degree of interference with the right.

The Court's review is an assessment of the interaction of all these factors. None of them is decisive on its own, although the loss of a basic means of subsistence is especially weighty. The outcome depends on how they play their role within the context of the case. These factors are also present in the Court's examination of partial reductions, as will be clear in the next section.

[157] ibid 76. Moreover, by keeping the job, the applicant continued to make contributions to the old-age system, which would improve the entitlement he already had whenever he decided to retire.

[158] I wrote elsewhere how such pattern distribution could be extrapolated to understand the problems caused by inflation in certain segments of the population, and what a consistent application of A1P1 would require for governments. Kevin Hartmann-Cortés, 'Should We Uprate Social Benefits for Inflation as a Matter of Article 1 Protocol 1?' (2022) 24 *European Journal of Social Security* 319.

[159] *Fábián v Hungary* (n 16) §83.The Court also examined the claim under Article 14. The applicant argued that only public sector workers were targeted by the measure, while private sector employees could continue to draw pensions alongside earnings. The Court rejected this claim, emphasising that differences between public and private employment fall within the discretion of the state. ibid §133.

ii. Partial Reduction of Benefits

Partial reductions of pensions are the most common interference under A1P1. Unlike total deprivations, these measures recalibrate existing entitlements rather than extinguishing them altogether. Partial reductions have been used recently in the context of the austerity measures undertaken by various Convention States as a way to rebalance the financial health of their social security systems in the context of the debt crisis of 2011.[160] These reforms were adopted in countries like Hungary, Portugal, Greece and Italy. Some of them were drastic legislative changes, resulting in a real reduction of pension amounts for those who were already entitled to claim and receive those benefits.[161]

The Italian pension reform of 2010 is particularly instructive. In the wake of the global financial crisis, Italy faced mounting public debt and an urgent need to consolidate public finances.[162] As pensions represented a large share of public spending, they became a primary target for reform. Alongside a rapidly ageing population and declining fertility rates, these pressures drove measures to contain costs and ensure long-term sustainability.[163] The reform included three relevant changes: a gradual increase in the retirement age, stricter criteria for early retirement, and a revision of the pension calculation formula.[164] The latter change led to a recalculation of pension entitlements for some of the beneficiaries.[165]

From this reform, two cases made it to the ECtHR: *Maggio and others v Italy*[166] and *Stefanetti and others v Italy*.[167] The applicants in both cases suffered a reduction

[160] Papadopoulos and Roumpakis (n 9); Theodoros Papadopoulos and Antonios Roumpakis, 'Democracy, Austerity and Crisis: Southern Europe and the Decline of the European Social Model' in S Romano and G Punziano (eds), *The European Social Model Adrift* (Routledge 2016); Sofia A Perez and Manos Matsaganis, 'The Political Economy of Austerity in Southern Europe' in A Jonston (ed), *Is the European Union Capable of Integrating Diverse Models of Capitalism?* (Routledge 2021); David Natali and Furio Stamati, 'Reassessing South European Pensions after the Crisis: Evidence from Two Decades of Reforms' in M Petmesidou and AM Guillén (ed), *Economic Crisis and Austerity in Southern Europe* (Routledge 2017); Karl Hinrichs, 'Recent Pension Reforms in Europe: More Challenges, New Directions. An Overview' (2021) 55 *Social Policy & Administration* 409; Manos Matsaganis and Chrysa Leventi, 'The Distributional Impact of Austerity and the Recession in Southern Europe' in M Petmesidou and AM Guillén (ed), *Economic Crisis and Austerity in Southern Europe* (Routledge 2017); Dafni Diliagka, *The Legality of Public Pension Reforms in Times of Financial Crisis: The Case of Greece* (Nomos Verlagsgesellschaft mbH & Co KG 2018) www.nomos-elibrary.de/index.php?doi=10.5771/9783845291574.

[161] Papadopoulos and Roumpakis (n 9); Papadopoulos and Roumpakis (n 160); Perez and Matsaganis (n 160); Natali and Stamati (n 160); Hinrichs (n 160); Matsaganis and Leventi (n 160); Diliagka (n 160).

[162] I Guardiancich and D Natali, 'German and Italian Pensions: Similar Roots, Different Reform Paths, Comparable Trajectories?' (2021) 30(3) *German Politics* 403–21.

[163] ibid.

[164] Giovanni Amerigo Giuliani, 'The Distributive Implications of Welfare Reform Packages. The Italian Case during and after the Great Crisis' (2021) 22 *European Politics and Society* 589.

[165] ibid. Over this point, an interesting finding in the literature suggests that increasing retirement ages allows for middle-age individuals to react to the longer working horizon by modifying their health-related behaviour. Marco Bertoni, Giorgio Brunello and Gianluca Mazzarella, 'Does Postponing Minimum Retirement Age Improve Healthy Behaviors Before Retirement? Evidence From Middle-Aged Italian Workers' (2018) 58 *Journal of Health Economics* 215.

[166] *Maggio and Others v Italy* (n 39).

[167] *Stefanetti and others v Italy* (n 51).

in their benefits. In *Maggio*, the reduction amounted to approximately 25 per cent[168] of their net benefit and in *Stefanetti* to about 67 per cent.[169]

The divergent outcomes of *Maggio* and *Stefanetti* can be explained by three interrelated factors that structure the Court's proportionality analysis under A1P1. The first signals how closely the Court should look at the case. It concerns the scale of the interference: the larger the reduction, the more demanding the scrutiny and the more reduced the margin of appreciation. The second identifies exactly what must be protected by A1P1 in cases of ad hoc reductions. It relates to the nature of the entitlement, particularly the distinction between contributory and non-contributory schemes, which reflects different forms of reliance. The third factor determines whose claim requires the most demanding justification from the government. It refers to the degree of dependency and vulnerability of the applicants, assessed in light of their position in the income scale and their capacity to maintain a minimum standard of living after the reduction. Together, these factors explain why some pension reforms fall within the margin of appreciation, while others are judged to have impaired the essence of the right. The following sections examine each of them in turn.

a. The Scale of the Interference

The first factor is the scale of the reduction. At first sight, the different outcomes in *Maggio* and *Stefanetti* might be explained by the numerical disparity between them. It would be tempting to infer that the Court drew a line between permissible and impermissible reductions somewhere between the two percentages of reduction. Yet the Court has been careful in not turning quantitative indicators into the 'essence' of the right itself. The size of the reduction matters not as a rule in itself, but because it signals the need for closer scrutiny of whether the reform preserved the substance of the entitlement. In fact, the Court has consistently reiterated that A1P1 does not guarantee any right to a pension of a particular amount.[170] Therefore, much as in cases of total deprivation, the fact of extinguishment frames, but does not resolve, the proportionality assessment. The size of the reduction matters only as one of the factors to define whether an interference impaired the 'essence' of the right under A1P1.

In *Maggio*, this distinction is explicit. Although the applicants lost about a quarter of their expected benefits, the Court emphasised that such a loss remained 'reasonable and commensurate', and thus compatible with the continued enjoyment of the entitlement:

> On the basis of these calculations the Court observes that the first applicant lost considerably less than half of his pension … [t]he Court considers that the applicant

[168] *Maggio and Others v Italy* (n 39) §38.
[169] *Stefanetti and others v Italy* (n 51) §57.
[170] *Maggio and Others v Italy* (n 39) §55. The ECtHR insisted in arguing that: 'Article 1 of Protocol No. 1 does not guarantee as such any right to become the owner of property … Nor does it guarantee, as such, any right to a pension of a particular amount'.

> was obliged to endure a reasonable and commensurate reduction … In consequence, the applicant's right to derive benefits from the social insurance scheme in question has not been infringed in a manner resulting in the impairment of the essence of his pension rights.[171]

Here, the numerical reduction operated as a contextual indicator of scale, but the judgment turned on whether the cut undermined the normative substance of the entitlement – adequacy, fairness and proportionality – rather than the figure itself. This is clarified in *Stefanetti*, where the scale of the cut prompted the Court to subject the reform to more demanding review. In that case, what proved decisive to determine that there was a breach of A1P1 was the inadequacy of the remaining benefits and the absence of safeguards ensuring a fair distribution of burdens. The Court underscored this point explicitly, drawing a comparison with *Maggio*:

> [I]n Maggio and Others, cited above, the fact that the applicant had lost considerably less than half of his pension, which therefore amounted to a reasonable and commensurate reduction, undeniably carried some weight in the finding that the provision had not been breached.[172]

And noticed that:

> Given the more substantial reduction in the present case and in view of the total contribution of the applicants, the Court must *reassess the matter and scrutinise the reduction more closely* in the context of the case.[173]

The closer scrutiny revealed that the applicants were left with pensions insufficient to guarantee a basic standard of living. The Court noted:

> Moreover, the Court observes that the government gave no information as to the quality of life one could expect to have on the basis of the sums received in pension by the applicants. In that light the Court cannot but find guidance in the conclusions of the European Committee of Social Rights and it therefore considers that if the sum of EUR 461 is inadequate as a minimum pension, the majority of the sums at issue, which do not exceed EUR 1,000 a month, must be considered as providing for only basic commodities. Thus, the reductions have undoubtedly affected the applicants' way of life and hindered its enjoyment substantially. The same can also be said of the higher pensions, despite them allowing for more comfortable living.[174]

On this basis, the Court concluded that the applicants:

> [F]ollowing a life-time of paying contributions, by losing 67% of their pensions the applicants had not suffered commensurate reductions but were in fact made to bear an excessive burden. Thus, despite the reasons behind the impugned measures, in the present cases, the Court cannot find that a fair balance was struck.[175]

[171] ibid §63.
[172] *Stefanetti and others v Italy* (n 51) §58.
[173] Ibid (emphasis added).
[174] *Stefanetti and others v Italy* (n 51).
[175] ibid §66.

The Court's reasoning demonstrates that the declaration of A1P1's violation did not emerge from the fact that the cut was two-thirds rather than one-quarter. The scale of the cut mattered because it triggered a more demanding review, which revealed three decisive weaknesses. First, the resulting pension was inadequate to preserve a dignified standard of living.[176] Adequacy is measured as a sufficiency threshold of the benefit entitlement relative to the total income of a given society, thereby reflecting the conclusions of the European Committee of Social Rights.[177] Second, the burden fell disproportionately on the claimants and was not sufficiently shared across society. Third, the long-standing balance between contributions and benefits was undermined. This last point implies that the Court reintroduces the distinction between contributory and non-contributory benefits as relevant for the 'fair balance test'. This point will be discussed in the following section.

b. The Nature of the Entitlement (Contributory versus Non-Contributory Pensions)

The second factor is the nature of the entitlement. In *Stefanetti*, the Court noted:

> The Court highlights that the present case concerns contributory benefits, and while it is true that the Court no longer makes a distinction between contributory and non-contributory benefits for the purposes of the applicability of the provision …, when assessing a reduction of social security payments, it is indeed of significance that such pensions were based on actual contributions paid by the applicants (transferred to the relevant disbursing authority), albeit lower than those paid by others, and that therefore they were not a gratuitous welfare aid solely funded by the tax-payer in general.[178]

At first sight, this reasoning may appear contradictory. Having abandoned the distinction for admissibility,[179] the Court nevertheless reintroduces it at the proportionality stage. This move could be seen, *prima facie*, as a doctrinal backlash. One might argue that it reinstates a hierarchy between entitlements, privileging those that resemble traditional 'private law' rights over non-contributory benefits, thereby echoing the Court's earliest distinctions about which claims merited protection.[180] However, this is not a case of doctrinal regression or inconsistency. The distinction is not reintroduced to establish a hierarchy but to clarify how arbitrariness should be understood in each scheme.

[176] ibid §64.

[177] There is not a single way of measuring such adequacy. It depends greatly on the type of objectives set by each social security arrangement. As explained by Sergio Nisticò: 'Assessment of the adequacy of pensions awarded to retiring workers should also be made in the light of the aim that the pension system seeks to achieve. One and the same average pension disbursed by a pension system can be considered either generous, if its aim is merely to prevent poverty among the elderly, or poor if disbursed by systems whose aim is to achieve consumption smoothing, especially in countries where average earnings are high. Moreover, seemingly low pensions could turn out to be fairly generous in a country where the elderly have access to various forms of support such as free health services, old-age care and housing allowances'. Sergio Nisticò, 'The Basic Concepts' [2019] *Essentials of Pension Economics* 5, 9.

[178] *Stefanetti and others v Italy* (n 51) §63.

[179] See chs 4 and 5.

[180] See ch 4 on the formalistic view of pensions as property at the admissibility stage.

Table 6.2 Defining the 'essence' of pension entitlements under A1P1

Scheme type	Essence trigger(s)
Non-contributory	**Adequacy** threatened (subsistence at risk)
Contributory	**Adequacy** threatened **or contribution–benefit proportionality** seriously undermined

Since A1P1 is fundamentally about protecting individuals against arbitrary governmental interference with their property, the question becomes how arbitrariness is defined in the context of pension entitlements. For the Court, the answer lies in the very justification that first led it to protect pensions as property: the degree of reliance of individuals on their benefits in modern welfare states.[181] Yet the nature of that reliance changes according to the type of benefit at stake. Table 6.2 synthesises exactly how to define the *essence* of pension entitlements under A1P1 as a function of the type of scheme.

Pensions are famously defined as claims to future output[182] and people in modern welfare states organise their future lives around them. Yet once retired, the nature of reliance on the pension system differs according to the type of benefit. Non-contributory benefits may be provided as a universal allowance, as in Beveridgean systems, or linked to an individual's earnings history, like in Bismarckian systems.[183] In either case, their primary purpose is to guarantee beneficiaries a minimum standard of living. Beneficiaries, therefore, do not expect a precise amount but instead rely on the state to preserve a benefit that meets an adequacy threshold. Contributory benefits, by contrast, have historically been structured around the proportionality of contributions and benefits at retirement. This proportionality was the central justification for the generalisation of these schemes across Europe.[184] Consequently, beneficiaries of such schemes can reasonably expect not merely some income in old age, but that this income preserves a reasonable proportion of what they had paid in.

Because reliance takes a different form in each scheme, the 'essence' of the right cannot mean the same across all pension entitlements. For non-contributory

[181] See ch 5 and the discussion of *Stec and Others v United Kingdom* (GC) ECHR 2006-VI (2006) 43 EHRR 47.

[182] This definition serves to reject a sharp distinction between PAYG and funded systems and can be found in the works of Nicholas Barr Nicholas Barr, *Economics of the Welfare State* (Oxford University Press, USA 2020); Nicholas Adrian Barr, *The Welfare State as Piggy Bank: Information, Risk, Uncertainty, and the Role of the State* (Oxford University Press 2001); Nicholas Barr and Peter Diamond, *Reforming Pensions: Principles and Policy Choices* (Oxford University Press 2008).

[183] Robin Blackburn, *Banking on Death: Or, Investing in Life: The History and Future of Pensions* (Verso Books 2002); Bruno Palier, *A Long Goodbye to Bismarck? The Politics of Welfare Reform in Continental Europe* (Amsterdam University Press 2010).

[184] Blackburn (n 183).

pensions, like in *Stec and Others v the United Kingdom*,[185] the essence lies in the degree to which a reform preserves adequacy, measured against an overall subsistence threshold. In the case of contributory pensions, the essence is dual: it consists of adequacy combined with the preservation of the contribution–benefit proportionality. Both *Maggio* and *Stefanetti* illustrate this point. In *Maggio*, the Court stressed that the reduction of a contributory pension remained 'reasonable and commensurate' precisely because the proportionality between contributions and benefits had not been undermined. In *Stefanetti*, by contrast, the sharp recalculation of contributory pensions meant that long-standing contributions no longer translated into a meaningful proportion of benefits, which the Court treated as a decisive element in finding a breach.

These examples show that the contributory/non-contributory distinction (...) is a matter of reliance instead of pure formal hierarchy: in contributory schemes, arbitrariness arises when proportionality between contributions and benefits breaks down. Yet reliance does not depend solely on the design of the scheme. It also varies with the individual's position within it, which is why dependency and vulnerability emerge as a third factor shaping the intensity of protection under A1P1.

c. The Vulnerability of the Applicant

The third and last factor is the vulnerability of the applicant. This factor captures the individualised dimension of the essence inquiry. While the scale of the reduction points to the objective severity of the measure, and the nature of the entitlement reflects the structural form of the beneficiaries' reliance, vulnerability addresses how these elements reflect in the claimant's concrete situation. It brings the analysis down to the level of the individual and determines whether, in practice, the essence of the right has been impaired.

Vulnerability is composed of two variables. The first is dependency, understood as the degree to which the pension constitutes the claimant's sole or primary source of income, and the availability (or absence) of alternative resources. Dependency was decisive *Stec and Others v the United Kingdom*,[186] where it justified extending A1P1's scope to all pension entitlements. The second element is the claimant's relative position in the income scale after the reform. This is measured against both the adequacy threshold of subsistence and, in the case of contributory schemes, the preservation of proportionality between contributions and benefits. Vulnerability is thus not only about how much has been lost but about what remains. Even a substantial cut may be compatible with A1P1 if the claimant is not dependent on the pension. At the same time, a modest reduction may be disproportionate if it pushes a highly dependent claimant below adequacy standards.[187]

[185] See ch 5 and *Stec and Others v the United Kingdom* (n 181).

[186] ibid. See ch 5.

[187] Over this idea I claimed somewhere else that A1P1 conveyed an underlying obligation for governments to uprate the benefits of people who were more vulnerable, even minor reductions in the real value of their benefit could potentially affect the 'essence' of their right and be declared disproportionate. See Hartmann-Cortés (n 158).

The Court has expressed this factor through what can be termed the 'means of subsistence' test. This test operates as a doctrinal device to assess whether the applicant retains sufficient income after the reform to secure basic living conditions. In practice, it links the abstract idea of adequacy with the claimant's concrete situation.

For non-contributory benefits, the test asks whether the remaining pension ensures access to essential goods and services necessary for subsistence. In *Stefanetti*, for instance, reductions of up to 67 per cent left applicants with pensions that the Court considered inadequate to cover more than 'basic commodities'. Referring to the European Committee of Social Rights, the Court found that such benefits failed to secure even a minimum quality of life, which led to a violation of A1P1. The same followed for cases of total deprivation. In *Ásmundsson*, the applicant's disability pension was permanently withdrawn, leaving him without any means of subsistence despite having relied on it for nearly two decades. The Court considered this a disproportionate burden that struck at the very core of the right.

For contributory benefits, the test further examines whether the reform preserved the proportionality between contributions and benefits, so that decades of contributions still translate into a reasonable share of retirement income. In *Maggio*, the Court emphasised that despite a 25 per cent cut, the proportionality remained intact and the reduced pension was still 'reasonable and commensurate'. By contrast, in *Stefanetti*, the recalculation destroyed this balance: long-standing contributions no longer yielded meaningful retirement income, which the Court treated as a decisive element in finding a breach.[188]

From the description of these three factors, it is clear that, as in cases of total deprivation, the Court does not treat a partial reduction as a breach in itself. It works with a set of factors that operate as levers in the fair balance test. Most are the same across both settings: the magnitude and duration of the cut, how the burden is distributed across beneficiaries, the timing and predictability of the measure, and, above all, what remains for the claimant in terms of means of subsistence. One lever plays a particularly distinctive role in partial-reduction disputes: the nature of the entitlement. For non-contributory schemes, the inquiry assesses adequacy against a subsistence threshold; for contributory schemes, it examines the contribution–benefit link and inquires whether proportionality has been compromised.

Taken together, these factors yield a single organising principle for identifying the essence of pension rights under A1P1. Compatibility under A1P1 is assessed against two constraints: that the claimant's benefit remain adequate, and, in contributory schemes, that the reform does not overturn the scheme's contributory nature. When either constraint is put at risk, the margin of appreciation narrows and the state's burden of justification increases. The following subsection frames this structure in normative terms, showing how the Court's analysis gives

[188] In *Fábián*, for instance, the suspension of the applicant's pension while he worked in the public sector was deemed compatible with A1P1, since his salary covered his living needs and the deprivation was temporary and conditional on his own choice.

greater weight to harms suffered by the most dependent claimants and how this *prioritarian* angle helps to explain the essence of the right in pension cases.

C. Prioritarian Reasoning and the Essence of Pension Benefits under A1P1

The case law on both total deprivation and partial reductions of pension benefits points to a single organising idea: the essence of A1P1 is defined contextually by three factors: (i) the scale of the interference, (ii) the nature of the entitlement and (iii) the vulnerability of the claimant. The same factors apply across both families of cases, and the Court adjusts the intensity of review by pulling the same levers to varying degrees as the facts change.

The margin of appreciation is generally wide in social-security matters, but it narrows, albeit exceptionally, when the interaction of these factors brings a measure close to arbitrariness. That occurs where adequacy is threatened, where proportionality between contributions and benefits collapses in contributory schemes, or where a claimant's subsistence is put at risk. In those cases, the Court moves towards a more demanding review and requires a higher argumentative burden from states.

On this view, the 'essence' of pension rights under A1P1 is not a fixed, abstract threshold. Instead, the essence is defined contextually, through the interaction of severity (scale of the measure), reliance (the scheme's design) and vulnerability (dependency and residual income). Taken together, these factors also reveal a normative rule within the Court's jurisprudence. The greater the claimant's vulnerability, the more demanding the proportionality review. In other words, as vulnerability increases, the margin of appreciation contracts. In that sense, the Court applies a form of *prioritarian* reasoning.

Prioritarianism is a principle of distributive justice that gives greater weight to benefits or protections for those who are worse off, even when the aggregate outcome is the same.[189] This distinguishes it from utilitarianism, which values all gains equally, and from sufficiency views, which focus only on whether a minimum threshold is met.[190] Applied to pensions under A1P1, this means that the Convention's property guarantee does not establish a flat property rule that applies equally to all claimants. Instead, it is calibrated to distributional effects. The intensity of protection tracks the interference's impact on the individual's situation, so harms to pensioners at or near subsistence call for stronger protection than equivalent harms to better-off claimants.

[189] Matthew D Adler and Nils Holtug, 'Prioritarianism: A Response to Critics' (2019) 18 *Politics, Philosophy & Economics* 101; Arneson (n 7); Richard J Arneson, 'Luck Egalitarianism and Prioritarianism' (2000) 110 *Ethics* 339.

[190] Adler and Holtug (n 189); Arneson (n 7); Arneson (n 189).

This reasoning suggests several policy lessons. Reforms are more likely to be compatible with A1P1 when they are temporary, moderate in scope, applied broadly and preserve a basic level of income. Even reforms establishing permanent cuts to benefits may be permissible if reductions are modest and individuals retain meaningful financial autonomy. By contrast, reforms that combine permanence, high magnitude, discriminatory targeting or the elimination of subsistence are almost certain to breach the Convention.

Certain aggravating factors, such as retroactivity, may still be tolerated when joined by mitigating elements like modest reductions, broad distribution or the preservation of income security. The overall assessment depends on how these features interact in a given case. Yet there is a hard limit: once a reform deprives individuals of the means to secure a basic livelihood, the 'essence' of the right is considered undermined, and no other configuration can justify the measure. In policy terms, this indicates that pension reforms are most likely to comply with A1P1 when they are temporary, proportionate, applied broadly rather than selectively and preserve a subsistence minimum. Where these conditions are absent, the scope of the margin of appreciation reduces, and the risk of A1P1's breach increases.

Two further implications follow for the design and justification of reforms. First, it confirms that A1P1's protection is functional. What matters is securing their function for an individual. In the case of non-contributory benefits, securing basic living standards, and, in the case of contributory entitlements, ensuring adequacy and proportional income replacement. Second, while A1P1 does not require states to guarantee a universal minimum to all,[191] it calibrates the strength of property protection as a function of the distributional effects of pension reforms on the beneficiary's specific situation. That means, concretely, that there are limits to the 'margin of appreciation' enjoyed by governments when designing their social policy.

The prioritarian reasoning of the Court imposes a burden on policymakers. Before legislating, they should undertake an ex ante distributional assessment with at least two elements: first, mapping dependency and residual income across affected cohorts, distinguishing contributory from non-contributory streams. Second, modelling post-reform adequacy against relevant subsistence benchmarks.

A reform must spread its burdens broadly, and less intrusive alternatives should be preferred. Transitional arrangements and targeted exemptions should be implemented to protect individuals at or near subsistence levels. For contributory schemes, the contribution–benefit relation should be monitored explicitly, with any recalibration justified as preserving the nature of contributory systems.

The previous analysis provides valuable guidance for applicants in framing their pension-related cases. Applicants can strengthen their case by demonstrating

[191] Leijten, 'The Right to Minimum Subsistence and Property Protection under the ECHR: Never the Twain Shall Meet?' (n 65).

high dependency, low residual income after the reform, and, where relevant, a breakdown of contribution–benefit proportionality. Evidence of selective burden-sharing or abrupt, retroactive changes could also support their claims. States, conversely, to avoid being held accountable for breaching A1P1, should present sufficient evidence about the broad burden-sharing of their reforms, the availability and evaluation of less restrictive options, the presence of transitional protections, and concrete proof that post-reform incomes remain adequate and, in contributory schemes, proportionate to lifetime contributions.

Finally, the Court's approach reflects a broader recognition that treating unequal cases alike can produce outcomes contrary to the Convention. By weighting its analysis according to the claimant's vulnerability, the Court avoids this risk. It ensures that those with the most to lose receive the strongest protection. This approach preserves the integrity of property rights while aligning their application with the principles of social justice. The prioritarian reasoning of A1P1's protection ensures that the necessary adjustments that most pension systems must introduce in the upcoming years do not come at the expense of those least able to withstand them.

Conclusions

This chapter examined how the ECtHR protects pension entitlements under A1P1. It uncovered two important adjudicative patterns that shape the Court's approach to pension-related claims.

The first pattern concerns the dual structure of the Court's reasoning. On one hand, the Court adopts a broadly liberal approach when defining what constitutes a 'possession' under A1P1. This has led to an inclusive approach to the recognition of all pension entitlements as interests that qualify for protection under the Convention's property clause. On the other hand, when assessing whether interferences with these entitlements are acceptable, the Court shifts to a more social-democratic logic. It does not treat pension rights as fixed or absolute entitlements but evaluates interferences in light of broader social and economic considerations. This logic is embedded in the acceptability test, which requires that any interference be lawful, serve a legitimate public aim, and strike a fair balance between the interests of the state and the rights of the individual. Within this framework, the Court grants states a wide margin of appreciation, particularly in areas involving complex policy decisions. However, it has also affirmed that this margin has limits: the core of the right must be preserved, and the disputed measures must not undermine the essence of the entitlement.

The second pattern concerns how the Court distributes the protection offered by A1P1. Contrary to the overall intuition on how A1P1 works, the Court does not apply the same intensity of review across all cases. Instead, its scrutiny increases when the interference affects individuals who are economically vulnerable or heavily dependent on their pension benefits. The jurisprudence shows that the Court is more willing to find a breach when a person is left without adequate means of subsistence or when the pension cut severely affects their standard of living. This reveals an implicit form of prioritarian reasoning: the Court's concern intensifies as the applicant's capacity to bear the burden diminishes. Although the Court does not explicitly articulate this principle, its decisions demonstrate a consistent logic in which the impact of a measure is weighed more heavily when it falls on those in weaker socio-economic positions.

These two patterns have two important implications. First, they show that a traditionally liberal right like property can serve distributive and protective functions within the welfare state. For legal doctrine, the findings suggest that greater clarity is needed in how the Court articulates the normative assumptions underpinning its proportionality assessments. A more explicit acknowledgement of the role of individual vulnerability and dependency could enhance the coherence and transparency of A1P1 case law. Second, policymakers, these insights point to a set of practical constraints. Pension reforms cannot simply be justified on grounds of fiscal necessity or public interest; they must also account for how their effects distribute burdens and gains, and ensure that those with the least capacity to adjust are not left worse off, or under a reasonable line of adequacy.

Ultimately, the ECtHR's jurisprudence under A1P1 does not prevent states from reforming their pension systems. While it is clear that the norm cannot function as an emancipatory tool for the poor, it can nevertheless constrain disproportionate regressive burdens on those in precarious socio-economic conditions. The requirements set by the case law guide policymakers on how those reforms should be carried out in a way that respects the basic material needs of the most affected individuals. It underscores fairness in both process and outcome, particularly when the stakes involve access to basic income and human dignity at old age.

Pensions as property under the European Convention on Human Rights reflects a vision of property rights that is responsive to the current context of modern welfare states. By combining formal recognition of entitlements with context-sensitive adjudication, the Court provides a model for how socio-economic rights can be meaningfully protected within the existing framework of the Convention. This model, though limited, offers valuable guidance not only for pension law but for the broader field of social rights adjudication in Europe.

General Conclusions

This book examined how the European Court of Human Rights protects pensions as property under Article 1 of Protocol No 1 (A1P1) and how this framing has shaped pension reform. Over the course of more than 50 years, the case law has evolved in terms of what pension interests are protected, when protection attaches and how intensely interferences are reviewed.

The property framework adds two valuable elements to pensions. First, a common normative ground for the analysis and interpretation of pensions and pension entitlements. Seen from this angle, a pension is a possession when it is legally grounded in domestic law, has economic value and protection attaches when eligibility is met or a concrete legitimate expectation exists. This shared characterisation highlights the role of pensions in securing individual autonomy and freedom. It also replaces fragmented labels, improves predictability and lets actors compare like with like across systems. Second, a standard method of judgement for evaluating reforms. Any interference with pension rights must be lawful, pursue a public interest and be proportionate. This method organises the burden of proof and the type of reasons the State must offer, and it gives legislators, administrators, courts and litigants a standard set of conditions for Convention-compliant reform.

Seen from the other side, pensions have also shaped the development of the property framework under A1P1. They brought back into focus the core function of the property guarantee: protecting personal autonomy and independence. The Court recognised that, in modern welfare states, pensions are legally grounded income claims on which people rely to live in conditions of dignity. Protecting that reliance is what A1P1 must secure, and that insight produced two doctrinal moves. First, it clarified the ambit of property protection by shifting from a formalistic, funding-based screen to a functional view of which legal interests fall within A1P1, thereby expanding its material scope. Second, it helped define the core of protection by organising proportionality around reliance and dependency. In doing so, the Court reviews the severity and duration of the interference in light of the nature of the entitlement and the claimant's vulnerability. The nature of the entitlement sets the metric of arbitrariness. In contributory schemes, it also highlights the contribution–benefit relationship, while vulnerability is measured by dependency and residual income after the reform.

The case law on pensions under A1P1 further challenges two common misconceptions about the private property framework. The first is that this framework is indifferent to inequality and distribution. The case law contradicts this view. The Court explicitly considers the distributive outcomes of pension reforms when assessing their compatibility with the Convention. In fact, measures that place heavy costs on individuals, especially vulnerable retirees, attract heightened scrutiny. Where burdens are broad, moderated and supported by targeted protection, the Court's scrutiny relaxes.

The second misconception is that property is a right enjoyed by everyone at the same intensity in the abstract. The case law suggests otherwise. In pension cases, the Court reasons in a *prioritarian* manner: as the severity of the measure increases and as dependency and residual income indicate greater vulnerability, it narrows the margin of appreciation and raises the State's justificatory burden. Where states do not meet that argumentative burden, the protection of the entitlement prevails, and the interference is found disproportionate. A1P1's protective scope thus tracks vulnerability rather than applying evenly, yielding a graded intensity of protection that determines who is protected and to what extent.

Tracking the doctrinal history of A1P1's material scope expansion from a formalistic to a functional approach is another significant contribution of this book to the literature. This expansion, however, did not translate into stronger protection of pension entitlements against governmental interference. The resulting paradox of broader inclusion with modest success follows from the balance the Court has maintained between two competing views of property that have guided its reasoning since the early years. A liberal approach governs admissibility: the Court interprets 'possessions' broadly to cover a wide range of pecuniary interests, reflecting a special commitment to safeguard individual freedom and autonomy against arbitrary interference. A social democratic approach governs the proportionality stage. It treats the regulation of property as the norm in social and economic policy. That is why states enjoy a wide margin of appreciation in designing and implementing welfare policies. Only in exceptional cases, where a fair balance is not maintained, does the Court find a breach of the Convention.

These doctrinal insights offer some policy guidelines for lawmakers. First, governments should conduct thorough *ex-ante* distributive impact assessments to evaluate how pension reforms may affect different groups of retirees. Meeting the proportionality requirement of A1P1 demands fair burden sharing, avoiding reforms that place excessive costs on those most dependent on their benefit. Where a measure risks such an unfair burden, policymakers should reconsider or redesign the proposal to avoid breaching the Convention. Second, A1P1 favours gradual reform over abrupt change. Sudden changes undermine legal certainty and can expose vulnerable retirees to economic insecurity. The Court's case law also suggests the importance of transitional or compensatory measures for those nearing retirement who lack the capacity to adjust plans late in life. That being said, it is also relevant to underscore that the property framework does not require states to guarantee a minimum pension to anyone, nor does it require states to ensure a specific pension level for anyone. Ultimately, A1P1 primarily serves as a limitation on state action.

This book opens several avenues for future research. For instance, exploring an intergenerationally sensitive property approach, given that current doctrine offers limited protection to those who have yet to meet the eligibility conditions. Moreover, comparative legal analysis could explore how different constitutional systems address this question, and whether doctrines such as legitimate expectations might evolve to offer some form of protection for future retirees. Finally, some doctrinal work might also expand this analysis to test whether other social goods, such as healthcare, can or should be pursued through property-based guarantees where directly justiciable social rights are weak.

Pensions as property provides a workable grammar of justice for pension reform and a discipline for government. In a period of demographic change and fiscal pressure, it sets substantive limits on state action by requiring lawfulness, public interest, proportionality and fair burden sharing, so that reforms do not shift costs onto those least able to bear them. It insists that policymakers honour reliance and legitimate expectations, and justify their choices to those who bear the burdens. It is not a framework for total emancipation. Yet, it serves as a reliable check against regressive policies, and one on which citizens of the Council of Europe's Member States can effectively rely.

BIBLIOGRAPHY

Ackerman B, *Private Property and the Constitution* (Yale University Press 1977)

Adler MD and Holtug N, 'Prioritarianism: A Response to Critics' (2019) 18 *Politics, Philosophy & Economics* 101

Alexander GS, *Commodity & Propriety: Competing Visions of Property in American Legal Thought, 1776–1970* (University of Chicago Press 2008)

——, *Property and Human Flourishing* (Oxford University Press 2018)

——, 'A Statement of Progressive Property' (2008) 94 *Cornell Law Review* 743

Alexander GS and Peñalver EM, *An Introduction to Property Theory* (Cambridge University Press 2012)

Alexy R, 'On the Structure of Legal Principles' (2000) 13 *Ratio Juris* 294

——, 'On Balancing and Subsumption. A Structural Comparison' (2003) 16 *Ratio Juris* 433

——, *A Theory of Constitutional Rights* (Oxford University Press 2010)

Allen T, *Property and the Human Rights Act 1998* (Hart Publishing 2005)

——, 'Liberalism, Social Democracy and the Value of Property under the European Convention on Human Rights' (2010) 59 *International & Comparative Law Quarterly* 1055

Alonso-García J, Boado-Penas M del C and Devolder P, 'Adequacy, Fairness and Sustainability of Pay-as-You-Go-Pension-Systems: Defined Benefit versus Defined Contribution' (2018) 24 *The European Journal of Finance* 1100

Altiparmakov N and Nedeljković M, '25 Years of Averting the Old Age Crisis in Eastern Europe' (2022) 22 *Global Social Policy* 84

Andersen TM and Bhattacharya J, 'The Intergenerational Welfare State and the Rise and Fall of Pay-as-You-Go Pensions' (2015) 127 *The Economic Journal* 896

Anderson D, 'Compensation for Interference with Property' [1999] *European Human Rights Law Review* 543

Arnardóttir OM, 'Res Interpretata, Erga Omnes Effect and the Role of the Margin of Appreciation in Giving Domestic Effect to the Judgments of the European Court of Human Rights' (2017) 28 *European Journal of International Law* 819

——, 'Res Interpretata, Erga Omnes Effect and the Role of the Margin of Appreciation in Giving Domestic Effect to the Judgments of the European Court of Human Rights' (2017) 28 *European Journal of International Law* 819

Arneson RJ, 'Luck Egalitarianism and Prioritarianism' (2000) 110 *Ethics* 339

——, *Prioritarianism* (Cambridge University Press 2022)

Arnold R, 'European Constitutionalism after the Second World War' in Susana Galera (ed), *Judicial Review, a Comparative Analysis inside the European Legal System* (Council of Europe 2010)

Barak A, *Proportionality: Constitutional Rights and Their Limitations* (Cambridge University Press 2012)

Baroness Hale, 'Common Law and Convention Law: The Limits to Interpretation' [2011] *European Human Rights Law Review* 534

Barr N, *Economics of the Welfare State* (Oxford University Press, USA 2020)

Barr N and Diamond P, 'The Economics of Pensions' (2006) 22 *Oxford Review of Economic Policy* 15

——, *Reforming Pensions: Principles and Policy Choices* (Oxford University Press 2008)

Barr NA, *The Welfare State as Piggy Bank: Information, Risk, Uncertainty, and the Role of the State* (Oxford University Press 2001)

Bates E, *The Evolution of the European Convention on Human Rights: From Its Inception to the Creation of a Permanent Court of Human Rights* (Oxford University Press 2010)

Beechey SN, *Social Security and the Politics of Deservingness* (Springer 2016)

Bentham J, 'The Theory of Legislation' in J Plamenatz (ed), *Readings from Liberal Writers* (Routledge 1950)
Bernhardt R, 'Human Rights and Judicial Review: The European Court of Human Rights' in DM Beatty (ed), *Human Rights and Judicial Review: A Comparative Perspective* (Brill Nijhoff 1994)
Bertoni M, Brunello G and Mazzarella G, 'Does Postponing Minimum Retirement Age Improve Healthy Behaviors Before Retirement? Evidence From Middle-Aged Italian Workers' (2018) 58 *Journal of Health Economics* 215
Besson S, 'The Erga Omnes Effect of Judgments of the European Court of Human Rights: What's in a Name?' in S Besson (ed), *The European Court of Human Rights after Protocol 14* (Schulthess 2011)
——, 'Subsidiarity in International Human Rights Law: What Is Subsidiary about Human Rights?' (2016) 61 *The American Journal of Jurisprudence* 69
——, 'In What Sense Are Economic Rights Human Rights? Departing from Their Naturalistic Reading in International Human Rights Law' in J Queralt and B van der Vossen (eds), *Economic Liberties and Human Rights* (Routledge 2019)
Bilchitz D, 'Socio-Economic Rights, Economic Crisis, and Legal Doctrine' (2014) 12 *International Journal of Constitutional Law* 710
Bingham T, *The Rule of Law* (Allen Lane 2010)
Blackburn R, *Banking on Death: Or, Investing in Life: The History and Future of Pensions* (Verso Books 2002)
Blackstone W, *Commentaries on the Laws of England in Four Books. Notes Selected from the Editions of Archibold, Christian, Coleridge, Chitty, Stewart, Kerr, and Others, Barron Field's Analysis, and Additional Notes, and a Life of the Author by George Sharswood. In Two Volumes*, vol 1 (JB Lippincott Co 1893)
Blanchet D and Villeneuve B, 'Que Reste-t-Il Du Débat Répartition-Capitalisation?' [1997] *Revue d'économie financière* 157
Boot ER, 'Public Interest' in *Oxford Research Encyclopedia of Politics* (Oxford University Press 2022)
——, 'The Public Interest: Clarifying a Legal Concept' (2024) 37 *Ratio Juris* 110
Boulhol H and Lüske M, 'What's New in the Debate About Pay-as-You-Go Versus Funded Pensions?' in N da Costa Cabral and N Cunha Rodrigues (eds), *The Future of Pension Plans in the EU Internal Market: Coping with Trade-Offs Between Social Rights and Capital Markets* (Springer 2019)
Bovenberg L and Van Ewijk C, 'Designing the Pension System: Conceptual Framework' in L Bovenberg, C van Ewijk and E Westerhout (eds), *The Future of Multi-Pillar Pensions* (Cambridge University Press 2011)
——, 'The Future of Multi-Pillar Pension Systems' in L Bovenberg, C van Ewijk and E Westerhout (eds), *The Future of Multi-Pillar Pension Systems* (Cambridge University Press 2011)
Boyle K, 'The European Experience: The European Convention on Human Rights' (2009) 40 *Victoria University of Wellington Law Review* 167
Brauch JA, 'The Margin of Appreciation and the Jurisprudence of the European Court of Human Rights: Threat to the Rule of Law' (2004) 11 *Columbia Journal of European Law* 113
Brems E, 'Conflicting Human Rights: An Exploration in the Context of the Right to a Fair Trial in the European Convention for the Protection of Human Rights and Fundamental Freedoms' (2005) 27 *Human Rights Quarterly* 294
——, 'Positive Subsidiarity and Its Implications for the Margin of Appreciation Doctrine' (2019) 37 *Netherlands Quarterly of Human Rights* 210
Brems E and Lavrysen L, '"Don't Use a Sledgehammer to Crack a Nut": Less Restrictive Means in the Case Law of the European Court of Human Rights' (2015) 15 *Human Rights Law Review* 139
Brudner A, Penner J and Smith H, 'Private Property and Public Welfare' in J Penner and H Smith (eds), *Philosophical Foundations of Property Law* (Oxford University Press 2014)
Bussiere E, 'The "New Property" Theory of Welfare Rights: Promises and Pitfalls' (2004) 13 *The Good Society* 1
Calabresi G and Melamed AD, 'Property Rules, Liability Rules, and Inalienability: One View of the Cathedral' in RA Epstein (ed), *Modern Understandings of Liberty and Property* (Routledge 2000)

Carbonnier J, 'Les Biens: (Monnaie, Immeubles, Meubles)' in J Carbonnier, *Droit Civil, Tome 3, Les Biens* 21st edn (Presses Universitaires de France, 2000)
Carone G and others, 'Pension Reforms in the EU since the Early 2000's: Achievements and Challenges Ahead' [2016] European Economy Discussion Paper
Cass RA, 'Property Rights Systems and the Rule of Law' [2003] Available at SSRN 392783
Cassese S, 'Ruling Indirectly. Judicial Subsidiarity in the ECtHR', paper for the Seminar on 'Subsidiarity: a double sided coin? 1. The role of the Convention mechanism; 2. The role of the national authorities', held to coincide with the ceremony marking the official opening of the judicial year of the European Court of Human Rights, 30 January 2015, Strasbourg
Castel R, *L'insécurité Sociale: Qu'est-Ce Qu'être Protégé?* (Seuil 2004)
——, *La Montée Des Incertitudes: Travail, Protections, Statut de l'individu* (Seuil 2009)
Chen T and others, *Inequality and Poverty across Generations in the European Union* (International Monetary Fund 2018)
Christoffersen J, *Fair Balance: Proportionality, Subsidiarity and Primarity in the European Convention on Human Rights*, vol 99 (Brill 2009)
Christoffersen J and Madsen MR, *The European Court of Human Rights between Law and Politics* (Oxford University Press 2011)
Cousins M, 'Legitimate Expectation and Social Security Law Under the European Convention of Human Rights' (2021) 23 *European Journal of Social Security* 24
Cremer H and Pestieau P, 'Reforming Our Pension System: Is It a Demographic, Financial or Political Problem?' (2000) 44 *European Economic Review* 974
Dagan H, 'The Social Responsibility of Ownership' (2006) 92 *Cornell Law Review* 1255
——, *Property: Values and Institutions* (Oxford University Press 2011)
De Mars B, Pieters D and Schoukens P, '"Security"' as General Principle of Social Security Law in Europe: Conclusions on Legislative Aspects' in B De Mars, D Pieters and P Schoukens (eds), *Security: A General Principle of Social Security Law in Europe* (Europa Law Publishing 2010)
De Schutter O, *International Human Rights Law. Cases, Materials, Commentary* 3rd edn (Cambridge University Press 2019)
de Szaszy E, 'Doctrine Des Droits Acquis En Droit Transitoire Ou Intertemporal, La' (1936) 17 *Revue de Droit International et de Législation Comparée* 406
De Witte K, *De juridische kwalificatie van het recht op pensioen* (KULeuven 2017)
Dembour M-B, 'Gaygusuz Revisited: The Limits of the European Court of Human Rights' Equality Agenda' (2012) 12 *Human Rights Law Review* 689
Denza E, 'The Relationship between International and National Law' (2014) 4 *International Law* 412
Detienne Q, *Droit Économique Européen et Systèmes de Pension de Retraite Nationaux. Quelles Influences Pour Quels Résultats?* (Presses Universitaires de Liège 2023)
Devolder P and De Valeriola S, 'Pension Design and Risk Sharing: Mixed Solutions Between Defined Benefit and Defined Contribution for Public Pension Schemes' in M Peris-Ortíz, J Álvarez-García, I Domínguez-Fabián and P Devolder (eds), *Economic Challenges of Pension Systems: A Sustainability and International Management Perspective* (Springer 2020) 311
Devolder P, Levantesi S and Menzietti M, 'Automatic Balance Mechanisms for Notional Defined Contribution Pension Systems Guaranteeing Social Adequacy and Financial Sustainability: An Application to the Italian Pension System' (2021) 299 *Annals of Operations Research* 765
Dewhurst E and Diliagka D, 'Increasing Pension Ages in Greece and Ireland: A Question of Legitimate Expectations' (2014) 16 *European Journal of Social Security* 225
Diamond M, 'The Meaning and Nature of Property: Homeownership and Shared Equity in the Context of Poverty' (2009) 29 *Saint Louis University Public Law Review* 85
Diamond P, 'Insulation of Pensions from Political Risk' in Salvador Valdes-Prieto (ed), *The Economics of Pensions, Principles, Policies and International Experience* (Cambridge University Press 1997)
Diliagka D, *The Legality of Public Pension Reforms in Times of Financial Crisis: The Case of Greece* (Nomos Verlagsgesellschaft mbH & Co KG 2018)

Dixon AD, 'The Rise of Pension Fund Capitalism in Europe: An Unseen Revolution?' (2008) 13 *New Political Economy* 249
Donnelly J, *Universal Human Rights in Theory and Practice* (Cornell University Press 2013)
Dorn JA, 'Pension Reform in China: A Question of Property Rights' (2003) 23 *Cato Journal* 433
Drahokoupil J and Domonkos S, 'Averting the Funding-Gap Crisis: East European Pension Reforms since 2008' (2012) 12 *Global Social Policy* 283
Duguit L, *Les Transformations Générales Du Droit Privé Depuis Le Code Napoléon* (Falcan 1920)
Dukeminier J and others, *Property* (Aspen Publishing 2017)
Dupeyroux J-J, Borgetto M and Lafore R, *Droit de La Sécurité Sociale*, vol 18 (Dalloz 2015)
Duxbury N, 'Ex Post Facto Law' (2013) 58 *The American Journal of Jurisprudence* 135
Dworkin R, *Law's Empire* (Hart Publishing 1998)
——, 'Rights as Trumps' in Jeremy Waldron (ed), *Theories of Rights* (Oxford University Press 2009)
Ebbinghaus B and Möhring K, 'Studying the Politics of Pension Reforms and Their Social Consequences' in K Nelson, R Nieuwenhuis and MA Yerkes (eds), *Social Policy in Changing European Societies* (Edward Elgar 2022)
Ebbinghaus B and Wiß T, 'The Political Economy of Pension Policy' in B Greve, A Moreira and M van Gerven (eds), *Handbook on the Political Economy of Social Policy* (Edward Elgar Publishing 2024)
Ely JW, *The Guardian of Every Other Right: A Constitutional History of Property Rights* (Oxford University Press 2008)
Epstein RA, *Takings: Private Property and the Power of Eminent Domain* (Harvard University Press 1985)
Esping-Andersen G, *The Three Worlds of Welfare Capitalism* (Polity 1990)
European Commission, 'European Semester Thematic Factsheet: Adequacy and Sustainability of Pensions'
Fabre C, *Social Rights under the Constitution: Government and the Decent Life* (Oxford University Press 2000)
Fallon Jr RH, 'The Core of an Uneasy Case for Judicial Review' (2007) 121 *Harvard Law Review* 1693
Feinberg J, 'Justice and Personal Desert' in M Friedman, L May, K Parsons and J Stiff (eds), *Rights and Reason: Essays in Honor of Carl Wellman* (Springer 1970)
Finnis J, *Natural Law and Natural Rights* (Oxford University Press 2011)
Follesdal A, 'The Legitimacy of International Human Rights Review: The Case of the European Court of Human Rights' (2009) 40 *Journal of Social Philosophy* 595
Fordham M and De La Mare T, 'Identifying the Principles of Proportionality' in J Jowel and J Cooper (eds), *Understanding Human Rights Principles* (Bloomsbury 2001)
Forsyth CF, 'The Provenance and Protection of Legitimate Expectations' (1988) 47 *The Cambridge Law Journal* 238
Fowkes J, 'Normal Rights, Just New: Understanding the Judicial Enforcement of Socioeconomic Rights' (2020) 68 *The American Journal of Comparative Law* 722
Freyfogle ET, 'Private Ownership and Human Flourishing: An Exploratory Overview' (2013) 24 *Stellenbosch Law Review* 430
Fried C, *Right and Wrong* (Harvard University Press 1978)
Friot B, *Le Travail, Enjeu Des Retraites* (Dispute (La) 2019)
Fuller L, *The Morality of Law* (Revised, Yale University Press 1969)
García Márquez G, *No One Writes to the Colonel* (Penguin UK 2014)
Gargarella R, *El Derecho Como Una Conversación Entre Iguales: Qué Hacer Para Que Las Democracias Contemporáneas Se Abran–Por Fin–al Diálogo Ciudadano* (Siglo XXI Editores 2021)
Gearty C, 'Human Rights: The Necessary Quest for Foundations' in Costas Douzinas and Conor Gearty (eds), *The Meanings of Rights: The Philosophy and Social Theory of Human Rights* (Cambridge University Press 2014)
Gérard M, 'Reform Options for Mature Defined Benefit Pension Plans: The Case of the Netherlands' (International Monetary Fund 2019) WP/19/22
Gerstenberg O, 'The Justiciability of Socio-Economic Rights, European Solidarity, and the Role of the Court of Justice of the EU' (2014) 33 *Yearbook of European Law* 245

Giuliani GA, 'The Distributive Implications of Welfare Reform Packages. The Italian Case during and after the Great Crisis' (2021) 22 *European Politics and Society* 589
Glackin SN, 'Back to Bundles: Deflating Property Rights, Again' (2014) 20 *Legal Theory* 1
Goldblatt B, 'The Right to Social Security' in M Langford and KG Young (eds), *The Oxford Handbook of Economic and Social Rights* (Oxford University Press 2022)
Gordley J, 'The State's Private Law and Legal Academia' (2008) 56 *The American Journal of Comparative Law* 639
Gosseries A and Hungerbühler M, 'Rule Change and Intergenerational Justice' in JC Tremmel (ed), *Handbook of Intergenerational Justice* (Edward Elgar 2006)
Gray K, 'Property in Thin Air' (1991) 50 *The Cambridge Law Journal* 252
Grech AG, 'Assessing the Sustainability of Pension Reforms in Europe' (2013) 29 *Journal of International and Comparative Social Policy* 143
Grech AG, 'What Makes Pension Reforms Sustainable?' (2018) 10 *Sustainability* 1
Green F, 'Legal Transitions without Legitimate Expectations' (2020) 28 *Journal of Political Philosophy* 397
Greer S, '"Balancing" and the European Court of Human Rights: A Contribution to the Habermas-Alexy Debate' (2004) 63 *The Cambridge Law Journal* 412
Greer SC, *The Margin of Appreciation: Interpretation and Discretion under the European Convention on Human Rights*, vol 17 (Council of Europe 2000)
Gretton G, 'The Protection of Property Rights' in C Himsworth and A Boyle (eds), *Human Rights and Scots Law: Comparative Perspectives on the Incorporation of the ECHR* (Hart Publishing 2002)
Hachez I, *Le Principe de Standstill Dans Le Droit Des Droits Fondamentaux: Une Irréversibilité Relative* (Bruylant 2008)
Hagemejer K, 'Rights-Based Approach to Social Security Coverage Expansion' in N Takayama, R Holzmann and DA Robalino (eds), *Closing the Coverage Gap: The Role of Social Pensions and Other Retirement Income Transfers* (World Bank 2009)
Hagemejer K and Schmitt V, 'Providing Social Security in Old Age: The International Labour Organization View' in SW Handayani and B Babajanian (eds), *Social Protection for Older Persons: Social Pension in Asia* (Asian Development Bank 2012)
Harris DJ and others, *Law of the European Convention on Human Rights* (Oxford University Press 2023)
Harris JW, *Property and Justice* (Oxford University Press 1996)
Hartmann-Cortés K, 'Should We Uprate Social Benefits for Inflation as a Matter of Article 1 Protocol 1?' (2022) 24 *European Journal of Social Security* 319
——, 'On Future Retirees' Legal Standing: Rethinking A1P1 Admissibility in Pension Reform Cases' (2025) 6 *The European Convention on Human Rights Law Review* 340
Hartmann-Cortés K, Herrera JF and Angarita GH, 'La'Privatización'de La Acción Pública de Inconstitucionalidad' [2021] *Revista Derecho del Estado* 203
Hassel A, Naczyk M and Wiß T, 'The Political Economy of Pension Financialisation: Public Policy Responses to the Crisis' in A Hassel and T Wiß (eds), *The Political Economy of Pension Financialisation* (Routledge 2020)
Hayek FA, *Law, Legislation, and Liberty*, vol 19 (University of Chicago Press 2022)
Hecker RJ, 'On the Subject of Property and Social Security: A Traditional Analysis' (2012) 7 *Liberty University Law Review* 143
Helfer LR, 'The New Innovation Frontier-Intellectual Property and the European Court of Human Rights' (2008) 49 *Harvard International Law Journal* 1
Hindriks J and Myles GD, *Intermediate Public Economics* (MIT Press 2013)
Hinrichs K, 'Recent Pension Reforms in Europe: More Challenges, New Directions. An Overview' (2021) 55 *Social Policy & Administration* 409
Hinrichs K and Jessoula M, *Labour Market Flexibility and Pension Reforms: Flexible Today, Secure Tomorrow?* (Springer 2012)
Hinz R, 'The World Bank's Pension Policy Framework and the Dutch Pension System: A Paradigm for the Multi-Pillar Design' in L Bovenberg, C van Ewijk and E Westerhout (eds), *The Future of Multi-Pillar Pensions* (Cambridge University Press 2011)

Hohfeld WN, 'Fundamental Legal Conceptions as Applied in Judicial Reasoning' (1917) 26 *The Yale Law Journal* 710
Holmes S and Sunstein CR, *The Cost of Rights: Why Liberty Depends on Taxes* (WW Norton & Company 2000)
Holzmann R, 'Global Pension Systems and Their Reform: Worldwide Drivers, Trends and Challenges' (2013) 66 *International Social Security Review* 1
——, 'Comments on Rethinking Pension Reform: Ten Myths about Social Security Systems by Peter Orszag and Joseph Stigliltz' in R Holzmann and JE Stiglitz (eds), *New Ideas About Old Age Security* (The World Bank, 2001)
Holzmann R, Hinz RP and Dorfman M, 'Pension Systems and Reform Conceptual Framework' (2008) 824 World Bank Discussion Paper
Honoré AM, *Oxford Essays in Jurisprudence* (Oxford University Press 1961)
Hyde M and Dixon J, 'A Just Retirement Pension System: Beyond Neoliberalism' (2009) 1 *Poverty & Public Policy* 1
Hyde M and Shand R, *Retirement, Pensions and Justice: A Philosophical Analysis* (Springer 2017)
Ireland P, 'Law and the Neoliberal Vision: Financial Property, Pension Privatisation and the Ownership Society' (2011) 62 *Northern Ireland Legal Quarterly* 1
Jackson JL, 'Broniowski v. Poland: A Recipe for Increased Legitimacy of the European Court of Human Rights as a Supranational Constitutional Court' (2006) 39 *Connecticut Law Review* 759
Jacobs AM, 'The Politics of When: Redistribution, Investment and Policy Making for the Long Term' (2008) 38 *British Journal of Political Science* 193
James E, Packard T and Holzmann R, 'Americas: From "Averting the Old-Age Crisis" to "Keeping the Promise of Old-Age Security" and Beyond' in SJ Kay and T Sinha (eds), *Lessons from Pension Reform in the Americas* (Oxford University Press 2007)
Jensen SL and Walton C, *Social Rights and the Politics of Obligation in History* (Cambridge University Press 2022)
Jones HW, 'The Rule of Law and the Welfare State' (1958) 58 *Columbia Law Review* 143
Kapuy K, 'Social Security and the European Convention on Human Rights: How an Odd Couple Has Become Presentable' (2007) 9 *European Journal of Social Security* 221
Kekes J, 'The Right to Private Property: A Justification' (2010) 27 *Social Philosophy and Policy* 1
Kent Jr MB, 'Public Pension Reform and the Takings Clause' (2017) 4 *Belmont Law Review* 1
Kleinlein T, 'The Procedural Approach of the European Court of Human Rights: Between Subsidiarity and Dynamic Evolution' (2019) 68 *International & Comparative Law Quarterly* 91
Kratochvíl J, 'The Inflation of the Margin of Appreciation by the European Court of Human Rights' (2011) 29 *Netherlands Quarterly of Human Rights* 324
Kuné JB, 'The Controversy of Funding versus Pay-as-You-Go: What Remains of the Debate?' (2001) 26 *The Geneva Papers on Risk and Insurance-Issues and Practice* 418
Lago CM, 'Evaluación de Cuatro Décadas de Privatización de Pensiones En América Latina, 1980–2020. Promesas y Realidades' [2021] *Revista General de Derecho del Trabajo y de la Seguridad Social* 28
Lamont J, 'The Concept of Desert in Distributive Justice' (1994) 44 *The Philosophical Quarterly* 45
Landau D, 'The Reality of Social Rights Enforcement' (2012) 53 *Harvard International Law Journal* 189
Landes X, 'How Fair Is Actuarial Fairness?' (2015) 128 *Journal of Business Ethics* 519
Langford M, 'Judicial Politics and Social Rights' [2019] *The Future of Economic and Social Rights* 66
——, 'The Impact of Public Interest Litigation: The Case of Socio-Economic Rights' (2021) 27 *Australian Journal of Human Rights* 505
Lautenbach G, *The Concept of the Rule of Law and the European Court of Human Rights* (Oxford University Press 2013)
Law DS, 'A Theory of Judicial Power and Judicial Review' (2008) 97 *Georgetown Law Journal* 723
Lehmann-Hasemeyer S and Streb J, 'Does Social Security Crowd out Private Savings? The Case of Bismarck's System of Social Insurance' (2018) 22 *European Review of Economic History* 298
Leijten I, 'From Stec to Valkov: Possessions and Margins in the Social Security Case Law of the European Court of Human Rights' (2013) 13 *Human Rights Law Review* 309

——, *Core Socio-Economic Rights and the European Court of Human Rights* (Cambridge University Press 2018)
——, 'The Right to Minimum Subsistence and Property Protection under the ECHR: Never the Twain Shall Meet?' (2019) 21 *European Journal of Social Security* 307
Lepage H, *Pourquoi La Propriété*, vol 287 (Hachette Paris 1985)
Letsas G, 'Two Concepts of the Margin of Appreciation' (2006) 26 *Oxford Journal of Legal Studies* 705
——, *A Theory of Interpretation of the European Convention on Human Rights* (Oxford University Press 2007)
Lindbeck A and Persson M, 'The Gains from Pension Reform' (2003) 41 *Journal of Economic Literature* 74
Lustig D and Weiler JH, 'Judicial Review in the Contemporary World: Retrospective and Prospective' (2018) 16 *International Journal of Constitutional Law* 315
Lutjens E, 'Invaren Pensioen: De Relevantie van Recht Op Eigendom' (2021) 10 *Tijdschrift voor Arbeidsrecht in Context* 3
——, 'Wet Toekomst Pensioenen: Wet Toekomst Pensioenen: Nieuwe Methode Pensioenopbouw: Een Onzekerder Pensioen En Een Fors Aantal Procedures' [2023] *Nederlands Juristenblad* 3046
Mackor AR, 'Explanatory Non-Normative Legal Doctrine. Taking the Distinction between Theoretical and Practical Reason Seriously' in M Van Hoecke (ed) *Methodologies of Legal Research. Which Kind of Method for What Kind of Discipline?* (Hart Publishing Ltd 2011)
Macpherson CB, 'Capitalism and the Changing Concept of Property' in Eugene Kamenka and Ronald Stanley Neale (eds), *Feudalism, Capitalism and Beyond* (Australian National University Press 1975)
——, *Property: Mainstream and Critical Positions* (University of Toronto Press 1999)
Marier P, *Pension Politics: Consensus and Social Conflict in Ageing Societies* (Routledge 2008)
Marochini M, 'The Interpretation of the European Convention on Human Rights' (2014) 51 *Zbornik radova Pravnog fakulteta u Splitu* 63
Matsaganis M and Leventi C, 'The Distributional Impact of Austerity and the Recession in Southern Europe' in M Petmesidou and AM Guillén (eds), *Economic Crisis and Austerity in Southern Europe* (Routledge 2017)
Maxwell D, *The Human Right to Property: A Practical Approach to Article 1 of Protocol No. 1 to the ECHR* (Bloomsbury Publishing 2022)
McCarthy F, 'Article One of the First Protocol to the European Convention on Human Rights: The Evolution of a Right in Europe and the United Kingdom' (PhD Thesis, University of Glasgow 2010)
McDougall HA, 'The New Property vs. the New Community' (1989) 24 *USFL Review* 399
McHarg A, 'Reconciling Human Rights and the Public Interest: Conceptual Problems and Doctrinal Uncertainty in the Jurisprudence of the European Court of Human Rights' (1999) 62 *Modern Law Review* 671
Melish TJ, 'Rethinking the Less as More Thesis: Supranational Litigation of Economic, Social, and Cultural Rights in the Americas' (2006) 39 *NYU Journal of International Law & Policy* 171
Merrill TW, 'Property and the Right to Exclude' (1998) 77 *Nebraska Law Review* 730
Mesa Lago C, 'La Privatización de Las Pensiones En América Latina. Promesas y Realidades' [2021] *Nueva sociedad* 15
Mesa-Lago C, *Evaluación de cuatro décadas de privatización de pensiones en América Latina (1980–2020): Promesas y realidades* (Friedrich Ebert Stiftung, FES 2020)
Meyerhoff AH and Mishkin JA, 'Application of Goldberg v. Kelly Hearing Requirements to Termination of Social Security Benefits' (1973) 26 *Stanford Law Review* 549
Michelman FI, 'Property as a Constitutional Right' (1981) 38 *Washington & Lee Law Review* 1097
——, 'Socioeconomic Rights in Constitutional Law: Explaining America Away' (2008) 6 *International Journal of Constitutional Law* 663
Minns R, *The Cold War in Welfare: Stock Markets versus Pensions* (Verso 2001)
Minoldo S and Peláez E, 'What Should Guarantee Pensions Systems Designed with a Human Rights Approach?' in F Rojo-Pérez and G Fernández-Mayoralas (eds), *Handbook of Active Ageing and Quality of Life: From Concepts to Applications* (Springer 2021)

Mola L, 'The Margin of Appreciation Accorded to States in Times of Economic Crisis. An Analysis of the Decisions by the European Committee of Social Rights and by the European Court of Human Rights on National Austerity Measures' (2015) 5 *Lex Social* 174
Monroy Cely DA, *Análisis económico del derecho Fundamentos y escuelas* (Universidad Externado de Colombia 2023)
Moriarty J, 'Desert-Based Justice' in S Olsaretti (ed), *The Oxford Handbook of Distributive Justice* (Oxford University Press 2008)
Mowbray A, 'A Study of the Principle of Fair Balance in the Jurisprudence of the European Court of Human Rights' (2010) 10 *Human Rights Law Review* 289
Moyn S, *The Last Utopia: Human Rights in History* (Harvard University Press 2012)
Muñoz Segura AM, *La Pensión de Vejez En Colombia. El Recorrido Histórico Entre La Exclusión y La Universalidad* (Universidad de los Andres 2019)
Munzer SR, *A Theory of Property* (Cambridge University Press 1990)
Murdoch JL, *Reed and Murdoch: Human Rights Law in Scotland* 4th edn (Bloomsbury Publishing 2017)
Murphy L and Nagel T, *The Myth of Ownership: Taxes and Justice* (Oxford University Press 2002)
Naczyk M, 'Agents of Privatization? Business Groups and the Rise of Pension Funds in Continental Europe' (2013) 11 *Socio-Economic Review* 441
Naczyk M and Domonkos S, 'The Financial Crisis and Varieties of Pension Privatization Reversals in Eastern Europe' (2016) 29 *Governance* 167
Naczyk M and Palier B, 'Feed the Beast: Finance Capitalism and the Spread of Pension Privatisation in Europe' [2014] Available at SSRN 2551521
Naczyk M and Seeleib-Kaiser M, 'Solidarity against All Odds: Trade Unions and the Privatization of Pensions in the Age of Dualization' (2015) 43 *Politics & Society* 361
Natali D and Stamati F, 'Reassessing South European Pensions after the Crisis: Evidence from Two Decades of Reforms' in M Petmesidou and AM Guillén (ed), *Economic Crisis and Austerity in Southern Europe* (Routledge 2017)
Nelson C, 'Judicial Review of Legislative Purpose' (2008) 83 *NYU Law Review* 1784
Nield S, 'Proportionality and the Vindication of Property Rights' in Heather Conway and Robin Hickey (eds), *Modern Studies in Property Law*, vol 9 (Hart Publishing 2017)
Nisticò S, *Essentials of Pension Economics* (Palgrave 2019)
Nobles R, 'Pensions as Property' (1994) 14 *Legal Studies* 345
Noveck SM, 'Is Judicial Review Compatible with Democracy?' (2007) 6 *Cardozo Public Law, Policy & Ethics Journal* 401
O'Cinneide C, 'Taking Horizontal Effect Seriously: Private Law, Constitutional Rights and the European Convention on Human Rights' (2003) 4 *Hibernian Law Journal* 77
OECD, *Pensions at a Glance 2019: OECD and G20 Indicators* (OECD 2019)
Orenstein MA, *Privatizing Pensions: The Transnational Campaign for Social Security Reform* (Princeton University Press 2008)
——, 'Pension Privatization in Crisis: Death or Rebirth of a Global Policy Trend?' (2011) 64 *International Social Security Review* 65
Oręziak L, *Pension Fund Capitalism: The Privatization of Pensions in Developed and Developing Countries* (Routledge 2022)
Orszag PR and Stiglitz JE, Rethinking Pension Reform: Ten Myths about Social Security Systems' in R Holzmann and JE Stiglitz (eds), *New Ideas About Old Age Security* (The World Bank 2001)
Ortiz I and others, 'Reversing Pension Privatization: Rebuilding Public Pension Systems in Eastern European and Latin American Countries (2000–18)' [2018] Available at SSRN 3275228
Ostrom E and Hess C, 'Private and Common Property Rights' in G De Geest (ed), *Encyclopedia of Law and Economics* (Edward Elgar Publishing Limited 2011)
Otting A, 'International Labour Standards: A Framework for Social Security' (1993) 132 *International Labour Review* 163

Padelletti ML, *La Tutela Della Proprietà Nella Convenzione Europea Dei Diritti Dell'uomo* (Giuffrè 2003)
Palier B, *A Long Goodbye to Bismarck?: The Politics of Welfare Reform in Continental Europe* (Amsterdam University Press 2010)
——, *Réformer Les Retraites* (Presses de Sciences Po 2021)
Palmer E, 'Protecting Socio-Economic Rights through the European Convention on Human Rights: Trends and Developments in the European Court of Human Rights' (2009) 2 *Erasmus Law Review* 397
Pamp O, *Political Preferences and the Aging of Populations: Political-Economy Explanations of Pension Reform* (Springer VS 2015)
Papadopoulos NA, 'Paving the Way for Effective Socio-Economic Rights? The Domestic Enforcement of the European Social Charter System in Light of Recent Judicial Practice' in C Boost, A Broderik, F Coomans and R Moerland (eds), *Myth or Lived Reality: On the (In) Effectiveness of Human Rights* (Springer 2021)
Papadopoulos T and Roumpakis A, 'Democracy, Austerity and Crisis: Southern Europe and the Decline of the European Social Model' in S Romano and G Punziano (eds), *The European Social Model Adrift* (Routledge 2016)
——, 'Rattling Europe's Ordoliberal "Iron Cage": The Contestation of Austerity in Southern Europe' (2018) 38 *Critical Social Policy* 505
Penner J, *The Idea of Property In Law* (Clarendon Press 1997)
Penner J and Otsuka M, *Property Theory: Legal and Political Perspectives* (Cambridge University Press 2018)
Penner JE, 'The Bundle of Rights Picture of Property' (1995) 43 *UCLA Law Review* 711
——, *Property Rights: A Re-Examination* (Oxford University Press, USA 2020)
Pennings F and Vonk G, *Research Handbook on European Social Security Law* (Edward Elgar Publishing 2023)
Perez SA and Matsaganis M, 'The Political Economy of Austerity in Southern Europe' (2018) (23(2) *Journal of New Political Economy*, Special Issue, Guest Edited by: Alison Jonston and Aidan Regan, Is the European Union capable of integrating diverse models of capitalism? 192
Pieters D, 'Security in Social Security: Reflections from a Legal Point of View' (2012) 67 *Pravnik* 21
Pistor K, *The Code of Capital: How the Law Creates Wealth and Inequality* (Princeton University Press 2019)
Praduroux S, 'Property and Expropriation: Two Concepts Revisited in the Light of the Case Law of the European Court of Human Rights and the European Court of Justice' (2019) 8 *European Property Law Journal* 172
Radin MJ, 'Property and Personhood' [1982] *Stanford Law Review* 957
Reich C, 'The New Property' (1964) 73 *Yale Law* 733
Reich CA, 'Social Welfare in the Public-Private State' (1965) 114 *University of Pennsylvania Law Review* 487
——, 'The New Property' (1964) 73 *Yale Law Journal* 733
——, 'Individual Rights and Social Welfare: The Emerging Legal Issues' in P Robson (ed), *Welfare Law* (Routledge 2020)
Riedel EH, *Social Security as a Human Right: Drafting a General Comment on Article 9 ICESCR-Some Challenges*, vol 26 (Springer Science & Business Media 2006)
Ripert G, Boulanger J-C and Planiol M, 'Traité de Droit Civil, d'après Le Traité de Planiol' in G Ripert and J Boulanger (eds), *Obligations, contrat, responsabilité, droits réels, biens, propriété*, vol 2 (Librairie Générale de Droit et de Jurisprudence 1957)
Rivers J, 'Proportionality and Variable Intensity of Review' (2006) 65 *The Cambridge Law Journal* 174
Riza Çoban A, *Protection of Property Rights within the European Convention on Human Rights* (Ashgate 2003)
Rodríguez-Garavito C, 'Beyond the Courtroom: The Impact of Judicial Activism on Socioeconomic Rights in Latin America' (2010) 89 *Texas Law Review* 1669

——, 'Empowered Participatory Jurisprudence: Experimentation, Deliberation and Norms in Socioeconomic Rights Adjudication in KG Young (ed), *The Future of Economic and Social Rights* (Cambridge University Press 2019)

Roubier P, *Le Droit Transitoire (Les Conflits de Lois Dans Le Temps)* 2nd edn (Dalloz 1960)

Rowland DT, 'Global Population Aging: History and Prospects' in P Uhlenberg (ed), *International Handbook of Population Aging* (Springer 2009)

Sackville R, 'Property, Rights and Social Security' (1977) 2 *UNSW Law Journal* 246

Salomon ME, 'Of Austerity, Human Rights and International Institutions' (2015) 21 *European Law Journal* 521

Savatier R, 'Les Métamorphoses Économiques et Sociales Du Droit Privé d'aujourd'hui' in R Savatier, *Approfondissement d'un droit renouvelé* (Dalloz 1959)

Schneider O, 'Reforming Pensions in Europe: Economic Fundamentals and Political Factors' CESifo Working Paper, No 2572, Center for Economic Studies and ifo Institute (CESifo), Munich

Schokkaert E and Van Parijs P, 'Just Pensions: Reply to Myles, Oksanen and Fornero' (2003) 13 *Journal of European Social Policy* 276

Schutte CB, *The European Fundamental Right of Property: Article 1 of Protocol No. 1 to the European Convention on Human Rights: Its Origins, Its Working, and Its Impact on National Legal Orders* (Kluwer 2004)

Schwelb E, 'The Protection of the Right of Property of Nationals under the First Protocol to the European Convention on Human Rights' [1964] *The American Journal of Comparative Law* 518

Shue H, *Basic Rights: Subsistence, Affluence, and US Foreign Policy* (Princeton University Press 2020)

Sicilianos L, 'The Rule of Law and the European Court of Human Rights: The Independence of the Judiciary', speech delivered in the Montenegrin Academy of Sciences and Arts, Montenegro, 28 February 2020

Simpson AWB, *Human Rights and the End of Empire: Britain and the Genesis of the European Convention* (Oxford University Press, USA 2004)

Singer JW, 'Democratic Estates: Property Law in a Free and Democratic Society' (2008) 94 *Cornell Law Review* 1009

——, 'Normative Methods for Lawyers' (2008) 56 *UCLA Law Review* 899

——, 'Property as the Law of Democracy' (2013) 63 *Duke Law Journal* 1287

Slingenberg L and Leijten I, 'Social Security in the Case Law of the European Court of Human Rights' in F Pennings and G Vonk (eds), *Research Handbook on European Social Security Law* (Edward Elgar Publishing 2023)

Smet S, 'Freedom of Expression and the Right to Reputation: Human Rights in Conflict' (2010) 26 *American University International Law Review* 183

Smits JM, 'What Is Legal Doctrine? On the Aims and Methods of Legal-Dogmatic Research' in R van Gestel, H-W Micklitz and EL Rubin (eds), *Rethinking Legal Scholarship: A Transatlantic Dialogue* (Cambridge University Press 2017)

Social Protection Committee, 'The 2018 Pension Adequacy Report: Current and Future Income Adequacy in Old Age in the EU. Volume I' (Social Protection Committee 2018)

Sonnevend P, *Eigentumsschutz Und Sozialversicherung: Eine Rechtsvergleichende Analyse Anhand Der Rechtsprechung Des Bundesverfassungsgerichts Und Des Ungarischen Verfassungsgerichts*, vol 185 (Springer-Verlag 2007)

Sorauf FJ, 'The Public Interest Reconsidered' (1957) 19 *The Journal of Politics* 616

Sorsa V-P and van der Zwan N, 'Sustaining the Unsustainable? The Political Sustainability of Pensions in Finland and the Netherlands' (2022) 32 *Journal of European Social Policy* 91

Spitz J-F and others, 'Why Private Property?' (2019) 73 *Raisons politiques* 119

Stern JY, 'Property's Constitution' (2013) 101 *California Law Review* 277

Stevens Y, 'The Silent Pension Pillar Implosion' (2017) 19 *European Journal of Social Security* 98

——, 'The Role of the Government in Creating or Enhancing the Access to Funded or Unfunded Pensions in the Modern Welfare State' in N da Costa Cabral and N Cunha Rodrigues (eds), *The Future of Pension Plans in the EU Internal Market: Coping with Trade-Offs Between Social Rights and Capital Markets* (Springer 2019)

——, *EU Pension Law* (Edward Elgar Publishing 2022)
Stoyanova V, 'Causation between State Omission and Harm within the Framework of Positive Obligations under the European Convention on Human Rights' (2018) 18 *Human Rights Law Review* 309
——, 'The Disjunctive Structure of Positive Rights under the European Convention on Human Rights' (2018) 87 *Nordic Journal of International Law* 344
——, 'Fault, Knowledge and Risk within the Framework of Positive Obligations under the European Convention on Human Rights' (2020) 33 *Leiden Journal of International Law* 601
——, 'Framing Positive Obligations under the European Convention on Human Rights Law: Mediating between the Abstract and the Concrete' (2023) 23 *Human Rights Law Review* 1
——, *Positive Obligations under the European Convention on Human Rights: Within and Beyond Boundaries* (Oxford University Press 2023)
Sweeney JA, 'A Margin of Appreciation in the Internal Market: Lessons from the European Court of Human Rights' (2007) 34 *Legal Issues of Economic Integration* 27
Sweet AS and Keller H, 'The Reception of the ECHR in National Legal Orders' in H Keller and AS Sweet (eds), *A Europe of Rights: The Impact of the ECHR on National Legal Systems* (Oxford University Press 2008)
Sweet C, 'Choses in Action' (1894) 10 *Law Quarterly Review* 303
Tasioulas J, 'Towards a Philosophy of Human Rights' (2012) 65 *Current Legal Problems* 1
Terré F, 'L'évolution Du Droit de Propriété Depuis Le Code Civil' [1985] *Droits* 33
Terré F, Simler P and Lequette Y, *Droit Civil: Les Obligations* 11th edn (Dalloz 2013)
Thaler RH and Sunstein CR, *Nudge: The Final Edition* (Yale University Press 2021)
Trahan J-R, 'Time for a Change: A Call to Reform Louisiana's Intertemporal Conflicts Law (Law of Retroactivity of Laws)' (1998) 59 *Louisiana Law Review* 661
Trykhlib K and Lemak V, 'Autonomous Interpretation by the European Court of Human Rights and Margin of Appreciation' (2022) 22 *International and Comparative Law Review* 135
Tsakyrakis S, 'Proportionality: An Assault on Human Rights?' (2009) 7 *International Journal of Constitutional Law* 468
Tushnet M, *Weak Courts, Strong Rights: Judicial Review and Social Welfare Rights in Comparative Constitutional Law* (Princeton University Press 2009)
Urbina FJ, 'A Critique of Proportionality' (2012) 57 *American Journal of Jurisprudence* 49
——, 'Is It Really That Easy? A Critique of Proportionality and "Balancing as Reasoning"' (2014) 27 *Canadian Journal of Law & Jurisprudence* 167
——, *A Critique of Proportionality and Balancing* (Cambridge University Press 2017)
Valdes-Prieto S, 'Securitization of Taxes Implicit in PAYG Pensions' (2005) 20 *Economic Policy* 216
Valentini L, 'In What Sense Are Human Rights Political? A Preliminary Explanation' (2012) 60 *Political Studies* 180
Van der Walt A, "Double'Property Guarantees: A Structural and Comparative Analysis' (1998) 14 *South African Journal on Human Rights* 560
van der Walt A and Walsh R, 'Comparative Constitutional Property Law' in M Graziadei and L Smith (eds), *Comparative Property Law* (Edward Elgar Publishing 2017)
Van der Walt AJ, *Property in the Margins* (Bloomsbury Publishing 2009)
Van Dijk P and Van Hoof GJ, *Theory and Practice of the European Convention on Human Rights* (Martinus Nijhoff Publishers 2023)
Van Drooghenbroeck S and Rizcallah C, 'The ECHR and the Essence of Fundamental Rights: Searching for Sugar in Hot Milk?' (2019) 20 *German Law Journal* 904
Van Gestel R and Micklitz H, 'Why Methods Matter in European Legal Scholarship' (2014) 20 *European Law Journal* 292
Van Hoecke M, 'Legal Doctrine: Which Method (s) for What Kind of Discipline?' in M Van Hoecke (ed), *Methodologies of Legal Research: Which Kind of Method for What Kind of Discipline?* (Hart Publishing 2011)
Van Limberghen G, 'In Min of in Meer: Wettelijke En Aanvullende Pensioenen' in Willy Van Eeckhoutte and Marc Rigaux (eds), *T. BOD, Het pensioenbegrip, Zwolle, Tjeenk Willink, 1994, 12* (Mys & Breesch 1996)

Van Parijs P, *Real Freedom for All: What (If Anything) Can Justify Capitalism?* (Clarendon Press 1995)
Varella MD, *Internationalization of Law Globalization, International Law and Complexity* (Springer International Publishing 2014)
Verbič M and Spruk R, 'Political Economy of Pension Reforms: An Empirical Investigation' (2019) 47 *European Journal of Law and Economics* 171
Vicente MN, 'Property Rights and Legitimate Expectations under United States Constitutional Law and the European Convention on Human Rights: Some Comparative Remarks' (2020) 26 *Comparative Law Review* 51
Waldron J, 'What Is Private Property' (1985) 5 *Oxford Journal of Legal Studies* 313
——, *The Right to Private Property* (Oxford University Press 1990)
——, *The Dignity of Legislation* (Cambridge University Press 1999)
——, 'Principles of Legislation' in Richard W Bauman and Tsvi Kahana (eds), *The Least Examined Branch: The Role of Legislatures in the Constitutional State* (Cambridge University Press 2006)
——, 'The Core of the Case Against Judicial Review' (2006) 6 *The Yale Law Journal* 1346
——, 'Legislation and the Rule of Law' (2007) 1 *Legisprudence* 91
——, 'The Concept and the Rule of Law' (2008) 43 *Georgia Law Review* 1
——, 'Property Law' in Dennis Michael Patterson (ed), *A Companion to Philosophy of Law and Legal Theory* (Wiley Online Library 2010)
——, *The Rule of Law and the Measure of Property* (Cambridge University Press 2012)
——, 'The Rule of Law in Public Law' in M Elliot and D Feldman (eds), *The Cambridge Companion to Public Law* (Cambridge University Press 2015)
——, 'Is the Rule of Law an Essentially Contested Concept (in Florida)?' (2002) 21(2) *Law and Philosophy* 137
Walsh R, *Property Rights and Social Justice: Progressive Property in Action* (Cambridge University Press 2021)
Wassenberg B, *History of the Council of Europe* (Council of Europe 2013)
Weinrib EJ, 'Corrective Justice in a Nutshell' (2002) 52 *The University of Toronto Law Journal* 349
Westerman PC, 'Open or Autonomous? A Debate on Legal Methodology as a Reflection of the Debate on Law' in Mark Van Hoecke (ed), *Methodologies of Legal Research* (Hart Publishing 2010)
White LE, 'Goldberg v. Kelly on the Paradox of Lawyering for the Poor' (1990) 56 *Brooklyn Law Review* 861
Wildhaber L, 'The European Convention on Human Rights and International Law' (2007) 56 *International & Comparative Law Quarterly* 217
Wills J and Warwick BT, 'Contesting Austerity: The Potential and Pitfalls of Socioeconomic Rights Discourse' (2016) 23 *Indiana Journal of Global Legal Studies* 629
Wolff M, *Private International Law* (Clarendon Press 1950)
World Bank, *Averting the Old Age Crisis: Policies to Protect the Old and Promote Growth. Summary* (The World Bank 1994)
Young KG, *The Future of Economic and Social Rights* (Cambridge University Press 2019)
Zaidi A, Gasior K and Sidorenko A, 'Intergenerational Solidarity: Policy Challenges and Societal Responses' [2010] Policy Brief, European Centre Vienna

INDEX

References are to page number.

www.ingramcontent.com/pod-product-compliance
Ingram Content Group UK Ltd.
Pitfield, Milton Keynes, MK11 3LW, UK
UKHW020819290926
15470UKWH00003B/1250

9 781509 986026